THE ART OF
ANCIENT AMERICA

CIVILIZATIONS OF CENTRAL AND SOUTH AMERICA

BY

HANS-DIETRICH DISSELHOFF

AND

SIGVALD LINNÉ

GREYSTONE PRESS/NEW YORK

Translated by Ann E. Keep

Frontispiece: a huge recumbent jaguar carved from volcanic stone, a
masterly symbol of savagery, barbarism and war. On its back is a
sacred *quauhxicalli* ('eagle's bowl') in which were placed the blood
and hearts of victims of human sacrifice. The inside of the vessel is
lavishly decorated with conventionally fashioned eagle feathers. The
relief on the base represents two deities seated opposite one another
and piercing their ears with bone daggers. Thus here even the gods
sacrifice their blood. One may admire the apparent ease with which
this huge jaguar has been carved with simple stone tools, and the relief
carvings on the sides and bottom of the cylindrical bowl, which measures 24½ in. in diameter and 10¼ in. in depth. This unsurpassed
masterpiece was discovered in the temple quarter of the city of
Tenochtitlán. *Museo Nacional, Mexico City.*
7 ft. 4½ in. x 3 ft. 11 in. x 3 ft. 1 in.

REVISED EDITION 1966
© 1960 BY HOLLE VERLAG G.M.B.H., BADEN-BADEN, GERMANY
LIBRARY OF CONGRESS CATALOGUE CARD NUMBER: 61-16973
MANUFACTURED IN THE UNITED STATES OF AMERICA

CONTENTS

List of plates and maps (5). List of figures (6). Acknowledgements (9).

PART I: THE ART OF MEXICO AND CENTRAL AMERICA
  by Sigvald Linné

  I. PREHISTORIC AMERICA AND THE EARLIEST
      INHABITANTS OF MEXICO   10

  II. THE ART OF THE WESTERN REGION   27

  III. TEOTIHUACÁN   30

  IV. THE ZAPOTECS   52

  V. THE CULTURES ON THE COAST OF THE GULF OF
     MEXICO   60

  VI. THE TOLTECS   76

  VII. MIXTECA PUEBLA CULTURE   81

  VIII. AZTEC ART AND CULTURE   84

  IX. MAYA CULTURE   107

  X. CENTRAL AMERICA: BRIDGE BETWEEN TWO
     CONTINENTS **122**

PART II: THE ART OF THE ANDEAN LANDS
  by Hans-Dietrich Disselhoff

  I. THE SETTING   131

II. GREATER PERU 135

The Chavín horizon (150). Paracas (151). Chavín (156). Moche culture (174). Nazca (184). Tiahuanaco (200). The age of city-builders and minor kingdoms (211). The Inca empire (214). The border provinces of the Inca empire: north-western Argentina and northern Chile (223). Ecuador (226).

III. THE EASTERN LOWLANDS 238

IV. COLOMBIA 241

V. SAN AGUSTÍN 246

CHRONOLOGICAL TABLE OF MESOAMERICA 250

APPENDICES 253

Glossary (254). Bibliography (263). Index (259).

LIST OF PLATES AND MAPS

PREHISTORIC AMERICA AND THE EARLIEST INHABITANTS OF MEXICO

Map of Mexico and Central America:
   principal sites 12-13
Female clay figures, Valley of Mexico 19
Figure of an athlete, Tlaticlo 20
Female figure, Nayarit 21

THE ART OF THE WESTERN REGION

Terra cotta figure of dog, Colima 22
Clay figure of dog, Colima 24
Hollow clay figure, Jalisco 25

TEOTIHUACAN

Pyramid of the Sun, Tetrihuacán 23
Mask of green stone 26
Detail of a mural, Tepantitla 43

THE ZAPOTECS

Clay figure, Monte Albán 44
Funerary urn 45

THE TOLTECS

Chac Mool, Chichén Itzá 46
Head of a parrot, Xochicalco 47

MIXTECA PUEBLA CULTURE

Xipe Totec, Otátes 48
Wooden gong 49

AZTEC ART AND CULTURE

Sacrificial bowl, Tenochtitlán   FRONTISPIECE
Atlatl 50
Tlazoltéotl giving birth to the Maize God 67
Xipe Totec: stone head or mask 68
Aztec shield with feather mosaic 69
Mask 70
'Plumed serpent' of stone. 71
Xipe Totec, Texcoco 74
Xolotl: nephritic stone figure 91

MAYA CULTURE

Frescoes from Bonampak 72-3
Kneeling ball-player: decoration in relief 92
Sacrificial vessel with representation of the
   Sun God 93
Clay figure, Jaina I. 94
Funerary urn, Mayapan 95

CENTRAL AMERICA

'Jaguar vessel', Nicoya peninsula 96
Tripod vase, Nicoya peninsula 97
Gold pendant, Costa Rica 98
Gold figure of shark, Costa Rica 139
Clay bowl, Coclé 140

GREATER PERU

Map of Greater Peru and Ecuador 134
Fragment of a cotton fabric, Ica 141

THE CHAVIN HORIZON

Shroud, Paracas Necropolis 142
Clay jar, Chavín culture 143
Clay vessel, Recuay style 144
Clay portrait vessel, Moche culture 145
Necklace, Etén near Chiclao 146
Clay figure jar, Moche culture 163
Head of fox, Moon Pyramid, Moche 164
Death mask, Moon Pyramid, Moche 165
Polychrome clay vase, Late Nazca culture 166
Magic fish: clay vessel, Pachacamac 167
Polychrome incense-vessel, Tiahuanaco style 168
Engraved incense-vessel, Tiahuanaco style 169
Encrusted ornamental plaque,
   Tiahuanaco style 170
Polychrome clay bowl, Tiahuanaco style 187
Head crowning a mummy pack,
   Tiahuanaco style 188
Kelim fabric, Pachacamac 189
Kelim fabric, Pachacamac 190

THE AGE OF CITY-BUILDERS AND MINOR KINGDOMS

Fabric woven in tapestry technique,
   Late Tiahuanaco 191
Bronze top of a ceremonial staff, Chanchán 192
Funerary gloves in gold 193

THE INCA EMPIRE

Polychrome clay jar, Inca style 194
Map: Expansion of the Inca Empire 215
Polychrome clay figure, Inca style 227
Sleeveless tunic with Inca design 228
Figure, silver with admixture of gold,
   Inca style 229

BORDER PROVINCES OF THE INCA EMPIRE

Gigantic fortifications, Sacsahuamán 230
Inca ruins, Pisac 231

ECUADOR

Sun Temple, Pisac   232

THE EASTERN LOWLANDS

Gateway with flight of steps, Sacsahuamán 233

COLOMBIA

Gold death mask, central Cauca Valley   234
Map: Colombia and adjacent territories   240

LIST OF FIGURES
I. THE ART OF MEXICO AND CENTRAL AMERICA

1 — Spear-head of flint-like material. *After Covarrubias*
2 — Clay figurine, Tlatilco. *After Groth-Kimball*
3 — Ceramic ware from Tlatilco. *Photo, Statens Etnografiska Museum, Stockholm*
4 — Ceramic ware from Tlatilco. *Photo, Statens Etnografiska Museum, Stockholm*
5 — Vessel in the shape of a fish, Tlatilco. *After Covarrubias*
6 — Clay vessel with incised ornamentation, Cerro de las Mesas. *Photo, Statens Etnografiska Museum, Stockholm*
7 — Flat clay figure, Higueras, Colima. *Photo, Statens Etnografiska Museum, Stockholm*
8 — Ceramic human figure, Colima. *After Groth-Kimball*
9 — Ball-player, Colima. *Stendahl Galleries, Hollywood*
10 — Schematic ground-plan of the ruin at Xolalpan
11 — Mask from Teotihuacán. *S. Linné Collection, Stockholm*
12 — Schematic sketch of mask in Fig. 11
13 — Sacred clay vessel, Teotihuacán. *Statens Etnografiska Museum, Stockholm*
14 — Sacred clay vessel, Teotihuacán. *Statens Etnografiska Museum, Stockholm*
15 — Sacred clay vessel, Teotihuacán. *Statens Etnografiska Museum, Stockholm*
16 — Ceramic ware from burial-place, Teotihuacán. *Statens Etnografiska Museum, Stockholm*
17 — Lid of a tripod vessel, Teotihuacán. *Statens Etnografiska Museum, Stockholm*
18 — Clay figure with movable arms and legs. *Statens Etnografiska Museum, Stockholm*
19 — Imported clay vessel. *Statens Etnografiska Museum, Stockholm*
20 — Bowl with annular base. Tlaxcala. *Statens Etnografiska Museum, Stockholm*
21 — Clay vessel from Teotihuacán. *Museo Regional de Teotihuacán*
22 — Detail of a mural from Teopancaxco. *After Krickeberg*
23 — Zapotec urn from Oaxaca. *Museo Nacional, Mexico City. After Linné*
24 — Urn, Monte Albán. *After Caso and Bernal*
25 — Entrance to a palace, Mitla. *After Holmes*
26 — Impression of a clay stamp, Veracruz. *After Enciso*
27 — Head from the coast of the Gulf of Mexico. *Museo Nacional, Mexico City. Photo, Statens Etnografiska Museum, Stockholm*
28 — Fragment of a sculpture (palmate stone). Central coastlands of the Gulf of Mexico. *Private collection, Mexico. Photo, Statens Etnografiska Museum, Stockholm*
29 — Ceremonial axe (?). Central coastlands of the Gulf of Mexico. *Private collection, Mexico. After Groth-Kimball*
30 — Yoke of polished greenstone from Boca del Monte, Oaxaca. *After Covarrubias*
31 — Detail from relief on ball-court, El Tajín, Veracruz. *After Covarrubias*
32 — Reverse side of schist mirror, Vega de la Torre, Veracruz. *After Bliss and Lothrop*
33 — Clay vessel with conical lid, Teotihuacán culture showing influence of Veracruz. *After Covarrubias*
34 — Clay bowl with decoration, Cerro Montoso, Veracruz. *After Krickeberg*
35 — Ceramic figure, coastlands of the Gulf of Mexico. *After Groth-Kimball*
36 — Ceramic figure, 'La Venta' culture. *After Krickeberg*
37 — Gigantic head from La Venta. *After Krickeberg*
38 — Figurine, Tabasco. *After Bliss*
39 — Mask of a jaguar in brown marble, Rio de las Balsas. *After Bliss*

40 — Polychrome clay vessel, southern coastlands of the Gulf of Mexico. *After Groth-Kimball*
41 — Column with bas-relief, Tula. *After Peterson*
42 — Column in form of a 'plumed serpent', Tula. *After Peterson*
43 — Painted Mazapan ceramic ware. *After Linné*
44 — Clay figure of the deity Xipe Totec, Mazapan culture. *Museo Regional de Teotihuacán. After Linné*
45 — Detail from a monument at Xochicalco. *Photo, Linné.*
46 — Jug with ornamentation, Mixteca Puebla culture. *Photo, Statens Etnografiska Museum, Stockholm*
47 — Detail of a Mixtec clay vessel. *Museum, Mitla. After Peterson*
48 — Carving on bone from 'Grave 7', Monte Albán. *After Covarrubias*
49 — Aztec bowl with painted decoration. *After Covarrubias*
50 — Aztec clay bowl with criss-cross incising on floor. *After Covarrubias*
51 — Clay bowl painted in black and orange, Valley of Mexico. *After Covarrubias*
52 — Incised decoration on a spindle-whorl, Teotihuacán. *Statens Etnografiska Museum, Stockholm*
53 — Impression of a clay stamp, Tenochtitlán. *After Enciso*
54 — Obsidian skull, Texcoco. *After Bliss and Lothrop*
55 — The gods Huehuetéotl and Tlaloc. *After Peterson*
56 — The goddess Xochiquetzal. *After Peterson*
57 — Mictlantecuhtli. *After Peterson*
58 — Man with blow-pipe, Maya culture. *After Peterson*
59 — Painted ornamentation on a clay vessel, Guatemala. *After Morley*
60 — Maya hieroglyphs. *After Covarrubias*
61 — Reverse side of a schist mirror, Guatemala. *After Bliss and Lothrop*
62 — Central part of a polychrome tripod vessel, Maya period. *After Bliss and Lothrop*
63 — Painted decoration on a tripod vessel. *From Expedition, Vol. 2, No. 2, 1960*
64 — Central figure from a polychrome clay bowl, Yucatán. *Formerly in the Staatliches Museum für Völkerkunde, Berlin*
65 — Cross-sections of Maya buildings showing corbelled arches. *After Peterson*
66 — Reconstruction of a temple pyramid, Guatemala. *After Proskouriakoff*
67 — Detail of painted ornamentation on a clay vessel, Guatemala. *After Morley*
68 — Caryatid from Zapatera I. *After Bovallius*
69 — Club-head from Costa Rica. *S. Linné Collection*
70 — Implement for grinding maize, Costa Rica. *After Joyce*
71 — Human figure, Costa Rica. *S. Linné Collection*
72 — Clay vessels from Chiriquí province
73 — Polychrome decoration on a bowl, probably from Coclé. *After Holmes*
74 — Clay vessel from a grave in Veraguas. *After Lothrop*
75 — Clay bowl from the Pearl Is. *After Linné*

II. THE ART OF THE ANDEAN LANDS

1 — Detail of knotted cotton threads from Asia cemetery, south of Lima. *After Fr. Engel*
2 — Painted design on the cotton swathing of a mummy. Early Paracas. *After Bird and Bellinger*
3 — Polychrome embroidery on a shroud. Paracas Necropolis. *After Bird and Bellinger*
4 — Double-spouted clay vessel. Late Paracas. *After Bennett*
5 — Painted clay bowl. Chavín horizon. *Museum für Völkerkunde, Berlin*
6 — Stone column with sculpture. Chavín style. *Photo, Rojas Ponce*
7 — Stone plaque in relief. Chavín de Huántar. *Private collection, Lima*
8 — Plaque in relief. Chavín de Huántar. *Photo, Rojas Ponce*
9 — Bas-relief on a stele. Casma Valley. *After Julio C. Tello*
10 — Engraved spatula. Central Peru. *Photo, Fr. Engel*
11 — Jar with stirrup spout. Chicama Valley. *After Larco Hoyle*
12, 13 — Clay flasks with incised and punched ornamentation. Chavín ceramic ware. *Collection of the Larco family, Lima. After Larco Hoyle*

14 — Vessel with stirrup spout. Salinar. *After Larco Hoyle*

15 — Double-bodied vessel with representation of a house. Gallinazo or Virú style. *After Willey*

16 — Fragment of a Moche vessel in the form of a house. *Museum für Völkerkunde, Berlin*

17 — Painted Moche vessel. *After Willey*

18 — Painted ornamentation on a stirrup-spouted vessel. Moche culture. *Museum für Völkerkunde, Berlin*

19 — Painted clay bowl. Moche culture. *Private collection, Switzerland. Photo, F. Anton*

20 — Jar with stirrup spout. Moche culture. *Museum für Völkerkunde, Berlin*

21 — Painted clay jar. Moche culture. *Private collection, Peru*

22 — Painted decoration on a stirrup-spouted jar. *Museum für Völkerkunde, Berlin*

23 — Detail of the painted decoration on the inside of a clay vessel. *Museum für Völkerkunde, Berlin*

24 — Painted decoration on a vase. Moche culture. *Museum für Völkerkunde, Berlin*

25 — Painted decoration on a stirrup-spouted vessel. Environs of Trujillo. *Museum für Völkerkunde, Berlin*

26 — Detail of the painted decoration on a stirrup-spouted vessel. *Museo Nacional, Lima. After a drawing by A. Jiménez Borja*

27 — Detail of the painted decoration on a Moche vessel. *After Rebeca Carrión Cachot*

28 — Painted decoration on a clay vessel. *Museum für Völkerkunde, Berlin*

29 — Detail of the painted decoration on the inside of a clay bowl. Moche style. *British Museum. After a copy by G. Kutscher*

30 — Painted decoration on a stirrup-spouted vessel. *Museum für Völkerkunde, Berlin*

31 — Scene on a vase. Moche culture. *Museum für Völkerkunde, Berlin*

32 — Scene on a vase. *Museum für Völkerkunde, Berlin*

33 — Painted decoration on a clay vessel. Moche culture. *Museum für Völkerkunde, Hamburg*

34 — Polychrome painting on a double-spouted clay vessel. Nazca style. *Gaffron Collection, now in Museum of Natural History, Chicago. After Ubbelohde-Doering*

35 — Polychrome clay bowl. Classic Nazca style. *Museum für Völkerkunde, Berlin*

36 — Painted clay vessel. Nazca style. *Museum für Völkerkunde, Berlin*

37 — Polychrome painted ornamentation on a double-spouted vessel. *Gaffron Collection. After Ubbelohde-Doering*

38 — Polychrome painted decoration on a clay vessel. Late Nazca style. *Museum für Völkerkunde, Berlin*

39 — Polychrome clay goblet. Late Nazca style. *Museum für Völkerkunde, Berlin*

40 — Polychrome pot. Interlocking style. *Museum für Völkerkunde, Berlin*

41 — Detail of relief on the Gate of the Sun. Classic Tiahuanaco style. *After M. Uhle*

42 — Detail of a tapestry. Tiahuanaco period. *Private collection, Switzerland. Photo, F. Anton*

43 — Sandstone sculpture. Tiahuanaco. *Museum für Völkerkunde, Berlin*

44 — Polychrome clay jar. Tiahuanaco style. *Museum für Völkerkunde, Berlin*

45 — Polychrome clay beaker *(kero)*. Tiahuanaco style. *Museum für Völkerkunde, Berlin*

46 — Polychrome clay potsherds. Pucara style. *After a reproduction in Handbook of South American Indians*

47 — Painted clay jug. Chancay. *Museum für Völkerkunde, Berlin*

48 — Double-bodied vessel of black clay with decoration in relief. Chimú culture. *Museum für Völkerkunde, Berlin*

49 — Painted jar with handle. Lambayeque style. *Museum für Völkerkunde, Berlin*

50 — Painted clay figure with ear-plugs. Chancay. *Museum für Völkerkunde, Berlin*

51 — Inca aryballus. *Photo, Archaeological Museum, Cuzco*

52 — Painted clay plate. Inca. culture. *Museum für Völkerkunde, Berlin*

53 — Carved wooden beaker. Ollantaytambo. *Museum für Völkerkunde, Berlin*

54 — Figurine of llama in gold. Inca style. *Museum für Völkerkunde, Berlin*

55 — Embossed silver beaker. Inca period. *Museum für Völkerkunde, Berlin*

56 — Sacrificial bowl in the form of a fish. Environs of Cuzco. *Formerly in the Museum für Völkerkunde, Berlin*

57 — Stone figure of an alpaca. *After Bennett*

58 — Rock engraving from Alto de la Guitarra. Chavín style. *Photo, H. D. Disselhoff*
59 — Rock engraving from Cerro Mulato. Tiahuanaco style. *Photo, H. D. Disselhoff*
60 — Rock engraving from Majes Valley. *Photo, H. D. Disselhoff*
61 — Rock engraving from Majes Valley, probably from the Inca period. *Photo, H. D. Disselhoff*
62 — Ornamental plaque in bronze. Diaguite culture. *Formerly in the Museum für Völkerkunde, Berlin*
63 — Urn with painted figures. Diaguite culture. *Museum für Völkerkunde, Berlin*
64 — Clay figure with engraved decoration. Environs of Tumaco. *Museum für Völkerkunde, Berlin*
65 — Stone seat. Manabí province. *Museum für Völkerkunde, Berlin*
66 — Engraved and painted clay urn. Màrajó I. *After Palmatary*
67 — *Tanga* of fired clay. Marajó I. *After Palmatary*
68 — Sacrificial figurine of gold. Muisca style. *After Bennett*
69 — Head of a clay figure. Muisca style. *Museum für Völkerkunde, Berlin*
70 — Clay figure in negative painting. Western Colombia. *Museum für Völkerkunde, Berlin*
71 — Polychrome clay bowl. Quimbaya area. *Museum für Völkerkunde, Berlin*
72 — Lid of a large urn. Mosquito style. *Museum für Völkerkunde, Berlin*
73 — Monumental stone figure. S. Agustín culture. *After H. Nachtigall*

ACKNOWLEDGMENTS

The following institutions and private persons kindly allowed reproduction of the coloured plates listed below:

Koninklijk Instituut voor de Tropen, Amsterdam 21, 96
Stöcker Collection, Amsterdam 68
Museum für Völkerkunde, Basle:
Lucas Vischer Collection 70, 74
Bernouilli Collection, Basle 143, 163
Museum für Völkerkunde, Berlin 43, 141, 144, 145, 146, 166, 167, 188, 191, 194, 227, 228, 229, 234
Fritz Buck, La Paz 168, 169
Miguel M. Gallo Collection, Lima (reproduced by kind permission of Messrs. Aurel Bongers, Recklinghausen) 193
Norbert Mayrock Collection 192
Sra. Machida Armila Collection, Mexico City 45

Museo Nacional, Mexico City FRONTISPIECE, 19, 24, 44, 46, 47, 48, 71, 92, 93, 94, 95,
Private Collection, Munich 140
Museum für Völkerkunde, Munich 98, 139, 142, 189, 192, 198,
Private Collection, Peru 177, 193,
Museo Nazionale Preistorico ed Ethnografico 'Luigi Pigorini', Rome 50
Lindenmuseum, Stuttgart 164, 165,
Lindenmuseum, Stuttgart (on loan from the Württembergisches Landesmuseum in the Museum für Länder- und Völkerkunde) 69, 91
Robert Woods Bliss Collection, Washington, D.C. 67
Private Collection, Zurich 170, 176, 203

The coloured illustrations listed below were kindly supplied by:

F. Anton, Munich 140
A. Assmann, Hamburg 168, 169
Photographisches Atelier Braumüller, Munich 142, 189, 190, 192
W. Bruggmann, Winterthur 3, 19, 24, 25, 44, 45, 46, 47, 48, 49, 67, 69, 70, 71, 74, 91, 92, 93, 94, 95, 143, 163, 170, 187
H.-D. Disselhoff, Berlin 231, 232

S. Linné, Stockholm 23
R. L. Mellema, Amsterdam 21, 50, 68, 96, 98, 139
J. Neumann, Paris 193,
M. Schliessler, Baden-Baden 230, 233
Photographisches Atelier W. Steinkopf, Berlin 141, 144, 145, 146, 166, 167, 188, 191, 194, 227, 228, 229, 234

Hella Appeltofft, Stockholm, was responsible for the drawings in Part I and Elisabeth Armgardt, Berlin, for those in Part II. The maps were drawn by Hannes Pixa, Baden-Baden, on the basis of data provided by the authors.

PART I: THE ART OF MEXICO AND CENTRAL AMERICA
by Sigvald Linné

I. PREHISTORIC AMERICA AND THE EARLIEST INHABITANTS OF MEXICO

"When we saw so many towns and villages built out over the water, and others on dry land and on the straight smooth causeway leading to Mexico, we were astonished, and declared that this was like the wonders related in the Book of Amadis, on account of the huge towers, pyramids and other buildings, all of stone, that rose above the water. Some of us soldiers even asked ourselves whether all we saw might not be just a dream."

Thus wrote the dauntless conquistador Bernal Diaz del Castillo when he accompanied Hernando Cortés on his ambitious enterprise, the conquest of the great empire of the Aztecs with a force of only 400 men.

His army had reached the Valley of Mexico and was drawn up on the southern shore of Lake Texcoco. Its line of march now lay along the causeway to Tenochtitlán-Mexico, the island city of the Aztecs, at that time probably one of the most populous cities of the world. So began the last and briefest chapter in the history of ancient Mexico. But when did the first act take place in the drama: the arrival of primitive man in America? And what took place between that early dawn and 8th November 1519, the day when the conquistadors caught sight of their destination, shimmering like a mirage far out on the lake?

Mexico can boast of a long and rich history, but the chapters of it that are recorded are fairly brief. The earliest discoverers of America were able to cross from north-eastern Asia to Alaska by the isthmus which is now the Bering Strait, without noticing that they had set foot on a different continent. The masses of ice that covered the earth during the Ice Age held so much water that the sea level was about 300 ft. lower than it is at present. 11,000 years ago the ice melted, the sea-level rose, and the isthmus became a strait. Later immigrants who came to seek their fortune in the New World had to use some sort of sea-going craft. But as even today the Bering Strait is only 53 miles wide at its narrowest point, and one can see across from one shore to the other, and as there are islands which afford convenient resting-places, the most primitive rafts were able to make the journey. It has been held that latecomers such as the Navaho (Navajo) did not arrive until 2000 years ago. Today their descendants are settled in Arizona, where their rapid rate of increase is giving rise to some concern. But long before their arrival immigration was taking place. One is continually coming across traces of these early adventurers. If the evidence of C-14 datings is to be believed, camp-fires were lit in Lewisville, Texas, some 37,000 years ago, and over 23,000 years ago there were primitive hunters living at Tule Springs, Nevada. These are just a few examples of the many that are available.

The radio-carbon dating method discovered by Willard F. Libby and later developed by other scholars is based on the following principles:

At high altitudes part of the nitrogen in the air is transformed by cosmic rays into C-14. C is the chemical term for carbon, and 14 is the radio-active isotope of carbon. This radio-active carbon is absorbed by plants in the form of carbon dioxide, and as animals and human beings live directly or indirectly off vegetation, all organic matter becomes radio-active. When death takes place, this assimilation process is halted. The radio-active carbon present disintegrates; the older a particular specimen of organic material is, the less radio-activity it will have. The disintegration of radio-active carbon takes place at a constant rate, with a 'half-life' of 5568 ± 30 years. [1] By comparing the radio-activity present in an archaeological find with that of the carbon to be found in a living plant the age of the material in question can be established. There is a new method of dating that is even more promising. This thermoluminescence technique was tested by Dr. Leon Knopoff, of the Institute of Geophysics in the University of California, on Mexican pottery of known date, and gave the actual date with a margin of error of 60 years. More thorough studies are not as yet available, but we may confidently expect other methods of determining the age and origin of archaeological finds to be devised.

The arrival of the first immigrants is coming to be backdated to the ever more remote past. This presents a difficult problem. According to the archaeologists American man is older than Siberian man, and there is little affinity between them. The term 'Mongoloid' is applied loosely. A number of scholars have claimed to have established Caucasian characteristics in the case of the anthropologically varied Indian peoples, and assumed that interbreeding took place while they were still in Asia. We are also confronted with the question where the differentiation of the 140 American languages occurred. There is no evidence that man immigrated prior to the last glacial period, or that seafaring peoples sailed across the ocean from South-East Asia in later ages.

Much time elapsed before remains of extinct animal species and well-shaped spear-heads provided conclusive evidence of human activity. A likely claimant to the title of 'Mr. Oldest American' is Midland man, who

Midland man

MEXICO

HUAXTECS

TOTONACS

TARASCANS

Tajín

Tula

Teotihuacán
Mexico ◯
Cholula

Xochicalco

TOLTECS
AZTECS

MIXTECS
Monte Albán

Mitla

ZAPOTECS

Tres Zapotes

La Venta

Ma...
Uxm...

Palenque

Bonampak

GUAT...
Kaminaljuyú

MEXICO AND CENTRAL AMERICA

featuring the present-day states and the principal Indian peoples now living there.
The sign ■▪■ denotes the ruined cities mentioned in the text. The main centres of
art in Panama, Chiriquí, Veraguas and Coclé, are also shown.

N

Chichén Itzá

BRITISH
HONDURAS

á

HONDURAS

LVADOR

NICARAGUA

COSTA RICA

CHIRIQUÍ VERAGUAS COCLE

PANAMA

13

FIG. 1 — *In 1925 bones of a species of bison (bison taylori) that later became extinct, and a spear-head of a special type, were found near Folsom, New Mexico. The latter was made of a flint-like material; it has a curved cutting edge and a broad groove along the centre on either side. Points such as these are among the oldest art objects in America. Approx. 10,000 years old. After Covarrubias.*

FIG. I

must have died some time between 13,700 and 11,300 B.C. Certain finds in Nevada, Texas and California, details of which have not yet been published, are said to be 37,000 years old. Of course, anything is possible, but more information is needed before these claims, apparently based on C-14 datings, can be accepted. In the south-western United States there are numerous finds about 10,000 years old of extinct animal species such as the mammoth, mastodon, prehistoric horse and camel, as well as a pre-historic species of bison, together with spear-heads and implements suit-able for cutting up venison. The oldest grave known to us dates from about 8000—6000 B.C. This is a grave containing remains of cremated persons. The body was interred in a tomb with a stone facing, together with his earthly belongings, stone scrapers and weapons with stone points. Twigs and brushwood were placed on top and then set on fire.

So far as we can tell the oldest Americans seem to have had a Palaeolithic hunter culture, although some of them were food-gatherers rather than hunters. Their diet consisted of seeds, grains, smaller kinds of fruit, roots and similar means of sustenance. Thus it is by no means surprising to find that millstones were used as long ago as 8000 B.C. They are thought to be two thousand years older than the earliest ones known in the eastern hemisphere.

Already at an early date the whole of America came under human occupa-tion. According to C-14 measurements men lived in Chilean caves 9000 years ago, and were contemporary with extinct animal species that lived in the southernmost part of South America 8000 years ago; it is thus not sur-prising that the oldest Mexican should have lost his life hunting mam-moth near Tepexpan in the Valley of Mexico as early as 10,000—12,000 years ago. The next oldest finds of primitive man in the Valley of Mexico come from a grave at San Vicente Chicoloapan, discovered in 1958; these remains date from about 4000—5000 B.C. The stone implements were crudely shaped but the size of the obsidian spear-heads suggests that they were javelins. The javelin-thrower (*atlatl*) may have been in use already at this time. That this characteristic means of increasing the leverage of one's arm was known at an early date can be deduced from the fact that the men who migrated into Australia when the Bering Strait was still an isthmus had spear-throwers. The bow had not yet been invented. As

FIG. 2 — *The advanced cultures of ancient Mexico had a predilection for the portrayal of gods or symbols associated with gods. Before the 'classic period' artists were not bound by such religious dogmas but showed far greater imagination. Tlatilco, Valley of Mexico. After Groth-Kimball.*

prehistoric Mexican man could also boast of fine grinding-stones, he is thought to be an intermediary type between a hunter and an agriculturalist. His predecessors were first and foremost hunters, but were also food-gatherers. He was first and foremost a food-gatherer, but was also a hunter. These are small patches of light in the darkness of Mexican prehistory. Some 3000 to 4000 years ago — the exact date is uncertain — the food-gatherers and hunters began to turn to agriculture. This earliest culture is known only in an advanced stage, the middle of the archaic pre-classic period, from 900 to 500 B.C.

ARCHAIC ART

The Indians were distinguished botanists. There was not a single cultivated plant of importance—maize, potatoes, manioc, tomatoes, pineapples, brown beans, ground-nuts, melons, chilli, tobacco, quinine, the coca plant, etc. — that was not already familiar to them before the coming of the Europeans. Tilling of the soil provided the basis for a new culture; for settlement and food-storage gave security and made possible an orderly community life. With this came the worship of new gods. Study of the rhythmic movements of the heavenly bodies provided the basis of astronomy, chronology and mathematics, and a form of writing was invented. Better types of dwelling were required both for men and their gods, and this led to the development of architecture. But the Tlatilco agriculturalists were not so different from us. They gathered edible berries and engaged in fishing and hunting. Their houses were built of sun-dried brick, *adobe,* which disintegrated and reverted to it original earthy state. The material used for building temples was the same and met the same fate. But the people themselves did not perish in this way. With agriculture and all the good things which it brought in its train for mankind the population grew, perhaps ten-fold, and continued to increase in spite of natural and man-made catastrophes.

This was the dawn of civilization. And now the sun suddenly rises.

At Tlatilco, a brick-kiln situated to the south of the Mexican capital, finds were discovered which gave its Aztec name, 'the place where something is hidden', a deeper meaning: delightful clay figurines, featuring cheerful scantily-clad girls performing a dance. Venus Tlatilco has taken a great deal of trouble over her hairdress and in painting her body in lieu of clothing. She is not an established deity, but personifies to the early agriculturalist the ideal of womanly beauty. For here there are no

FIG. 2

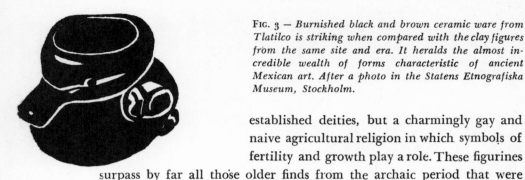

established deities, but a charmingly gay and naive agricultural religion in which symbols of fertility and growth play a role. These figurines surpass by far all those older finds from the archaic period that were discovered earlier in the Valley of Mexico. Artists belonging to this same people have also produced astonishingly well-designed vessels in the form of fish and birds; although these are only represented in outline, they are vividly portrayed and frequently manifest a humorous touch which is otherwise, apart from a few exceptions, hardly the *forte* of Indian art. Only the advanced peoples of the Peruvian coast can claim to have produced anything comparable. But their work lacks the playfulness, naiveté and humour found in that of the Tlatilco artists. In north-western Mexico archaic art may have survived right up to the Spanish conquest; here still greater scope was allowed to the imagination, creative ingenuity flourished, and there was a wealth of spontaneous humour. The potters here abounded in original inspiration, and their work shows that their fate was in the hands of benevolent spirits.

This is the picture presented to us by the primitive era. But the earliest cultures are fully developed, and each of them is a world of its own. The differences between them can be so pronounced that it is difficult to find a common denominator for their artistic ideals. But precisely this is characteristic of ancient America.

If we leave out of account 'culinary culture', i.e. the kitchen and all that goes with it, and also the fact that the utensils invented in antiquity are (with some exceptions) the same as those used nowadays, each culture appears to be a chapter unto itself. The situation could be illustrated by

FIG. 3, 4, 5, 6

FIG. 7

FIG. 4 — *The swimming duck (Fig. 3) and this bird, staring ahead foolishly, testify to a close observation of nature and an ability to perceive detail and capture essentials. Valley of Mexico. After a photo in the Statens Etnografiska Museum, Stockholm.*

FIG. 5 – *This vessel in the shape of a fish is an example of the creative talent of the potters of Tlatilco. After Covarrubias.*

an analogy drawn from the world of drama: the curtain rises, the play is acted out, the curtain falls, only to rise again. The actors are new, but the drama is the same.

In part, perhaps, there are new gods, new ideals of beauty and a different attitude to life. The stage-manager has an easy task Of the dramatic properties of prehistoric times the most important have survived: *metate,* a stone slab on which boiled maize was ground with a *metla-pilli* (metate's son, who does the grinding); bowls for grinding Spanish pepper with criss-cross incising on the floor; kitchen ware and some stone implements and spearheads.

At Cuicuilco, not far from Tlatilco, an early settlement lay hidden beneath a great stream of lava from a volcano in the mountains skirting the valley to the south. This modest counterpart to Pompeii met its doom in 500 B.C. From the layer of lava there rises a circular building of the stepped variety, once the base of a sanctuary. From an architectural point of view this monument is of no particular interest, but it must be America's oldest known building.

It is one of the tasks of the archaeologist to trace the development of a culture and the stratification of successive cultures. Those who study the advanced cultures of ancient Mexico will, as has been mentioned, find that the earliest cultures are fully-fledged in their main features (i.e. both in the material

FIG. 6 – *Clay vessel from Cerro de las Mesas in the state of Veracruz, an ancient hitherto unexplored city in which cultures and styles of different periods blended with one another. This elegant vase has spirited decoration incised with absolute sureness of hand. It can equally well be assigned to 'Olmec' as to archaic culture. After a photo in the Statens Etnografiska Museum, Stockholm.*

FIG. 7 — *Flat clay figure of a very primitive type akin to the human figures of the 'archaic period' from the Valley of Mexico. Two perforations in the area of the neck indicate that it was worn as a pendant ornament. Higueras, Colima. After a photo in the Statens Etnografiska Museum, Stockholm.*

aspect and to some extent in the spiritual aspect as well). And wherever the evidence comes to a stop, archaeologists have drawn analogies with parallel cultures in South America, which sometimes involve fantastic journeys in space and time. But it was not until the discovery of the finds at the brick-kiln of Tlatilco that the questions they raised could be given a positive answer.

Those scholars who devoted themselves to the study of Peruvian antiquities — I am thinking here in particular of Dr. H.-D. Disselhoff, Director of the Ethnological Museum, Berlin, and his predecessor, Prof. Walter Krickeberg, doyen and leading expert in the field of American studies — discovered a startling affinity between the pottery of Tlatilco and of the pan-Peruvian Chavín culture in regard to the shape of some vessels and their decoration. This has been established by Dr. Disselhoff after many years of study, during the course of which he has carried out a number of excavations. The latest information shows beyond all doubt that the advanced civilizations of ancient America have a common root and go back to a time when the various features that later became characteristic of Central America and the Central Andes had not yet become differentiated.

The art of the earliest Monte Albán culture and of the early Gulf Coast culture coincided in time with the dissemination of domesticated plants, in particular of maize and cotton. Some scholars hold that Peru was the centre of origin, while others adhere to the view that it was Mexico that influenced South America.

By making a cross-section of a settlement, or a place where a village or temple was situated, the student can arrange the art objects and artefacts he finds by strata — it is as though one were reading a book written in the soil. Sometimes the text makes for easy reading, as for example in the Valley of Mexico, but at times confusion arises where one comes across a culture that has not yet been defined or classified, in which case no interpretation is possible.

1   In the latest research the figure given is 5760 ± 30 years.

Female clay figurines with remains of painted decoration, from Tlatilco and other sites in the Valley of Mexico. Such figures date from the late archaic period and can be divided according to their style into several groups. For during the lengthy archaic period the various peoples developed their own generically related styles which, though difficult to distinguish, can serve as a guide in ascertaining the origin of their products. These figures are neither representations of gods nor portraits, but an attempt on the part of primitive agriculturalists to obtain a plentiful harvest by invoking the aid of magic forces. In a similar way fields in Africa are said to have been 'manured' by magic figures. *Museo Nacional, Mexico City.*

This whimsically modeled terra-cotta figurine of an athlete, a relic of the Zacatenco culture, was unearthed at Tlatilco and dates from about 800 B.C.

This stoutly-built female figure, with thick legs and thin arms, is a fine example of the ancient art still practised in the state of Nayarit. It is not a representation of a goddess but of some unspecified woman. Female figures such as this are not unusual. The skirt has an attractive design and the body is sparsely painted. Round the ears are several rings. The hair — or the false plaits common among women in archaic times and still met with among Zapotec wo nen in Oaxaca — is artistically dressed. *Koninklijk Instituut voor de Tropen, Amsterdam. Height 99 in.*

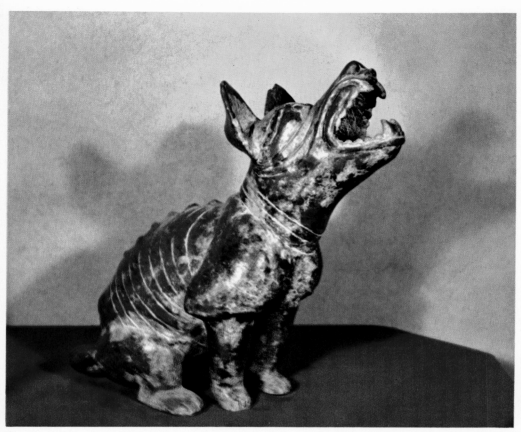

Howling dog in red terra-cotta, a relic of the Colima culture of western Mexico. The Colima, Nayarit and Jalisco cultures were cut off from the major pre-Columbian cultures of Mexico by the formidable Sierra Madre Occidental. Because of this isolation, their arts developed more slowly than those of the central Mexican cultures.

The Pyramid of the Sun at Teotihuacán, the largest building in America after the damaged pyramid at Cholula. It has suffered greatly from deliberate damage, centuries of neglect and well-intentioned but unskilful restoration work. The crowning temple is missing. It is 213 ft. high; the sides measure over 720 ft. and the total volume is 1,300,000 cubic yards. It has lost its painted stucco facing, which ran parallel to the surface at a distance of several feet. Stone and cement have now given it a durable, but false surface. The pyramid has thus been reduced in size. Several tunnels have been driven into it, which have shown that the work was carried out all at once.[1] The Cholula pyramid near the town of Puebla, which was larger in volume than the Cheops pyramid, contained a large number of different pyramids built over one another at different periods, as has been shown by tunnelling: the total length of the tunnels is about four miles. The innermost and therefore oldest pyramid dates from the same period as the Pyramid of the Sun, and may be even older still.

Dog in clay, from the state of Colima. This charming canine breed is nowadays almost extinct. Such dogs were hairless and unable to make any sound whatever. When fattened for the table, they were regarded by the ancient Mexican epicure as the daintiest of morsels, and were relished much more keenly than jaguars, which were unpalatably tough. These *techichi* were sold on the market at Tenochtitlán-Mexico together with other food-stuffs. The Spanish conquistadors also developed a taste for this delicacy, which after the destruction of Tenochtitlán was mainly sold at the present-day town of Acolman, northeast of the capital. *Museo Nacional, Mexico City. 16½ in. x 9¾ in.*

Hollow clay figure from the state of Jalisco, representing a hunchback holding in his left hand a staff ▶ which rests on a fish with a head at either end. The man is probably a mythical or legendary figure. In certain parts of ancient America hunchbacks were a common motif in ceramic ware. They were also found in the households of the prince of Tenochtitlán in Mexico and the Inca rulers in Peru — a custom paralleled in the princely courts of Europe at the time, where the jester was frequently a hunchback. *Museo Nacional, Mexico City. 16½ in.*

Mask encrusted with mosaic of green stone. The mosaic consists of square pieces of turquoise and small pieces of red shell. Masks of this kind are referred to by some authors as funerary masks. They may have been used in burial ceremonies and death rites. But so far not a single mask has been found which clearly indicates what purpose they served. The mask shown is thought to originate from the present-day state of Guerrero. Since this state, twice the size of Belgium in area, has hardly been explored by archaeologists, many debatable problems have been disposed of by assigning works to this area. A string of light red beads in affixed to the pierced ears. There is however some doubt as to the authenticity of this association. *Museo Nacional, Mexico City. Height 9 in.*

II. THE ART OF THE WESTERN REGION

Western and north-western Mexico are areas that have aroused less interest among archaeologists than among looters. It transpired that the art objects made here could fetch high prices on the international market. Only a few systematic studies have been carried out, but plunderers have been only too active in making excavations of their own. Although Mexico seems to be an almost inexhaustible treasury of monuments of ancient cultures, the time has surely come to take a keener interest in Nayarit, Jalisco, Colima and Michoacán. For in those areas archaeologists have so far confined themselves to conjectures and vague generalizations about the likely course of events. So long as only few facts are available, or none at all, to assign objects to the period 500—1521, as is sometimes done, is almost worse than to forego any attempt at dating whatsoever.

The secular art of antiquity originated, as has been mentioned, in western and north-western Mexico, in the states of Nayarit, Jalisco, Colima and Michoacán. The vast wealth of material, mainly human and animal figures, may be classified into three groups: the Nayarit style (finds from Nayarit and the adjacent parts of Jalisco), the Colima style (from Colima and the adjacent parts of Jalisco), and the Michoacán style (from the third area mentioned). A fourth area, Guerrero, may also be distinguished. In some parts this region of the country is little known, but in other parts the road leads the visitor directly to well-known places frequented by wealthy tourists. The pillage carried on and the skilful reproductions of stone implements made in Guerrero cause Mexican archaeologists much consternation. So far as the other areas, which have yielded thousands of clay figures, are concerned, conditions are scarcely any better. Here, too, in most cases looters have been at work.

In western and north-western Mexico the archaic style survived over a long period, while in central Mexico even the most recent of the pre-classic styles had already been superseded by the beginning of our era. What is the reason for this? The answer may be that the states of Guerrero, Michoacán, Colima, Nayarit and Jalisco lacked contact with those religions which in the south gave regularity and system to artistic production. It is possible that the cultures in the west existed from the 4th century onwards, but all such chronological and cultural data must be treated with a good deal of reserve.

Taking as our criterion the art they produced, these cultures may by and large be classified in two groups: Nayarit and Colima. But artistic centres

PLATE P. 21

PLATES PP. 24, 25

FIG. 8 — *Men carrying clay vessels on their shoulders or backs are among the most popular figures in the ceramic ware from Colima. But in this instance a humorous note is struck: the jar would fall off the back of the crawling child were it not for the strap around its forehead. After Groth-Kimball.*

are of course not marked off from one another by political boundaries. The Nayarit style is also to be found in those parts of Jalisco situated close by, and the Colima style is also indigenous in the regions of Jalisco adjacent to Colima. It is nothing short of a national scandal that this area has been totally neglected by Mexican archaeologists and that a great deal of pillage has been allowed to occur. This also applies to most other areas, in particular perhaps to Guerrero and Oaxaca.

In spite of the great distances in space and time involved, the art of this vast area is closely interrelated, and bears no resemblance to that of any other area of Mexico. But with its human characteristics it is so much closer to our own conceptions than the refined elegance of the high cultures, with their profound symbolism. We have to go all the way to Peru to find pottery in which human and animal figures are fashioned so vividly as they are here; in Peru, however, the models convey an attitude of Indian stateliness.

The art of everyday life

Pyramids on which temples — the abodes of the gods, as it were — were erected are lacking in this part of the country. In art the commonplace prevails; the expert potter is still unconcerned with theological problems and is free from religious ties and the constraining effect of tradition; his work therefore does not comprise deities in human guise but expressive timeless representations of the present moment. The artists of antiquity display little profundity, but devote themselves entirely to portraying the simple things of life. This enduring reflection of private joys and sorrows makes for a human style closer to our conceptions than the exclusive refinement of the high cultures.

The small figures, mostly solid, of the archaic period are followed by large hollow ones with an aperture on the crown of the head. As there was now risk of fragmentation during the drying and firing process, it was possible to make larger figures and to obtain the size one desired.

28

The artists were enabled to imbue their sculptures with lifelike vigour and to free themselves from the limitations of frontal symmetry. They concentrated upon the essential and characteristic features, making simplifications as they thought fit, without regard for naturalistic representation. Each figure has a personal touch; it is filled with life, and differs completely from the human beings and gods of later periods, which are uniform in character—slavishly exact copies of images of deities fashioned by artists of virtuosity in clay, stone or in sacral pottery, with the gods and demons depicted in perfunctory fashion, often reduced to mere ornamentation.

Some of the heterogeneous pottery overflows with youthful vigour. The Nayarit style arrests our attention by the way in which grotesque features have been deliberately exaggerated. One also comes across caricatures, no doubt kindly in intent. The Colima style is more refined; the figures convey a sense of elegance and Indian repose, but also bear a certain resemblance to the works of the Nayarit sculptors. The fact that they are not simply the result of faulty observation of nature is shown by the accurate representation of such animals as dogs, armadillos, ducks and snakes. The dogs, which are of the hairless breed and have a certain charm about them, belong to a species that is practically extinct today. PLATE P. 24 A well-fed hairless dog, *techichi* or *tepescuintli,* was no doubt regarded by an ancient Mexican epicure as the very king of beasts; and the Spanish conquistadors, too, appreciated this delicacy. But the dog also had a higher function to fulfil: he was his master's guide into Hades, and on his death followed him into his grave. Already at Tlatilco such *techichi* were found in graves.

Not all the figures, however, depict men slavishly carrying out their daily routine. Frequently, wearying of inert frontal symmetry, men are portrayed demonstrating their virility with club, helmet and harness, as mighty warriors, or playing ball, summoning up all their strength for the final blow. One man, a hunchback, is represented standing on a most curious fish with a head at each end. Here we leave the everyday world for that of myth and mystery. Unfortunately we have little hope of learning anything about this individual, propelling himself forwards with the aid of a fish which zoologists would certainly not accept as a real creature.

FIG. 9 — *This figure wearing a fan-like ornament on his back is thought to be a ball-player holding a ball in his right hand. He has also been identified as a man in close combat hurling a stone, but his cheerful and genial expression suggests that he is a ball-player rather than a warrior. Colima. Stendahl Galleries, Hollywood.*

III. TEOTIHUACÁN

The various unnamed peoples of archaic times have their own discernible artistic peculiarities. In the course of centuries the differences between them became ever greater. Already before the beginning of the Christian era there was erected in the Valley of Mexico a circular pyramidal structure of the stepped variety. It provides the first evidence of the power exercised by the priestly caste. The priests observed and studied the movements of the heavenly bodies and secured their power by acting as intermediaries between men and their gods. From a host of anonymous deities the first ones to become prominent were the god of fire and the rain god — the oldest of the hidden forces that gave the farmer his daily bread.

In the first centuries A.D., after gathering strength during a late archaic epoch which can be subdivided into several periods, the high cultures of Mexico suddenly burst into life. This first golden age, the 'classic epoch', is marked by an incredible amount of activity, a great quickening of the pace of cultural development. The question naturally arises as to its causes. The cultivation of a new kind of edible plant may possibly have afforded leisure time, which could be used to exorcise evil demons. The use of leisure is indeed an ever-present problem. Curiously enough each cultural centre can boast of an individual style of its own: Teotihuacán, Tajín (terms given later to denote the political and religious centres of two unknown peoples) and the Zapotecs in Oaxaca and the Maya in northern Guatemala, south-eastern Mexico and western Honduras. It is not known how and why these cultures developed, or what accounts for the total disappearance of the peoples to whom the two first-mentioned cultures owe their development. The Zapotecs and Maya live on today, have languages of their own, and are increasing in numbers.

Each culture has its own distinct style and artistic ideals. Everything, from ornaments to pyramids, bears witness to the fact that expert hands were at work. Just as one can trace the development of Spanish painting from the Renaissance to our own day in the work of a handful of artists of genius, who stood out from a more or less undifferentiated mass, so also in ancient Mexico there must have been great artists who left a lasting imprint upon the style of their people. Later these men found emulators, and as their work was carried out under the supervision of a powerful priesthood, major deviations from the basic orthodox style were not permitted.

The city of pyramids

Teotihuacán is situated in the Valley of Mexico, about 30 miles northeast of Mexico City. Apart from two exceptions from a later period in northern Yucatán, Teotihuacán is the only real city in ancient Mexico; all the other towns were no more than religious centres. Once a place of pilgrimage, it is today the most important point of interest in the country, a centre of attraction for countless tourists. This crumbling city covers an area of some seven square miles. The remains of the secular buildings are hidden beneath fields of maize, plantations of cacti and simple dwellings. When the city was destroyed and later abandoned the roofs and walls collapsed. The sun-dried brick *(adobe)* of which it was built reverted to earth and fields of maize. The sacred area contains two imposing pyramids, of which the crowning temples have unfortunately been lost, as well as a gigantic plaza in which ceremonies were performed and a splendid processional avenue, forming the north-south axis of the city, flanked by temples and ruined palaces; all these edifices were built in a uniform style of *adobe* daubed with dazzling white or red stucco; this often formed the ground for extensive murals.

In 1932, assisted by the owner of a plot of land and some of his friends, I unearthed the ruin of a small house or palace which lay beneath a field of maize. I was led to make this excavation by the fact that I had caught a glimpse of fine flooring in white and red shimmering through the earth at the roadside, where the ground had been worn down with the passage of

FIG. 10 — *Schematic representation of the ruins at Xolalpan, Teotihuacán. The west side is 102 ft. and the south side 131 ft. long. A low altar stands in the centre of the courtyard, which is surrounded by four platforms, with flights of steps leading down into it. Behind these are rooms and inner courtyards, with depressions in the centre of the rooms.*

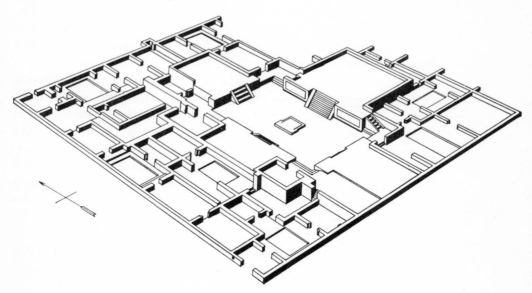

time; the owner of Xolalpan complained about the hard floors which he had to break up to obtain a hole large enough to plant *maguey* or nopal cactus. The first-mentioned produces pulque, the latter a fruit full of seeds and rich in vitamins. The complex of Xolalpan measured some 1200 square yards in area and consisted of several dwellings grouped around a courtyard, in the middle of which was an altar that no doubt served a religious purpose. From the point of view of comfort, neither the owner's hut dating from 1932, nor his newly-built house with electricity laid on, were comparable to the ancient palace. In 1934 and 1935, together with some old friends of mine, I examined the remains of another complex, Tlamimilolpan. This was a conglomeration of 175 rooms built around a rather large number of courtyards, as well as a network of corridors; it gave the impression of a rectangular village pressed in on all sides. The part of the site which we excavated was 4000 square yards in area.

Excavations at Teotihuacán We began work in a section which we took to be the centre and continued our excavations until the rains made them impossible, without reaching an external wall. As in the complex we had excavated first, so also here the rooms, which had no windows, were arranged around a central area with an opening in the roof. Under this opening was a depression in which rain-water could collect; this was then drained off beneath the floors and out of the house. When rain-water was to be collected in this basin, the conduit could be closed by stopping it up with finely-polished stone plugs. Such plugs were found *in situ*. We can be almost certain that these houses had no upper storeys, and that the flat roofs sloped inwards towards the inner court where the water collected. From time to time these unusual dwellings were reconstructed; but, so far as I could make out, there were no practical reasons for moving the walls, or covering the fine floors, still in perfect condition, with a filling upon which new floors were then laid.

These two houses are suggestive of hotels rather than permanently inhabited dwellings. Teotihuacán, like all the towns of those days, was a place of pilgrimage frequented by countless people at religious festivals and at market-time. But it also seems to have had some permanent inhabitants. Later the existence of larger houses was proved, above all at Zacuala. These ruins, unearthed between 1955 and 1957, cover an area of some 5000 square yards. They contain a large number of lavish murals depicting many deities who appear at Tenochtitlán at a later date. This is not surprising, as it was hardly possible for the inhabitants to vanish completely, even though the city did lose its former importance. The ruler of Texcoco, Nezahualcóyotl (*d.* 1470), regarded himself as a successor of the priest-kings of Teotihuacán.

At least two deities, those who played the most important part in agriculture, the rain god Tlaloc and the god of fire Huehuetéotl, held a higher rank among the host of deities at Teotihuacán, but the number of gods was increased by the inclusion of minor deities. Water and fire were more important than anything else, for there was sunshine in abundance. The oldest deities fulfilled the same functions from ancient times until the introduction of Christianity, and they have certainly not been completely displaced even now. Some gods may have been born and have 'hibernated' in this area until the Aztecs of Tenochtitlán took them over from the descendants of the priest-kings of Teotihuacán and incorporated them into their great pantheon. Others may have been born in Teotihuacán, but have come to Tenochtitlán by way of Tula, which was inhabited by the Toltecs. This group may perhaps include Quetzalcóatl, Chalchihuitlicue.— the female counterpart to Tlaloc — and Yacatecutli, the god of merchants.

The Pyramid of the Sun is the largest monument in ancient America. It was built within a single architectural period, as has been established with the aid of tunnels driven into the pyramid. [1] The sides measure over 720 ft. and it is 213 ft. high. Vast amounts of building material must have been carried to the site, since neither wheeled vehicles nor draught animals were available. For the construction of the Pyramid of the Sun over 1,300,000 cubic yards of *adobe* were needed; including all the other buildings, the total quantity required will have been several times greater than this. When restoration was carried out between 1905 and 1910 the top layers of the pyramid, which had been badly damaged by vegetation and rain, were removed. Originally the surface was painted and faced with stucco. The Pyramid of the Sun has thus been reduced in height and the surface has taken on an utterly strange appearance, that of the stone-casing which is thought to have run parallel to the original surface and about 13 ft. beneath it. To prevent rain-water disintegrating the *adobe* under the surface, Leopold Batres, who was in charge of the restoration work, had the interstices between the stones filled in with mortar. Worse still was the fact that the upper part of the monument assumed a different shape. Of the crowning temple, which must have been of considerable size, not a vestige is left. In spite of everything this gigantic edifice is most imposing.

The unusual interest in architecture shown by the ancient Mexicans is a matter for astonishment, and raises the question how it was possible for the rulers of the country to persuade their impoverished peasant subjects to engage in such heavy toil to carry out their will — that is to say, the will of the gods. The work must probably have been performed by

Pyramid of the Sun

mobilizing the whole population to defend the state from the powers of evil. The administrative mechanism by which food, drink and accommodation was provided for those employed in building and decorating the city deserves as much admiration as the workers and artists themselves. Both the Pyramid of the Sun and the smaller Pyramid of the Moon only acquired their names at a later date. It is not known which gods they were erected to honour. They probably had nothing to do with the sun or moon.

The great temple plaza The architecture of the temple plaza is austere and practical. There is a pyramid, in the same style as the embankment walls of the square complex of buildings, which are surmounted by a platform and are 440 yards long. This pyramid, which is built in front of and over another stepped pyramid, is lavishly decorated with figures in relief and great heads sculptured in the round, such as those of Quetzalcóatl, 'the plumed serpent', and Tlaloc, the god of rain and water. The writhing body of the serpent is chiselled in relief between sea-shells and snails, and forms a background to the splendid heads, alternately of the serpent and of the rain god. Below this imposing frieze is the writhing body of a plumed serpent with its head modelled in relief. The occurrence of molluscs suggests that they, too, live in the water.

The pyramid consists of six platforms of decreasing size, all decorated in a completely identical manner. As all sides bore the same vividly-coloured ornamentation, and a thin coating of stucco, the whole monument must have been a stately and unbelievably splendid symphony in honour of the life-giving power of water, and at the same time a constant prayer to the water gods from a land parched by the sun's rays. These highly-stylized heads possess a disquietingly barbaric beauty. Even though we are not able to understand fully the mysteries of the plumed serpent, of its abode and function, nevertheless this magnificent monument from early Teotihuacán tells of the immense amount of labour and devotion expended on it by the men who fashioned these gigantic heads and complex reliefs with simple stone tools. There are many stages in the development of Stone Age art, and this edifice unquestionably dates from one of the phases when it reached an apogee.

The more recent terraced pyramid was constructed in the same way but was ornamented solely with paintings. In style it follows the other monuments of the temple plaza, or 'ciudadela' as it is called. The façades of the terraces have an austere and rigid form which recurs everywhere in Teotihuacán — also in the dwellings, hotels and small palaces which we unearthed.

Teotihuacán is built of *adobe;* the walls are made of stone and clay, and the stairways, too, are of the same material. The top layer of mortar and plaster bound it all together. When it was destroyed everything made of earth disintegrated and turned into earth again. There are not many remarkable examples of monumental sculpture. Although we may harbour feelings of respect for the so-called 'Diosa del agua' figure, measuring 10 ft. 4 in. in height, which was found close to the Pyramid of the Moon, we do so rather for its size than for its artistic merit. On the front face of the massive single square block of lava a female figure has been roughly carved out. This figure represents a goddess, as is shown by the short shoulder cape of the meticulously chiselled *quechquemitl*, a garment still worn today in some remote villages of the central Mexican plateau. As early as 1889 this figure, weighing 23 tons, was taken to the National Museum in Mexico City. It must be one of the most ancient giant statues of Mexican gods, but it is exceeded in size by the giant statue at Coatlinchán near Texcoco, carved in the same style. This figure measures 23 ft. x 14 ft. 6 in. x 12 ft. 6 in., but is unfinished and has not been carved quite free from the rock in which it was hewn.

The stone masks of Teotihuacán are ageless. Carved in natural size, they are graceful and, in a true Indian manner, devoid of any emotional expression. They are believed, for no very good reason, to originate from the state of Guerrero, to the west of the Valley of Mexico, where in days of yore skilled stone-masons carried on their craft. Their modern successors carve in much the same way as they used to; they make, in addition to simple tourist trophies, stone masks which bear such a close resemblance to the old ones that they are often taken for genuine antiques. The same material, the same motifs — and fashioned by the descendants of the ancient artists! Since they know well how to conceal the traces, they nowadays use labour-saving tools. What then is genuine art? I personally prefer to regard myself one of the doubters. For practical purpose Guerrero is still a blank patch on the archaeological map of Mexico, and it is easy to dispose of works of disputed origin by ascribing them to this area. But with what mastery — despite simplification and stylization — have these sculptors succeeded in reproducing Indian racial characteristics which no camera can really capture.

Teotihuacán masks

FIGS. 11, 12

A predominant place in Teotihuacán ceramic art is taken by the hundreds of thousands of small clay figurines and cylindrical vessels, mounted on three hollow feet, mostly rectangular and with a flat base, a conical lid is sometimes added as well. The designs were either incised or painted on a thin coating of finely tempered stucco. This fragile chalky surface forms an excellent foundation for mineral colours, usually yellow, red and green. The 'classic' Teotihuacán tripod is a rare phenomenon among ceramic

FIGS. 13, 14, 15, 17

FIG. 11 — *Stone 'mask' with teeth and eyes of shell and mica. It may be a portrait of an inhabitant of Teotihuacán or the image of an unknown god venerated by an unknown people. S. Linné Collection, Stockholm.*

objects the world over. In shape it resembles a copy in clay of a metal vessel. A potter would shudder at the idea of making a vessel in such a shape. This type of pottery is so characteristic that even a small potsherd discovered far away from Teotihuacán reveals close affinities with it. In a grave found beneath the bottom floor at Tlamimilolpan were buried a large number of cylindrical tripods; some of them were not decorated and were 'classic' in style, but for the most part they had thick walls with a projecting curved rim, conical feet and geometric designs, and were in a primitive style that may be considered 'pre-classic'.

The clay figurines differ in type, although only within certain limitations. Some of them no doubt represent certain deities. The head-dress varies, but this always excited the imagination of the artist, especially when he had an opportunity to reproduce a feather ornament. One type that occurs frequently is completely devoid of any decoration at all. As with most of these figures, it is mould-made and lightly worked over. Although these are factory products the heads, measuring some 1¼ in. in height, show considerable artistic achievement; they are, as it were, monuments in miniature. Unique in character are the figures with movable limbs. Perforations were bored right through the body, and on the arms and legs as well; with the aid of cords the limbs could thus be attached to the torso. Usually the heads were fashioned at the same time as the body, moulds

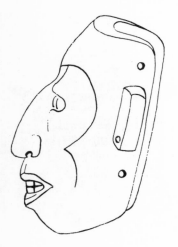

FIG. 12 — *Schematic sketch of the 'mask' depicted in Fig. 11, showing the depression on the back and the four perforations on the sides. This 'mask' must have been affixed to something, but to what, how and why we do not know. S. Linné Collection, Stockholm.*

FIG. 13 — *Sacred clay vessel from Teotihuacán. These had no practical function. Since we have to rely for our knowledge of religious concepts entirely upon monuments and artefacts, interpretation must await detailed iconographic studies. Xolalpan, Teotihuacán. Statens Etnografiska Museum, Stockholm.*

generally being used. The function of the figures is not known, but it is not beyond the bounds of probability that they may have been used as toys. The fantastic number of heads, arms and legs points to their use in some magic ritual. In a child's grave at Xolalpan from the Teotihuacán culture I did, however, discover two figures fashioned in the same mould, which may well have served as toys.

Moulds were also used for making small decorative details, which were affixed to the vessels while still damp. I have also discovered hemispherical bowls completely covered with an extremely complicated design.

In 1932, when excavating the graves below the floors at Xolalpan, we found 'classic' clay vessels and also pottery that was in complete contrast to these vessels. The former bore ornamentation that had been scratched after firing and the grooves filled in with cinnabar. The practice of ornamentation with figures is no doubt connected with rain and water rites. The scenes were composed in such a way that it was possible to see the whole of each group, extending over about a third of the surface of the vessel. The ideas that motivated these designs have long been forgotten; an attempt to ascertain them is a fascinating adventure, comparable to trying to solve an equation with several unknown quantities. We have to make Aztec mythology our starting-point and proceed by way of the Toltecs to arrive at that of the Teotihuacán people.

But the rain god Tlaloc, as has been mentioned, can be traced throughout all periods. He is not represented in disguise, but is recognizable by his face, his

FIG. 14 — *A comparison between the murals and ornamentation on pottery from Teotihuacán with the religious motifs of the Aztecs shows that this clay vessel must have been dedicated to the rain god Tlaloc, the god of a peasant people. Xolalpan, Teotihuacán. Statens Etnografiska Museum, Stockholm.*

serpent's tongue, his snakes and flowers, the rings round his eyes, and his various other attributes — all constant prayers addressed by the agriculturalists of that early period to the life-giving rain god.

Pottery from other areas

FIGS. 19, 20, 21

But, as mentioned above, a completely different type of pottery was also found in the graves below the floors at Xolalpan. Most of this consisted of small bowls upon which was incised a design in the form of an 'S' with dots. The most characteristic feature, however, was the material: this was thin and hard, either yellowish-red or light orange in colour. This ware would repay more detailed study. It undoubtedly dates from the 'classic' period, between 200 and 600 A.D. Mineralogical tests kindly carried out by colleagues of mine at the Natural History Museum in Stockholm showed conclusively that they were imported. Identical finds from Kaminaljuyú near Guatemala City have been analysed in North America. Everything tallied except the results — or, to be more accurate, nothing tallied until it became clear that both we in Stockholm and Dr. Anna O. Shepard, the leading American authority on archaeological pottery, were referring to the same thing in different petrographic terms. The Gordian knot was untied without resort to drastic measures. But the following problem still remains: the light orange colour spread outwards by trade from a centre that has yet to be identified where there were expert free-lance potters. Where were these works produced, and how were they exported? Why did this type of pottery form an independent group, with designs having no connection with the aesthetic ideals illustrated by the clay vessels from the other culture of that time? This export trade continued over a long period and extended to places situated far from the area where the pottery was produced, such as Tlaxcala, Teotihuacán, Tula, Jalisco and Colima, southwards to Monte Albán and Mitla in Oaxaca and south-east as far as Kaminaljuyú and Copán in Honduras. These products were the work of men who were not only skilled in the potter's art but were also gifted merchants. It was indeed a major feat to export such fragile ware across vast distances on the backs of human porters; they might have had to cross 'iron curtains', i.e. areas inhabited by peoples who spoke different languages and

FIG. 15 — *Some decorative elements can easily be identified, but others show a strong conventionalism, indicating that these peoples had made great strides from representation towards abstraction, from the image to the hieroglyph. Xolalpan, Teotihuacán. Statens Etnografiska Museum, Stockholm.*

FIG. 16 — *Ceramic ware which in style anticipates 'classic Teotihuacán' was found in a tomb under the lowest of the three floors in the palace at Tlamimilolpan, Teotihuacán. Statens Etnografiska Museum, Stockholm.*

belonged to different cultures, who, if not actually at war, as a rule mistrusted one another. It is not surprising that this yellowish-red pottery should be popular and in great demand: these bowls were exceptionally fine, elegantly shaped and of exquisite material, thin, hard and smooth; they were fashioned in shapes that departed from the tradition of the uniform tripod vessels and those designed for everyday use. It was, so to speak, the 'genuine Chinese porcelain' of ancient Mexico.

It is remarkable that the material used, as petrographic tests have shown, originated not from Teotihuacán or the plateau region, but from some tropical area. One Mexican scholar claims to have located the actual spot: Ixcaquixtla, in Tepexi department, South Puebla. But so far no information about these unusually important findings has been published.

From Central America we as yet know only of about 20 'whistling vessels' — double-bodied jars connected by a vent at the base. One vessel is open, and the other closed except for a whistle fashioned in the shape of a bird, for example. When water is poured into the open vessel and runs into the closed one air is expelled, thus operating the whistle. Such vessels also occur in the yellowish-red material mentioned above. As they were produced between 200 and 600 A.D., this raises another interesting problem: the whistling vessels of South America, of which thousands have been discovered, are coastal ceramic ware dating from 1000 to 1450

FIG. 17 — *The eternal god of rain, and probably of wind, is portrayed on this lid of a cylindrical tripod found empty, as is the case with all funerary vessels, in a tomb under the lowest floor of the ruins at Xolalpan, Teotihuacán. Statens Etnografiska Museum, Stockholm.*

A.D. There are, to be sure, also some dating from an earlier period, but they were not so widely distributed at that time. This suggests that the two inventions were made independently in Mexico and in South America. The connections that existed between South America on one hand and Central America and Mexico on the other during pre-Spanish times are as yet far from clear. But it is known that south-western Mexico was open to stimuli from the south and that the coastal area of Ecuador was influenced from the north.

PLATE P. **43**

The cosmic powers and gods that performed secret functions or scudded across the face of the earth on rain-clouds must have been a friendly and agreeable band. The paradise of the rain god, Tlalocan, as it is depicted in a mural found in 1943 at Tepantitla near Xolalpan, not far from the Pyramid of the Sun, gives the impression of one of the better-class tourist advertisements. This is not art of high quality, but it is cheerful, genuinely naive, and for this reason arresting; in this land of the dead it overflows with life, movement and happiness. Men, trees and flowers are painted in different colours on a red ground. From the lake in the centre of the land of the dead two rivers flow in different directions. Here grow sapota and cacao-trees, bushes and maize; here life is lived to the full; people dance, sing and bathe — the different styles of swimming suggest lack of practice! — but these apparently asexual people show no feelings of tenderness. One can imagine voices acclaiming in word and song Tlaloc's mercy and the glory of his domain. He was no doubt the mightiest of the gods, who every year could send the rain that was so essential for a farming people.

Fig. 19 — *Clay vessels of thin yellow and red material with fanciful ornamentation and a form completely alien to Teotihuacán have been found in tombs in association with Teotihuacán tripods (cf. Figs. 13—5, 17). Petrographic analysis shows that they were imported from a tropical region. Statens Etnografiska Museum, Stockholm.*

FIG. 20 — *Bowls with an annular base and elongated S-shaped lines and dots, applied before firing, comprise the greater part of the finds at Xolalpan and Tlamimilolpan, Teotihuacán. This is borne out by a site dating from the Teotihuacán period in the state of Tlaxcala, where the soil is yellow and red over a wide area owing to the large amount of ceramic ware which the peasants smashed while ploughing the fields. Statens Etnografiska Museum, Stockholm.*

The Aztecs believed that those who were drowned or killed by lightning entered Tlaloc's domain, as did many unfortunates who suffered from internal injuries, contagious diseases, gout or similar ills. But now all their sufferings are eased, all their ailments cured. From the right a man can be seen on his way to paradise, but he does not enter it. Well-meaning commentators have suggested that he is exulting at having reached his goal and is shedding tears of joy — he is perhaps a healer reunited with his patients. Normally an angular line from the mouth is used to suggest speech and song; all the figures in this mural are speaking or singing, but the man going to paradise has five such 'signs of speech', which are moreover adorned with flowers and butterflies. Mexicans versed·in such matters have said that he may be a politician, to whom paradise remains closed despite all his fair words.

When, how and for what reason Teotihuacán was transformed from a flourishing city into a ruin we do not know. Probably a slow decline set in, until eventually an alien people took possession of part of the city, and were followed in turn by Aztec settlers. The first people to arrive there were Toltecs, who came from the north. Their capital, situated north of the Valley of Mexico, is said to have been in existence between 856 and 1168. But a fairly long time must have elapsed between the abandonment of the town and its settlement by the Toltecs. In unearthing the ruins of houses near Xolalpan dating from the period of efflorescence

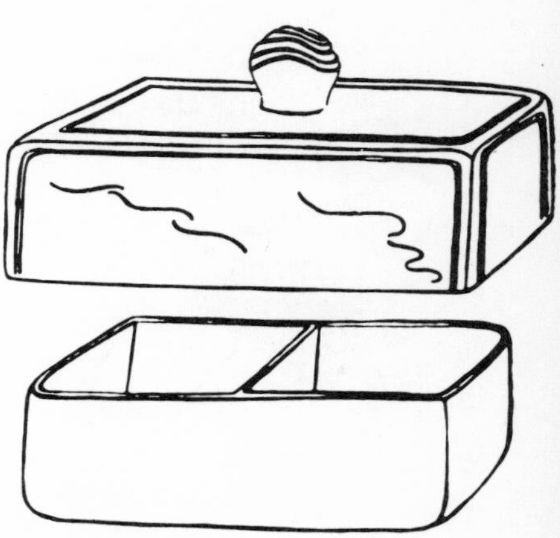

FIG. 21 — *This little chest with two compartments and a lid is one of the most interesting clay vessels from Teotihuacán. It is a practical object with a timeless quality about it, such as one might find on sale, made of modern material, in any store. Museo Regional de Teotihuacán.*

FIG. 22 — *In a ruin dating from Teotihuacán's age of grandeur are some paintings of great interest. The murals from Teopancaxco show, inter alia, two priests standing opposite one another in lavish attire and wearing magnificent head-dresses. Signs of speech leading from their mouths indicate that they are chanting sacred or benedictory songs. After Krickeberg.*

I was able to establish that the new settlers were not familiar with the walls only about 3 ft. high that were found below a low hill on which they had settled. Their houses were mainly built of *adobe*. That the town was unimportant in Aztec times is clearly shown by the fact that, with very few exceptions, Teotihuácán is not mentioned by any of the chroniclers; and where a reference to it does exist, this is only in order to relate some improbable legend. Only in our own day, some one thousand years later, has this town again become a place of pilgrimage. January 1960 saw the launching of a bold and optimistic plan of exploration, excavation work and restoration which, if it materializes, will probably yield exceptionally valuable results. Everyone with an interest in the history of art and culture, and of town planning as well, will eagerly await the information that emerges from this ancient city as it is brought to light.

A mound fairly close to Xolalpan, where the author unearthed the ruins of a house in 1932. It contained collapsed walls with extremely well preserved murals. Of particular interest among these murals is one depicting the Paradise of the Rain God, or perhaps the Land of the Dead. It is indeed a veritable paradise, the dream-land of a peasant of those early times. All the figures are cheerful; they are playing and dancing, and are all shown in movement — a sharp contrast to the rigid and punctilious stone or clay human figures in ancient Mexican art. This illustration shows the central part of the painting. Tepantitla, Teotihuacán. *Size of detail 33½ x 39⅜ in.*

The Zapotecs, who created one of the most important civilizations of ancient America, were preceded by two peoples who lacked their vitality and power of resistance and who subsequently intermingled with them. Two thousand years ago the Zapotecs were a powerful martial people, and even today they are still full of vigour, industrious, go-ahead and independent-minded. Benito Juárez (1806—1872), Mexico's most eminent statesman, who repelled the French invaders and laid the foundations of modern Mexico, was a pure-blooded Zapotec. The figure depicted above comes from Monte Albán and dates from the second epoch, i.e. immediately prior to the efflorescent period of Zapotec culture, a few centuries after the beginning of our era. The man's face, particularly his mouth, suggests a certain affinity with the Olmecs, who venerated the jaguar. *Museo Nacional, Mexico City. Height 24½ in.*

Funerary urn, a fine example of the fully-fledged type evolved during the classic **epoch of Zapotec** culture, in or about the middle of the first millennium A.D. In spite of the number of finds that have been made we still do not know what this cylinder-shaped receptacle contained or the purpose for which it was used. The human figure represents a deity and wears all the appropriate splendid ornaments. In his left hand he holds a bag for incense. The principal ornament consists of feathers, moulded in clay. and the large head of a bird. *Sra. Machido Armila Collection, Mexico City. Height 25½ in.*

According to comparatively reliable archaeological data, the fairly tranquil centuries of the classic period were brought to an end by drastic changes. The Maya emigrated, the Zapotecs were driven out by the Mixtecs, and Teotihuacán, a city built of *adobe*, reverted once more to earth. The Toltecs who immigrated from the north built their city of Tula in what is now the state of Hidalgo; it lay to the north of the Valley of Mexico, on the border between the advanced civilizations of the south and the hunter tribes of the north. It was here that the Toltecs introduced new architectural elements such as gigantic figures and square columns with carved figures of warriors and plumed serpents, used to support the lintel over the entrances to their temples. Also of Toltec origin is this recumbent idol from Chichén Itzá, which has been given the meaningless Maya name of 'Chac Mool'. All such images of deities bear a resemblance to this figure. It is not known what purpose was served by the bowl which the god holds with both hands, resting it on his chest and the upper part of his thighs. But it is certain that this unknown deity had some function to fulfil in the supply of water from heaven. Under the heavy pressure of primitive and warlike kindred tribes from the north the Toltecs were gradually compelled to leave Tula and move towards the south. Though their temples were thoroughly ravaged and destroyed, their gods followed them on their trek, and the Maya city of Chichén Itzá in northern Yucatán flourished more vigorously during its Toltec period than any other city. *Museo Nacional, Mexico City. 41¼ in. x 58¾ in.*

Head of parrot, from the ruined city of Xochicalco in the state of Morelos. A sculpture of recent date, from the Toltec period. The form is greatly simplified and deliberately stylized to give the effect of compactness. The pierced eyes, nostrils and mouth make this a particularly lifelike impression of a fully-grown *ara* parrot, with its great beak. The contrast between this static sculpture and the dynamic and forceful plumed serpents in the reliefs on the central altar testify to the unbounded creative abilities of the Toltecs. *Museo Nacional, Mexico City. Height 22½ in.*

Head of a large clay figure of Xipe Totec, 'The Flayed Lord', the god of growth and vegetation, whose power was renewed by the skin of the human beings sacrificed to him. Their power was believed to lie in their skin, which was donned by the priest, who thus transferred the power to the god. Xipe Totec is common to the Zapotecs, Mixtecs and other southern peoples. The head above was discovered at Otátes, Veracruz. *Museum für Völkerkunde, Berlin. Height 8 in.*

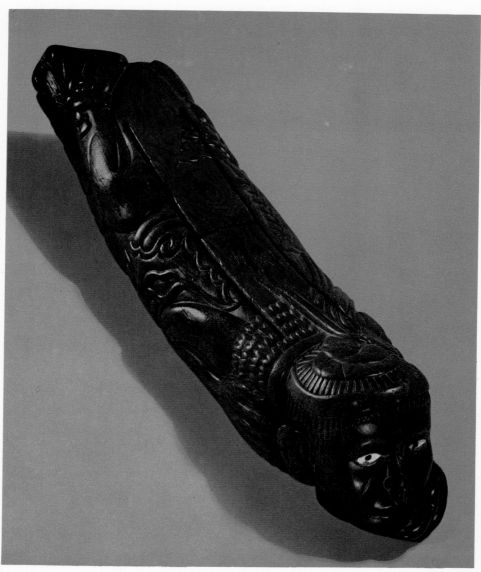

Wooden gong (Aztec: *teponaztli*), probably from the city of Tlaxcala. It is fashioned from a hollowed-out tree-trunk. The base is open, and on the top are two tongues of wood, each of which produces a different note when struck. The gong, one of two which have been preserved, is lavishly decorated with ornaments; the eyes are inlaid with mother-of-pearl and pyrite. The orchestras of ancient Mexico only had a small number of different instruments, such as rattles and conch-shells of various kinds, pan-pipes and whistles, several types of trumpet, and standing drums (*huehuetl*) with membranes of skin; stringed instruments were entirely unknown. The gong above is a magnificent product of Mixteca Puebla culture. *Museo Nacional, Mexico City. 23½ in. x 6 in.*

Spear-thrower (Aztec: *atlatl*). Part of it is lavishly decorated with sculptures and covered with a thin sheet of gold. The specimen above is an exceptionally well preserved example of an Aztec ceremonial weapon; it was probably produced by Mixtec craftsmen for the Aztec prince who ruled over them. For this reason such spear-throwers are associated with the extremely vague term 'Mixteca Puebla culture'. But it was the inventive Toltecs who actually introduced the *atlatl* as a weapon for use in battle and for ceremonial purposes. This precious object was most probably in the collection sent by Cortés in 1519 to the Emperor Charles V, or at any rate must have been brought to Europe shortly after the Spanish conquest of Mexico. *Museo Nazionale Preistorico ed Etnografico 'Luigi Pigorini', Rome. Length 22⅜ in.*

But it was not only Teotihuacán that could boast of such violent and explosive development. The same phenomenon also occurred in Oaxaca – at Monte Albán, the sacred town of the Zapotecs, and along the Atlantic coast, where the cultural centre of Tajín still keeps its secrets, and among the Maya, who were a world unto themselves.

All manner of conjectures have been advanced regarding the antiquity of the remarkable culture of Teotihuacán. But since reliable data are lacking, these ideas have necessarily remained tentative. It is true that common sense and comparative studies have enabled some headway to be made, but the goal was only within sight when radio-carbon (C-14) dating began to be applied to finds of wood and charcoal. Unfortunately there were considerable inconsistencies between the various measurements. In the grave in the ruin of Tlamimilolpan mentioned above, in which clay vessels of an archaic type prevailed, a large amount of charcoal, as well as charred baskets, fabrics, etc., were discovered. The deceased person was cremated in a chamber in the ruin complex, and the grave may date from the beginning of the classic epoch. Filling was added up to the level of the top of the grave, and on all this a floor was laid some 2 to 4 in. thick. As is always the case at Teotihuacán, the floor was almost as hard as cement. Later reconstruction took place, fresh filling was inserted, and a new floor laid. The whole procedure was then repeated a second time.

The grave was air-tight and protected from any influences that could have had an effect upon the radio-carbon tests carried out by the laboratory. The result was an age assignment of 1720 ± 65 years "before the present" (1956), i.e. A.D. 236 ± 65 years. The margin of error of 65 years indicates that there is a 68% certainty that the correct date lies between 171 and 301 A.D. If the margin is trebled a 99.73% certainty is obtained for a date between A.D. 41 and A.D. 431.

All this has little to do with art, but illustrates how the C-14 method works. For the purpose of dating it is an exceptionally valuable device of which archaeologists and art historians could scarcely dare to dream before 1950. But this method is not free from error. In order to establish the date of Teotihuacán accurately one would need to undertake a fresh examination of new material from other parts of this ancient city. Our study only shows that its golden era, or 'classic epoch', began after 236 A.D., or to be on the safe side, sometime after A.D. 41 but before A.D. 431.

---

[1] Recently, however, two further tunnels have been driven into the pyramid, and the excavator reports having found a construction of earlier date than the large pyramid.

IV. THE ZAPOTECS

Near Oaxaca, the capital of the state of that name, there rises a mountain called by the Spaniards Monte Albán, which stands 1312 ft. above the level of the three fertile valleys that converge at this point. The climatic conditions here are excellent. On the top of this mountain, 6560 ft. above sea-level, are the ruins of the sacred city and place of pilgrimage of the Zapotecs. Its situation was ideal from several points of view, cultural even more than military. There were no fortifications, but through the subtropical valleys roads led from far and wide to this spot, the central place of worship of the Zapotecs. And communications are the key to civilization. The summit of the whole mountain, covering an area of over fifteen square miles, gives the impression of having been remodelled at the hands of the diligent and god-fearing Zapotecs. The part which has now been excavated, measuring 656 x 1082 ft., consists of a plaza surrounded by monuments and with other structures in the centre. This alone makes an unforgettable impression upon the visitor: in the silence of the mountain-top, high above the pulsating life in the valleys below, temple after temple stands guard over the mysteries of past ages. The gods once venerated here are now dead — but perhaps not quite, for during the excavations some very modern-looking pottery was unearthed. Among the pieces found was a large vessel with a handle, which shows that even in our own day the inhabitants of Oaxaca secretly come to make sacrificial offerings to the powers revered by their forefathers.

In the course of centuries the temples have fallen into ruin. But the silent fragments of primeval splendour have enabled Mexican scholars to gain an insight into the deeds that were performed at this site. The pyramids arranged around the main courtyard, as well as the ball-court that has been excavated after being buried under vegetation for centuries, are imposing in their splendid architecture and in the skilful manner whereby they are adapted to the environment. They give the impression of having been carved out of the summit of the mountain. The ball-court is an object of respect for all sportsmen, as it must be one of the oldest in America, the home of the rubber ball. The rules of the game are not as yet known. Later the courts were surrounded by vertical walls. High up in the centre of each longitudinal wall there projected a stone ring, through which the ball had to be propelled with one's back.

The architects of ancient America were particularly expert at building stairways, but these were not designed for purposes of communication.

They doubtless served a decorative purpose in religious ceremonies and processions. The lateral sides of the principal courtyard, on the north and south, are bounded by ruined monuments of imposing dimensions, and in the north there are also very complex edifices and other structures of various epochs. This temple area is reached by a stairway 141 ft. wide and 46 ft. from top to bottom. It is said to be the broadest in America — but whether this claim is made from patriotic exaggeration or not it is difficult to say.

Looking at all these temple platforms, we inevitably ask ourselves what purpose they can have served. Except for one monument which may have had some astronomical or astrological function, they all closely resemble one another. They are like houses in the streets of old cities, but yet at the same time each house has its own distinctive character. It is very probable that each larger town in Zapotec territory had a sanctuary where pilgrims were able to assemble for certain religious festivals — as is still the case today in several places in Mexico. Even near the church of Santiago de Tlatelolco in Mexico City, a metropolis of over one million inhabitants, at certain festivals Indian dancers foregather to fulfil a pledge to pay homage in this way to some saint who has afforded them some assistance — doubtless an Aztec god in disguise.

The Zapotecs are one of the oldest civilized peoples of Mexico. When the Spaniards arrived they could already look back upon 2000 years of history. Even more curious, however, is the fact that they are still rich in numbers and in vitality. So far as their cultural development is concerned, their golden age dates from the period 200 — 800 A.D. On Monte Albán we can distinguish five epochs. It is still an open question who the people or peoples were who gave rise to the culture of the first and second epochs. It has been held that the first buildings can be traced back to the 7th century B.C. The culture of the third and fourth epochs belongs to the Zapotecs. It is an age of unparalleled expansion, a golden age without gold. Finally there are the Mixtecs, who have an abundance of gold. Mexican scholars have for many years been attempting to establish the connections between the earlier and later periods.

2000 years of Zapotec civilization

This is an important task, but unfortunately it is rarely possible to obtain definite evidence. Two standing figures from a tomb on Monte Albán originate from the second pre-classic period, immediately before Zapotec culture reached its peak. In appearance they are extremely vital and energetic — one might say they are as unapproachable as overburdened policemen on traffic duty! Somehow they do not seem to belong to the other Zapotec clay figures, which are serene and stately. They are, as it were, strangers who do not know how to behave in better-class society.

Their eyes and mouths suggest that the mysterious Olmecs, the people of the 'La Venta' culture, also exercised great influence upon the area of Zapotec culture. Even more alien are the unique figures in relief known as 'Danzantes', supposedly representative of the earliest period on Monte Albán. Their affinity with the 'La Venta' culture is obvious, as is the fact that they originate from the epoch Monte Albán I. The dates assigned to these ancient cultures are continually in need of amendment. C-14 datings necessitate drastic revision of the chronological tables laboriously built up by common-sense methods. The accepted dating now given by Mexican scholars to the earliest period on Monte Albán is between 600 and 300 B.C. Monte Albán II, which can boast of a number of new elements and which in style differs completely from its predecessors, is generally by-passed. One prefers to linger on epochs III and IV, which are now believed to have lasted from 500 to 1000 A.D. This is the classic age of the Zapotecs. It was then that the sacred city of Monte Albán was enlarged to its present size — although now it lies in ruins; it was then that Zapotec culture developed in all the valleys of Oaxaca.

It has been established that during the latter part of the third period more than 200 archaeological sites in this area were inhabited. Many of them must have been sizable communities of diligent farmers. They no doubt brought prosperity to the sacred city and made it possible for art and architecture to flourish there.

Personally I am inclined to assign an earlier date to this period. The Zapotecs were now in close contact with Teotihuacán and probably with

advanced cultures in other parts of the country as well. They nevertheless retained their artistic individuality. Judging from paintings found in a vault on the slopes of Monte Albán, there can be no doubt that Teotihuacán artists lived and worked here, or else exerted such a strong influence upon their Zapotec fellow-artists that they became 'Teotihuacanized', so to speak.

FIG. 23 — *This Zapotec urn was given to the Museo Nacional, Mexico City by a Swedish business man from Oaxaca. The body is treated with greater naturalism than is otherwise the case with Zapotec human figures of this kind. The chest, upper arms and cylindrical legs show notched ornamentation. San Lorenzo Albarradas, Oaxaca. After Linné.*

FIG. 24 — *Urn, painted after firing, affixed to the back of a large screen. The face is authoritatively said to represent the god '5F' (Alfonso Caso's classification). The urn was found in a tomb on Monte Albán. After Caso and Bernal.*

For an archaeologist who has worked in the sacred city of Teotihuacán this would certainly seem a most edifying notion. But it is not borne out by the chronological evidence, unless an earlier date is assigned to the 'golden age' of Teotihuacán; but this, on the other hand, does not tally with my C-14 dating. Several studies in the field, authentic archaeological finds, and many dates reliably ascertained by C-14 analysis have, however, succeeded in bringing at least some order into the confusion that existed hitherto.

The Zapotec artists did not excel in the technique of making pottery. They specialized entirely in 'funerary urns': cylindrical vessels with a standing or seated figure affixed to the front like a guard. Occasionally these two component parts were blended to form a hollow figure, usually of a human being. The urns were not modelled, but were made up of several parts; occasionally the faces were mould-made. It is astonishing that these compositions, which were often very complex, should have stood up to firing. The Zapotecs were better architects than they were sculptors. To call these vessels funerary urns is only partly correct. In most cases they were discovered acting as guardians in front of the entrances to graves and stone sepulchral chambers.

But these urns were also encountered in temples, without any association with burials. One day we shall perhaps find out more about their social function. But although we are faced with an unsolved problem here, we are still able to appreciate these urns, in the form of human beings and gods, with their half-open mouths and heads larger than life-size; we may approach them with respect and gratitude, as objects of magnificent beauty from the distant past of a distant land.

No other ancient American human figures are quite so lavishly decorated as are some of the large urns in the shape of seated figures. In this case it is not a matter of artistic excess, as is best illustrated by the groups of Zapotec dancers, whose art has been handed down from one generation to the next and is peculiarly their own: they perform a dance in Oaxaca City at certain religious festivals, wearing imposing head-dresses decked out with gaily-coloured feathers. What purpose these urns served, and what they were supposed to represent, we do not know; and nothing is said about them by the Spanish chroniclers. As has been mentioned, they are met with both in (or in front of) sepulchral chambers and in temples, as sacrificial offerings; it seems that in both cases they were fashioned by the same artists. There is no recorded instance of anything having been found inside these urns.

Links between pottery and religion

It is strange that, once ceramic art ceases to have a purely utilitarian purpose, it is completely identified with religion, i.e. with death rites. For the fact is that these fine objects, which took so much skill and labour to produce, were destined to be buried in sepulchral chambers under mounds of earth.

On the basis of detailed studies carried out on the enormous number of urns to be found in museums and private collections, or which have been reproduced pictorially, Mexican archaeologists have been able to classify them into certain categories. Here, as everywhere else in ancient Mexico (apart from the north-western region, which is the exception that proves the rule), artists were the servants of religion. It appears that the deity most frequently portrayed is the rain god. Then comes the god of maize, and after him Quetzalcóatl, perhaps as a manifestation of the wind god. For in an agricultural religion rain, wind and seed are naturally the most vital secret forces; and from the earliest times to the present agriculture has been more important to man than anything else.

The image of Quetzalcóatl, portrayed as a rattlesnake decked out with rare and costly feathers, is indisputably one of the strangest representations of a deity known to the history of art. The name is equally curious. *Quetzal* is the name of a bird that has unusual lustrous green tail-feathers. *Cóatl* simply means snake, the mystical death-dealing rattlesnake. As a deity Quetzalcóatl is the king of snakes. All kinds of philosophical theories have been propounded with regard to his origin, but I wonder whether the correct interpretation may not be that which sees in him the God of Heaven (the feathers) and Earth (the snake). This dualism may then be carried further *ad lib.*: light and darkness, good and evil, rain and drought, and so on.

Figures shown wearing head-dress composed of elements identical from one period to the next may very well be associated with the veneration of some deity that is still unknown to us and probably always will be. Some gods appear already in the first period, but it is not until the third that they are present in all their splendour. In many cases one of the most important components of the head-dress, in addition to a variety of feathers, is the head of a bird.

At the end of the 10th century Monte Albán (which according to all the calculations that have been made must have extended over the whole ridge, as well as the mountain slopes where the graves were found) ceased to be a religious centre. The reason why this was so has yet to be clarified. But the sacred city, even when dead, did not lose its significance entirely. The vaults found on the slopes of the mountain, of which there are 200, are magnificent pieces of architecture, subterranean sepulchral chambers in stone. Some of them are decorated with murals, and as has been mentioned some of these paintings are executed in a late Teotihuacán style, suggesting that they may have been painted by artists from this great centre of culture, which reached its apogee at approximately the same time as Monte Albán.

Their appearance is more heavy and their lines less flowing. The funerary urns, bearing rigid and immobile seated figures, may have stimulated Zapotec painters to carry into effect, acting on their own initiative and using their own creative imagination, the intentions of their fellow-artists from the north.

The Mixtecs immigrated from the mountainous area of the north, drove the Zapotecs out from many districts, and themselves settled at several places in the valleys near Monte Albán. In the same casual way as occured frequently in Europe, the stronger tribes also took over the vaults of the weaker ones. In one of the Zapotec vaults — one from which, luckily enough, the contents have not been removed, thus enabling its origin to be established and a date to be ascribed to it — a most important Mixtec personality was interred, together with some companions on his journey to Hades. He was also well provided with precious articles which, it was hoped, neither moth nor any other corruption of time could destroy. Unfortunately that is the limit of our information. But we must be grateful for what has been preserved in this famous 'Grave 7', which was discovered on 9th January 1932, and was fortunately enough immediately examined by Dr. Alfonso Caso, the most distinguished antiquarian in the country. It is the most precious archaeological treasure ever to have been unearthed in America. *Huaqueros,* as they are called, who began to rifle graves already 450 years ago, and who are more active than ever nowadays, when even very simple clay vessels fetch high prices, discovered, in Peru at least, graves that yielded large quantities of gold. To pillage graves in those parts of Mexico where they are to be found is a most lucrative leisure occupation which seems quite blameless to those who pursue it. From a cultural point of view, however, it is disastrous, especially when the plunder at once appears on the international market through some mysterious channels, apparently without any obstacles being put in the way of this traffic. As it is, foreign archaeologists have trouble in acquiring even second-rate replicas for their institutes.

'Grave 7'

In 'Grave 7' on Monte Albán Caso discovered, among other things, a large amount of jewellery and ornaments in gold, mother-of-pearl, jadeite, agate, turquoise, bowls of rock crystal and onyx, silver and alabaster, as well as some tastefully-carved jaguar bone — all the work of Mixtec artists.

Already in the 11th century the Mixtecs, who lived in the mountainous areas of western Oaxaca, began to harass their Zapotec neighbours. The Zapotecs retreated, leaving behind them even their cultural centre on Monte Albán. That their withdrawal was complete is best illustrated by the fact that the newcomers were able to take possession of their sepulchral chambers. Thus from 1300 onwards, or shortly before, up to the arrival of the Spaniards in 1521 the most important sanctuary of the Zapotecs was under Mixtec control.

Mitla, probably the best-preserved historical monument in Mexico, became the Zapotecs' new cultural centre. The architecture at Mitla differs completely from that of Monte Albán, as well as from that of all other ancient cities. Open courts are surrounded by long buildings erected on low terraces; flat roofs are supported by six monolithic pillars in an arcade; and some buildings are subdivided into smaller chambers by interior walls. The decoration of the walls is a characteristic feature of Mitla. Both the interior and exterior walls, even in chambers where there was hardly any lighting, were embellished with specially cut stones affixed to the wall. These were arranged to form compositions, most frequently FIG. 25 with designs *à la grecque* or with zigzag and scalariform patterns, of which the dimensions are calculated exactly. They are of exceptional beauty, changing according to the position of the sun. And in spite of the enormous labour entailed in fashioning a mosaic of some one million stones with the aid only of stone tools, it must be said that the exquisite result made the effort well worth while. However much we admire these stone-

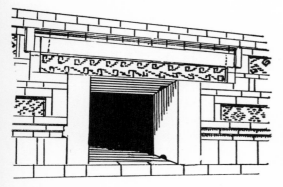

FIG. 25 — *Lavishly decorated entrance to the palace of an ancient priest-king. The construction of the palace, with enormous monoliths serving as lintels and door-posts, is characteristic of the buildings at Mitla. After Holmes.*

masons, we should not forget their colleagues who hewed out of the rock door-lintels weighing as much as 23 tons and transported them to the building sites.

After about a thousand years of slow but on the whole uninterrupted development the Zapotecs were driven to the south by the Mixtecs. Monte Albán, Mitla and many other important places had to be abandoned. But the Mixtecs were not able to enjoy the fruits of their victory for long. Soon the Aztecs carried out their successful campaigns, incorporated the country into their empire, and subjected it to crippling taxation, and then the Spanish conquest put a sudden stop to any further development of Indian culture. But although their culture was destroyed the people themselves live on; they are expanding in numbers and today form an important element of the Mexican population.

Only part of Monte Albán has been cleared of vegetation, restored, and studied by archaeologists. Mitla, on the other hand, will probably have few surprises to offer. Yagul, situated between these two sites, has been excavated in recent years, and much has been brought to light of interest to those in the field. But apart from this we know little of the antiquities in Zapotec territory. It may still yield fresh art objects of various kinds and of high quality. The soil of Mexico seems to be an almost inexhaustible hunting-ground for the things of beauty fashioned by primitive peoples when soliciting the favour of their gods.

V THE CULTURES ON THE COAST
OF THE GULF OF MEXICO

The fertile tropical region along the coast of the Gulf of Mexico saw the rise and fall of three remarkable cultures. From the point of view of the history of art they differ greatly from one another, and all we know about the peoples responsible for them is limited to whatever information can be derived from the material remains they left behind them.

The classic era of the culture of this area may be dated to approx. 200–1000 A.D. One of its most characteristic features are exquisitely-shaped stone objects that served some purpose difficult to determine. The decorative elements on these figures consist of stylized human or animal figures, scrolls and whorls. These mysterious objects are usually subdivided into four groups. Since it is not known to what use they were put, they have been named after articles to which scholars believed they bore some resemblance: 'yokes', 'palmate stones', 'ceremonial axes' and 'padlocks'.

FIGS. 27–30 In size and shape the modelled 'yokes' recall the yokes of horses. They are embellished with masterly carvings of human faces, the mask of the rain god, reptiles and toads. The 'palmate stones' (or 'palmas') are shaped in the form of a paddle and have a concave base. The 'axes' consist of thin slabs portraying a human head in profile with a simple border at the bottom, and frequently with the same border at the back. The 'padlocks' resemble abstract sculptures, with perforations and projecting buds and bulbs. The purpose of these stone figures has been the subject of much conjecture, but no clear picture has as yet emerged, chiefly because there is an almost complete lack of information as to the circumstances in which these finds were made. It is commonly assumed that the 'yokes' were used in a ceremonial ball-game, but I cannot subscribe to this view.

FIG. 26 — *Impression of a fired clay stamp. It may represent a hieroglyph in the Aztec calendar. Clay stamps such as these were used to decorate fabrics and also the human body; in the latter case this replaced the painted ornamentation normally applied to the skin. Veracruz. After Enciso.*

FIG. 27 — *It is not known for certain what this head was used for; it may be a 'ceremonial axe', although the idea seems far-fetched. Central coastlands of the Gulf of Mexico, from an unknown site. Museo Nacional, Mexico City. After a photo in the Statens Etnografiska Museum, Stockholm.*

There were two types of ball-court: it was either roughly in the shape of the letter 'I' or of two 'T's' placed base to base, and was surrounded by a wall. With the Totonacs, Maya and Zapotecs the longitudinal sides were slanting, whereas with the Toltecs and Aztecs they were vertical. The goal was a stone ring fixed vertically high up in the middle of each longitudinal wall. This ball-game was an extremely arduous sport. The players had to put through the ring a massive rubber ball weighing about 4 lbs. One was not allowed to use one's hands or feet, but only one's back and hips. The players wore pads on their backs and knees, as is clearly shown by the famous round stone slab from Chincultic, a ruined city in the state of Chiapas. The ornamentation of this relief consists of a band of hieroglyphs which show, among other things, a certain day in 590 A.D., as well as a ball-player in a kneeling posture. Both the Maya gods and, a thousand years later, Aztec professional teams played the same sort of game with massive rubber balls that was immortalized in this monument.

It seems absurd to provide a player with an ornament weighing 40 lbs. or more worn round the waist. But in Tajín there are figures in relief which appear to be wearing such ornaments. They must have been made of some lighter material; stone ornaments can only have been worn for parades or ceremonies.

On the other hand accounts of the ball-game dating from the time of the Spanish conquest and later tell of the manner in which it was played in the central Mexican highlands at that time, and compel one to believe that the rules of the game were as stated, i.e. that heavy balls were used. We have several descriptions by reliable eye-witnesses from the early colonial period which prevent us from dismissing out of hand the archaeological evidence relating to the ball-game. It is a historical fact that such games took place. No doubt they had a religious significance.

FIG. 28 — *What a 'palma' represented we do not know; nor do we know why the hands are lifted up as if in prayer. It is certainly not a fragment of a large sculpture, but an independent work in its own right, and one that manifests considerable power of observation. Central coastlands of the Gulf of Mexico. Private collection, Mexico. After a photo in the Statens Etnografiska Museum, Stockholm.*

The player depicted will probably have been honoured not as victor but as a mediator between man and the celestial powers, as the emissary of the gods.

These stone figures used once to be associated with the Totonacs, who lived in the coastal zone when the Spaniards arrived. But they have also been found far from the area inhabited by the Totonacs. They may be the work of their predecessors, but it is more likely that they derive from the same people that built the large city of Tajín on the coast near Misantla, north of Veracruz. Professor Walter Krickeberg, who is the leading authority on the Totonacs, ascribes this city and these stone figures to them. Tajín is a gigantic old city, of which only a part has so far been examined. One monument has been known since the late 18th century, and since 1935 others have been brought to light during the course of the excavations and restoration work that has been carried on. But unfortunately funds are insufficient for work on this vast area to go ahead as fast as one might like. In its day this ancient city could vie with Teotihuacán, Monte Albán and the Maya coastal towns. Its relations with Teotihuacán were so close that the tripods characteristic of this culture could be decorated in pure Tajín style. But one swallow does not make a summer, as they say, and except among specialists surprisingly little interest has been shown in this ruined city. The only pyramid known to have existed at Tajín before systematic studies were undertaken is completely different from any other in the whole of Mexico. It has seven steps, and niches were carved into the risers of each step. It is not accidental that the total number of steps comes to 364.

FIG. 33

FIG. 30 — *'Yoke' of polished greenstone from Boca del Monte, Cincatlán, Oaxaca. As far as can be ascertained the ornament features a butterfly god, pointing to Teotihuacán influence. After Covarrubias.*

Fig. 31 — *Detail of a relief from the ball-court at El Tajín, Veracruz. The priest is raising his hand, in which he is holding a flint knife, ready to strike his sacrificial victim; the latter is leaning backwards, and is held fast by an assistant. After Covarrubias.*

The calendar is an important element in the religion of the people who built this pyramid, and evidence of this sometimes appears where it is least expected. This monument was above all else the place where rites FIG. 31 were performed by a powerful priesthood before a devout but ignorant congregation; for it was the priest-king who was invested with supreme power, if not in heaven then at least on earth. Here as elsewhere religion permeated all arts and crafts.

The Huaxtecs, who lived along the lower reaches of the River Pánuco, were an outpost of the high culture to the north. Even today they still speak the same language as the Maya, although a long time ago they lost contact with their kinsfolk in the south. For this reason they were not familiar with Maya hieroglyphics and did not possess their calendar or astronomical knowledge — the brilliant product of abstract thought. The

FIG. 32 — *Reverse side of a schist looking-glass, decorated in the typical early classic Veracruz style. The mirror side consists of haematite disks. A man wearing a loin-cloth and neck-band is kneeling between loops indicating snares. A sign of speech leads from his mouth, and he seems to be turning towards a bird perched in the snares. Vega de la Torre, Veracruz. After Lothrop and Bliss.*

Huaxtecs were brave warriors who put up a dogged defence against Aztec attacks, with the result that they were never conquered by the latter.

The oldest finds of ceramic ware show great affinities with the earliest Maya pottery, both from the standpoint of style and of technique, but the Huaxtecs developed an individual style of their own. They were an independent people in every respect, who transmuted — 'Huaxtecized', so to speak — all extraneous influences. Their pottery thus has a completely individual quality and owes nothing to neighbouring peoples. The skilled Huaxtec potters fashioned original vessels in animal shape and other vessels resembling teapots; a characteristic feature is their effective black decoration on a cream-coloured ground. As sculptors the Huaxtecs were unable to vie with, say, the Totonacs in the south, but some of their reliefs and sculptures in the round are of remarkable beauty. The so-called 'Youth of Tamuín' is one of the most interesting monuments of Mexican sculpture. In the south one encounters along the coast remains of a very ancient and original culture which, like that

FIG. 33 — *Clay vessel, which to judge from its shape belongs to the pure Teotihuacán culture. This flat-bottomed vessel has hollow rectangular supports, slightly concave cylindrical sides and a conical lid. The scrolls and loops of the ornament show Veracruz influence, but the deities and aesthetic elements originate from Teotihuacán. After Covarrubias.*

of the Maya, appears fully-fledged, without any preliminary stages being evident. This may be due to the fact that vast stretches of Mexico are still blank patches on the archaeological map. It is also possible that man developed his artistic talents first by working softer materials, such as wood, thus perfecting his style and technique before he went on to stone.

The most important finds hitherto discovered originate from the ceremonial centre of La Venta, in what is now the state of Tabasco. Today this is an uninhabited area of marshy land, mangrove forests and impenetrable swamps, the habitat of obnoxious insects and all kinds of dangerous animals. At two other sites close by, Cerro de las Mesas and Tres Zapotes, the discovery was made of similar remains of an ancient people, since vanished.

According to Aztec tradition the Olmecs, a people from the rubber-growing country, lived in a Garden of Eden on the coast. But it is far from certain that this legendary people had any connection with the ancient culture found

FIG. 35 — *A specimen of the 'smiling faces' which occur frequently in most museum collections of ancient American art. They seem to originate from looted graves, for no archaeologist has yet reported finding such a figure. Intact specimens are very rare. From the Totonac part of the Gulf of Mexico coastlands. After Groth-Kimball.*

FIG. 36 — *Figure from the Olmec or 'La Venta' culture. Since this culture had long been extinct when the Spaniards arrived there is no tradition to help us to identify these strange figures, which have no apparent connection with other works of sculpture in Mexico. After Krickeberg.*

here. For this reason the term 'La Venta' has been adopted, since it was this locality that yielded most of the treasures, and the best, that this culture had to offer. Sculptors and stonemasons of incomparable talent were already at work in this area as early as 800 B.C. For these imaginative craftsmen, unsurpassed in Stone Age art, no stone was too hard or too fragile, no dimension too large, no source for their material too remote. Perhaps the finest examples of their creative talent are the great heads with no bodies attached, nor even necks, that rested on stone platforms erected before their pyramids, which were remarkably simple and unpretentious. The largest monolith of this kind is one of the four gigantic heads found at La Venta. It measures 8 ft. in height and 20 ft. 9 in. in circumference, and has been estimated to weigh at least 14¾ tons, possibly as much as 29½ tons. This points to the existence of populous communities and powerful priest-kings, such as ruled over all Mexican peoples at some time or other. If Moctezuma (Montezuma) had not been the religious leader of his people, Hernando Cortés could not have conquered Mexico.

Characteristic of this mysterious culture is a rather repellent combination of the face of a jaguar and that of a child. These round faces are to be found on the gigantic heads. The close-fitting headgear resembles a modern crash-helmet. But the dwarfish companion figures are represented resting in the arms of apparently normal-sized and asexual human beings.

FIG. 37 — *The 'La Venta' culture presents many unsolved — and, indeed, insoluble — problems: for example, how could these people, living amidst swamps and mangrove forests, transport blocks of stone weighing up to 20 tons from quarries situated some 60 miles away? After Krickeberg.*

One of the most curious motifs known to the history of art: Tlazoltéotl, the 'Mother of God', giving birth to the maize god Centéotl. At the harvest festival a priest donned the skin of a female victim who personified Tlazoltéotl, crouched on the ground before the flight of steps leading to the main temple, and went through the motions of giving birth to the infant deity. To a people for whom maize is the most important article of food this was the main event of the year. It is not very strange to find that Tlazoltéotl is also the goddess of child-birth; but it is all the more curious that she was also able to take upon herself the sins of mankind and absolve them. For the name Tlazoltéotl also means 'eater of dirt', and the priests of this goddess were able to forgive the sins of those who confessed them and atoned for them by penance. But this was possible only once in a lifetime, and for this reason confession was often postponed until old age, when most sins had lost their force of attraction — so, at any rate, we are told by the great scholar and explorer Fray Bernardino de Sahagún, who lived and worked among the scribes of the Valley of Mexico shortly after the Spanish conquest. The site where this remarkable work of art was found is not known, but it probably lies in the Valley of Mexico. *Robert Woods Bliss Collection, Washington, D.C. Height 8¼ in.*

The energetic, ruthless and bellicose nature of the Aztecs, characteristics that may have been inborn but which in any case became more pronounced during their early days in the Valley of Mexico, found varied expression in many striking works of art. As the last tribes to immigrate into Mexico from the north, they were at first treated harshly by their kinsfolk and the other inhabitants of the valley. But they soon took over control and began to rule over the area in a despotic manner. Their art, frequently brutal in character and lacking in moderation, stands in contrast to the restrained and refined quality of the earlier high cultures. This stone head — possibly a mask — is thought to portray the god Xipe Totec. *Stöcker Collection, Amsterdam. Height 4⅛ in.*

Aztec shield decorated with a feather mosaic. Various types of shield were used by the Aztecs: solid plain ones by ordinary warriors, and others with feather ornamentation by commanders and chiefs. There existed yet a third type for parades, dances and the embellishment of idols. This kind, shown above, consisted of small hard sticks of wood, set close to one another by means of fine twisted cotton threads. Lying diagonally across them were stouter sticks, to which were affixed the 'handles' for the bearer's hand and arm. The shield is mounted on leather, and the feather mosaic is stuck on to a kind of paper made by beating out the bark of certain sorts of wood. The shield above originates from the Valley of Mexico and dates from the Aztec period. Whether it was a product of the Aztecs or imported from the area of Mixteca Puebla culture will probably never be conclusively established. *Lindenmuseum, Stuttgart: loaned by the Württembergisches Landesmuseum in the Museum für Länder- und Völkerkunde. Height 29½ in.*

69

Mask of greyish-green stone, which may have been an unusually fine, sympathetic and lifelike portrait. The eyes, which now appear crudely worked, were furnished with inlays, probably of snail-shells and pyrite. Some Aztec masks, as well as those from the Teotihuacán culture, are hollowed out and perforated at the back, indicating that they must have been affixed to something. The finest Aztec masks are also decorated with sculptures on the reverse side. The mask above is part of the collection built up by L. Vischer, a merchant from Basle, in Mexico between 1828 and 1837. We thus know that it is a genuine mask, which is important in view of the number of fake 'antiquities' produced nowadays. Unfortunately Vischer never stated where he made his acquisitions. This mask is probably Late Aztec or Mixtec. *Museum für Völkerkunde, Basle. Height 4¼ in.*

A coiled 'plumed serpent', in stone. The snake played a great part in ancient Mexican religion; nowhere else are so many reptile figures to be found in the form of sculptures, or as functional or decorative elements in architecture. Rattlesnakes in stone, awesomely lifelike, coiled up and poised for the attack, are a feature of Aztec culture. But the chief Mexican reptile is unknown to natural history: the 'plumed serpent', a rattlesnake embellished with the brilliant green tail-feathers of the matchlessly beautiful *quetzal* bird (*pharomacrus mocinna*). In religious beliefs and ritual ceremonies snakes were generally connected with rain or thunderstorms and formed one of the attributes of the rain god. The 'plumed serpent' above is a fairly small specimen of this common type, and seems to be coiled in repose. The place of discovery is not known, but all the evidence points to the Valley of Mexico. *Museo Nacional, Mexico City. 8½ in. x 15¾ in.*

In 1964 the town of Bonampak in the state of Chiapas was rediscovered after 12 centuries. In one of the ▶ buildings the walls were covered with a series of murals portraying various aspects of the Maya civilization. Battle scenes, religious sacrifices, processions are all depicted.

This stone figure, which has been identified as Xipe Totec, the god of spring and sowing and the 'Flayed Lord', probably does not represent the god himself but rather the priest who served as an intermediary between god and man. The visible parts of the body are painted red; the other parts were covered with the skin of a human victim. Right across the chest there runs a sewn-up scar, through which the victim's heart was torn out of his body in a ritual manner and then sacrificed to the god. Xipe (cf. p. 72) was accepted into the Aztec pantheon under the 6th chief ('king'), the bellicose and victorious Axayacatl (1469—1483). Texcoco, Valley of Mexico. *Lucas Vischer Collection, Museum für Völkerkunde, Basle. Height 15¾ in*

FIG. 38 — *The enigmatic Olmecs could boast of sculptors able to produce fine small-sized as well as large-sized works. They scorned clay, and carved figures from hard jadeite, which was then polished, an example of which is this acrobatic dancer. Tabasco. After Bliss.*

It is clear that the jaguar must have had some connection with the religious concepts of this distant and ancient people.

FIG. 39

They not only erected fine altars and stelae, and carved figures of warriors and jaguars, but also treated the hard material of jadeite with complete assurance. Their human figures belong to a peculiar race. Thick-set, plump and broad-shouldered, they give an impression of rotundity; their arms and legs are short and fat. With apparent ease, as though they were modelling in a plastic material, the artists fashioned exquisite ornaments and figures from jadeite, amethyst, rock-crystal and obsidian; jadeite appears to have been at all times the costliest of stones. The Spaniards, too valued it highly — not least, perhaps, as an effective remedy against sciatica.

FIG. 38

The influence of this unique culture, that could boast of a highly-developed art a thousand years prior to the beginning of the age of classic culture — the first efflorescent period in Mexico as a whole — is to be found over a wide area. Tlatilco and other sites in the Valley of Mexico and in the adjoining area, in Guerrero and Oaxaca abound in evidence of the stylistic influence exerted by La Venta. It is possible that the legendary people of the Gulf Coast had an influence upon Maya culture and that it was from them that the latter adopted the calendar and the rudiments of mathematics, but this cannot be proved. It is sometimes quite a hazardous undertaking to attempt to establish tenuous affinities between two cultures the early origins of which are in each case shrouded in darkness. And 'La Venta' culture is, and will perhaps remain, one of the truly great mysteries of that land of mystery, ancient Mexico.

FIG. 39 — *This jaguar mask of brown marble is not quite typical of Olmec art, but it has been ascribed to this culture by Dr. Lothrop on account of the energy with which it is charged and its peculiarly stylized naturalism. Rio de las Balsas, Guerrero. After Bliss.*

VI. THE TOLTECS

Gradually the art of the classic age grew sterile, and the map of Mexico underwent radical changes. An era ruled over by humane gods gave place to one in which the spiritual climate was harsh and brutal. The curious cult of the dead, signs of which had been apparent already in earlier times, now began in earnest; it survives even today in Mexican folk art on All Souls' Day, not least in Mexico City with its population of more than one million. Formerly peace and tranquillity had prevailed; now there were wars and migrations of whole peoples. Where once benign agricultural deities had held sway there now appeared gods of malevolent intent.

The new civilization of the Toltecs

Between 856 and 1168, so the chroniclers record, a vigorous people, the Toltecs, developed a new civilization in the central Mexican highlands. It is thought that they immigrated from the north by way of Jalisco and Guanajuato, and that on their way they paused in their city of Tula, in the state of Hidalgo north of the Valley of Mexico, 50 miles from the capital. At Tula they had plenty of time to absorb much of the heritage of their predecessors; to a certain extent they were the heirs to the Teotihuacán culture, but they introduced into its art new elements of such revolutionary significance that we can say that they inaugurated a new era. Their was a new art with new ideals. Nothing is known, however, about the origin and development of Toltec civilization.

Tula, their cultural and political centre, has been excavated, but we are still in the dark with regard to the factors that made this people and their city so important.

FIG. 40 — *Clay vessel in black rust red, orange and white on a cream-coloured ground; it rests on three globular feet. In the middle of the bowl a fantastic figure — a curious combination of insect and ape — is performing a dance. Southern coastlands of the Gulf of Mexico. After Groth-Kimball.*

At Tula pyramids of moderate height were erected, which however had crowning temples of considerable dimensions, if one may judge by the four atlantes 15 ft. 9 in. tall which, together with square columns, supported the lintels. A new element thus found its way into Mexican architecture. Other innovations are pillars with carved warrior figures and round columns decorated with the 'plumed serpent' motif. These are not monoliths but have been carved in sections; a cone projecting from the centre of the lower section corresponds to a recess in the one above. Both the atlantes and the pillars are in three sections. This method of joining together sections to form a whole was common in the Old World from ancient times, but the Toltec architects must have discovered it independently. The atlantes and the figures carved on the columns represent warriors — yet another innovation. Particularly fanciful are the columns featuring Quetzalcóatl, the 'God of the Plumed Serpent'. They are cylindrical in shape and decorated with chiselled feathers; the head is depicted with the mouth wide open and resting upon the ground, while the tail, also squared off, supports the lintel. There are also some small atlantes carrying loads on their heads and in their outstretched hands. From Chichén Itzá we know that they supported altar slabs. The wall decorations, the reliefs featuring jaguars, coyotes and eagles tearing out each other's hearts express the mood of the new era. New conceptions are also manifest in a frieze decoration comprising rattlesnakes — reduced to head and tail — in the act of devouring skeletons. Even in the case of such exalted phenomena and figures as the planet Venus and Quetzalcóatl, the Toltecs' favourite god, we have to conclude that the benevolent deities of this new era resemble nothing so much as their antitheses.

The most remarkable sculpture in the round is a reclining figure found *in situ* in one of the three large chambers arranged round an inner court, the roof of which was supported by double rows of columns. Referred to by the meaningless Maya name of Chac Mool, this unusual and fascinating figure actually represents a Toltec. Wherever it is to be found it signifies that Toltecs lived and worked in the area. This is the case, for example, at Michoacán, Veracruz, east of the Valley of Mexico, and even as far

Fig. 41 — *Column from Tula, Hidalgo. Square columns such as these, decorated with warrior figures in bas-relief, are one of the strangest innovations made in the whole history of Mexican art. The Toltecs were also the first to make use in their architecture of caryatids and columns in the shape of serpents. After Peterson.*

to the south as El Salvador; there are also a good many at Chichén Itzá. The figure is always represented in the same posture: the man lies on his back with his knees drawn up and his body slightly raised, resting on his elbows; on his stomach he holds a bowl in his hands; his head is turned towards the onlooker, and he wears a challenging expression on his face. When the treasures of the Mexican museums were exhibited in Paris and Stockholm in 1952, and in London in 1953, the collection included a large PLATE P. 46 Chac Mool figure from Chichén Itzá. In Stockholm (where the number of visitors to the exhibition reached the astonishingly large total of 212,431) I had to warn visitors not to put offerings in Chac Mool's bowl, since he is thought to be a rain god. But unfortunately this advice was not taken seriously, and when the exhibition closed Chac Mool had a personal bank account amounting to 468.72 Swedish crowns. And the autumn of that year turned out to be exceptionally rainy!

An ancient Mexican would say that all bad things come from the north. It was thence that the Toltecs came, as their predecessors had done. But it was not until the 12th century, when the food-gathering and hunting stage of cultural development had been left behind, that their encounter with the local inhabitants led to insoluble conflict. In 1168, when the pressure became intolerable, Tula was evacuated and its people moved southwards. Some of them remained in the Valley of Mexico; others went on as far as Nicaragua, passing through Cholula; others again may have made their way to Yucatán and have united with kindred tribes who had fought on the winning side in the civil war and received as their reward Chichén Itzá.

Not until Tula was explored in 1941 was it possible to prove that they had an outpost in Teotihuacán. But as early as 1931-2 it had been established that, after Teotihuacán had been destroyed by the action of man, the wind and the weather, and when its former grandeur was no more than a legend, a people settled there whose ceramic ware was somewhat inferior artistically to that of their predecessors. It was then that the distinguished American archaeologist George C. Vaillant, unhappily no longer with us, and I carried out excavations in the area of Mazapan.

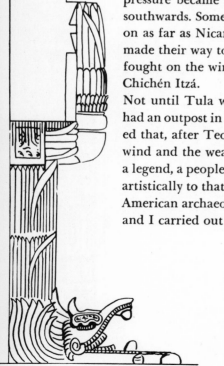

FIG. 42 — *Column in the shape of a 'plumed serpent' in the ruined city of Tula. The plumed serpent, Quetzalcóatl, was a very ancient god of water and vegetation, and also the symbol of a high priest. After Peterson.*

FIG. 43 — *Clay vessel of the so-called Mazapan type, from Teotihuacán. Before firing it was painted in a style radically different from that of clay vessels from the classic period. Vaillant and I assign this ware to the time between the Teotihuacán culture and the Aztec ascendancy. Later excavations have shown that Mazapan ceramic ware originated with the Toltecs in Tula. After Linné.*

The ancestors of the Toltecs, the architects of the city of temples that was Tula, probably attacked and destroyed Teotihuacán after it had ceased to be a powerful city. From the 10th century to 1168 they were the principal people on the central Mexican plateau. Although they adopted something of the ancient culture, they were a creative race, who excelled both as architects and sculptors; they introduced new elements, notably atlantes and columns in the shape of plumed serpents. According to tradition the Toltecs were the 'supermen' of a past golden age.

Quetzalcóatl, their leader, ruler and god, presents a very complex historical problem. There is one clue: a commander of this name led his people to the south when Tula had to be abandoned. He became a mythological figure, an old god who promised to return and rule over his sorely afflicted peoples and bestow upon them peace and prosperity. This legend became reality for the Aztec ruler Moctezuma the day Cortés landed at Veracruz. The strangers came from the east on the very day tradition designated. Cortés was undoubtedly Quetzalcóatl. Had he been an invader, neither he nor his followers would have remained alive for long.

A considerable time before the Toltecs had been forced to move on by the pressure of ruthless and barbarian tribes, other groups had also migrated

FIG. 44 — *In the ruin near Xolalpan our expedition found a large clay figure from the Mazapan culture representing the god Xipe Totec. This figure was literally in a thousand pieces, and it was only with great effort that my wife managed to piece it together again. Museo Regional de Teotihuacán. After Linné.*

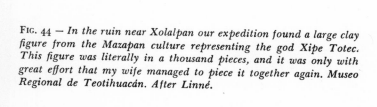

79

southwards. Chichén Itzá, a Toltec city in northern Yucatán, deserves particular mention; it is another Tula, but on a larger and more grandiose scale. To this town the Toltecs came at the end of the 10th century. But they also left traces of their passage in other places nearby, such as Xochicalco, situated in the state of Morelos, an area that is today almost completely barren. This ruined city, which always lay high above running water, was subjected to influences from Teotihuacán rather than Tula. But the plumed serpent, which played such a prominent part in Tula, is the dominant feature in the magnificent reliefs on the central monument at Xochicalco. These are powerful and dramatic representations, pulsating with life and vigour. By contrast the plumed serpents of Teotihuacán on the stepped pyramids of the 'ciudadela' seem quite unpretentious.

PLATE P. 47

FIG. 45 — *Only a single monument in the ruined city of Xochicalco bore any ornamentation: a small building which must have been the central altar. Here Quetzalcóatl, the plumed serpent, wears a particularly expressive and challenging aspect. After a photo by Linné.*

VII. MIXTECA PUEBLA CULTURE

The descriptions of Spanish chroniclers and the evidence of artefacts preserved from the time of the conquest or later enable us to reconstruct the cultural pattern in the Aztec capital of Tenochtitlán. Many masterpieces of mosaic and feather-work, pottery and pictographic codices, and last but not least ornaments in gold, that were found there were imported from Mixteca Puebla.

Most of the art objects sent to Emperor Charles V by Cortés in 1519 were probably the work of Mixteca Puebla artists. These treasures included those described by Albrecht Dürer with unaffected admiration in his diary of his journey to Holland in 1520; at that time they were exhibited in Brussels. But already in 1519 Bartolomé de las Casas, the liberator of the Indian slaves, had the opportunity of studying them in Spain. He found them "dream-like, and not fashioned by human hands."

The Emperor is also said to have given the Pope a silver fish inlaid with gold. The Holy Father showed it to Benvenuto Cellini, one of the greatest goldsmiths of all time, who was unable to fathom how it was made. It must be admitted that this makes the story seem somewhat apocryphal, for the technique was probably a relatively simple one. And even if this were not the case a man of Cellini's self-possession would scarcely have conceded that anyone could outdo him.

Among the five hundred or more precious objects discovered by Dr. Alfonso Caso in 'Grave 7' on Monte Albán in 1932 were remains of skeletons that had probably been buried there in the late 15th century. As well as the objects mentioned above that were discovered there — Mixtec jewellery in gold and silver, pearls, semi-precious stones, rock crystal, etc., and also inlaid work — the excavators found a skull entirely inlaid with turquoise, a macabre but nevertheless exquisite trophy, and furthermore 35 narrow tablets of bone, covered with carved figures.

The level of perfection attained by these craftsmen may be judged from the fact that they could fashion fine works of art out of even the hardest natural material, rock-crystal, using only stone tools, for they had neither iron nor steel.

Many Mixtec pieces of jewellery would be proudly worn by ladies of fashion in our own day. One would have to make an exception — for the

FIG. 46 — *The Mixtecs were the most advanced people in Mexico at the time of the Spanish conquest. According to Bernal Díaz de Castillo Moctezuma's table-ware originated from Cholula and was alternately black and red in colour. This jug may have belonged to the royal set. After a photo in the Statens Etnografiska Museum, Stockholm.*

time being, at any rate — in the case of the attractive and elaborate lip-ornaments, which were affixed to a disk passed through a hole in the lower lip.

Xipe Totec, 'The Flayed Lord', a deity probably originating from Oaxaca, is represented in 'Grave 7' by a small gold mask. Here divine majesty is depicted with a considerable degree of human naturalism. A man's strength was believed to lie in his skin (just as that of Samson was thought to lie in his hair); the priest would flay the skin off his victim while he was still alive, and by covering himself with it transfer its strength to the god. Women of today would probably be less eager to wear this small gold mask if they knew something of its background!

One of the deceased persons in the grave was an elderly man who must have been an important priest; the others were probably priests, too, for they have no weapons with them. But the elderly man had more pieces of jewellery than the others. Among these was a gold diadem with a plume hammered into a thin leaf. It has been put forward as a serious proposition that this ornament may have been imported from Peru, where these were worn as insignia. But all the other objects found in the grave are of Mixtec workmanship.

The traces left behind by the Mixtecs in Tenochtitlán and on Monte Albán are evidence of a mobility unusual in ancient Mexico. The term 'Mixteca Puebla culture' embraces several peoples resident partly in Oaxaca and Puebla and partly in Tlaxcala and Guerrero. But the dominant element in this cultural group were the Mixtecs, 'the people of the land of clouds', who lived in the mountainous areas of what is today western Oaxaca and who played an exceptionally important role in the time immediately preceding the Spanish conquest. Their rise to power began after the Toltecs left Tula. Some Toltecs, as we know, moved south while others remained on the central Mexican plateau. Whether they had much to offer the peoples of the countries to which they went is doubtful, but they may perhaps have acted as a catalyst, generating new

FIG. 47 — *At Teotihuacán the plumed serpent (the god of water which the Toltecs in Tula represented as a column in the shape of a serpent) lies coiled between shells and snails. On a Mixtec clay vessel in the museum at Mitla are writhing plumed serpents, showing that Toltec influence extended as far south as Oaxaca. After Peterson.*

impulses. The barbarians who forced them to leave Tula were bowmen. But was it possible for the Toltecs to have spread the bow elsewhere? Their weapon, after all, was the javelin. It is difficult to obtain an impression of their calendar system. The importance of the Toltecs is generally overestimated. It is not to them that we owe the introduction of metal-working, which came from the south, from Costa Rica or Panama. The technique gives the impression of being fully-fledged, as though the rough work had been done already. Was this done in South America, or was metal-working introduced by contact across the Pacific Ocean, between the so-called Dongson culture in China and the west coast of Peru? These are important questions which as yet we are unable to answer.

The most remarkable feature about the Mixtecs is perhaps the unique success they achieved as artists, despite the fact that they cannot boast of a very long recorded history. Their books are made of leather, frequently deerskin, or of paper from bast or bark, such as is still produced nowadays in remote villages (but exclusively for magic purposes). Most of the books preserved from pre-Spanish times are Mixtec in origin, and treat either of religious mysteries, rites and cults, or else of historical problems. Those of the former type are magnificent, and are painted in a style reminiscent of the colourful figured ceramic ware from Cholula, in the modern state of Puebla. The distinguished German Americanist Eduard Seler is renowned for his expertise in interpreting these codices. His scholarship and intuitive understanding have given his epoch-making findings lasting validity. In our own day these studies are being continued by the English scholar Cottie A. Burland. But the interpretation of the codices dealing with history and genealogy has been undertaken largely by Dr. Alfonso Caso. He has, for example, been able to trace the fortunes of the Mixtec rulers from approximately 670 to 1521, when codices of this sort ceased to be compiled. They are actually genealogical lists, giving dates of birth, marriage and death, as well as various other historical data. They are not simply dry chronicles, for the chronology of events is interrupted by accounts of the workings of supernatural powers. If these historical data can be relied on, the Mixtecs were not only heirs to the Teotihuacán culture but were also greatly influenced by the Toltecs. This, too, is a point of dispute among scholars. On their way to Tula the Mixtecs must have fertilized the culture of all the peoples with whom they came into contact.

FIG. 48 — *In 'Grave 7' on Monte Albán 30 carvings on bone were found. Here six seated figures are witnessing the birth of Quetzalcóatl. After Covarrubias.*

VIII. AZTEC ART AND CULTURE

The art of the Maya is noble and composed, of a truly Indian stateliness. In every respect it is measured and restrained. This is true also of their vital and dynamic murals. Their art keeps strictly to traditional rules, and their craftsmanship is beyond all praise.

But in an exhibition of ancient Mexican art that of the Aztecs strikes one at once as something completely different. Aztec sculptures are dramatic, full of primitive vigour and elasticity. Their art is loud; it thrusts itself forward brutally at the onlooker, who experiences, as it were, a cold blast from a harsh and cruel primitive world. Aztec art is the art of a very young, energetic and successful people; it contains elements derived from previous cultures and also more recent works in keeping with their religion — a religion that honoured the powers of death and destruction, and paid homage to despotic gods who lived off the sacrifice of human hearts and blood.

The Maya have been called the Greeks of ancient America. The Aztecs might still more justifiably be compared to the Romans. They were a small and impoverished tribe, with an unprepossessing culture, ill-treated by hostile neighbours; they were given land that nobody else wanted — small islands far out on the shallow Lake Texcoco. They were a rough and barbarous people some one thousand strong, who used the same language as the inhabitants of the densely populated towns and large villages along the shores of the lakes that lay in the Valley of Mexico.

The building of a mighty empire From these poor fishing villages they expanded their power by force of arms, skilful diplomacy, ingenious alliances and lucrative commercial connections. They were men of action, enterprising and successful administrators and empire-builders, open to external influences. But they were unable to build a genuine empire out of the multifarious peoples of the country, who spoke different languages and were at varying levels of cultural development. But from the Atlantic Ocean down to southern Mexico and Guatemala one tribe after another came to pay them tribute. Taxes poured in, and the Aztec master-race became prosperous; for their armies were merciless, feared more anxiously than fire or plague. A decisive part in Mexican warfare may have been played by the *tortilla,* a thin oatcake made of boiled or finely chopped maize. The fact that each soldier was able to carry with him his own rations, which were nutritious and needed no troublesome preparation, enabled the Aztec troops to undertake long forced marches across impassable country.

The financial authorities in the capital of their empire worked out precise and comprehensive tables of the taxes that were due; these had to be paid and delivered punctually, for one's life depended on it. Copies of the tax-tables in use when the Spaniards arrived have been preserved. They cover everything from food and clothing to rubber balls and gold. The Valley of Mexico was from an early date the goal of migrating peoples, and later it became an exceptionally rich matrix of culture. It was here that hunters and food-gatherers became the peasants who left their mark at Tlatilco. Teotihuacán arose in an epoch of cultural formation. It was here that Mexico witnessed its first efflorescent period, here that the capital of the empire was to be situated. Even today it is the focal point of culture, the capital of the United States of Mexico, a metropolis with several million inhabitants.

Until the Europeans conquered the country this valley must have afforded a fine example of what nature could offer in the way of favourable conditions for agriculture: large lakes, fresh water in abundance, wooded slopes with land suitable for tilling, and an excellent climate, with brilliant sunshine during the dry season and moderate precipitation during the rains. Today the forests have been cleared and a great deal of damage has been caused by erosion. On the shores of the largest lake, Lake Texcoco, were the settlements of people who at first made life difficult for the Aztecs but later became their allies, and finally their subjects. In our day these settlements have become suburbs of Mexico City.

The lakes have been drained off by channels dynamited through the mountains that border the valley to the north. The ground-water has been pumped up, and the bottom of the lake on which most of the city lies has dried up. The town is slowly sinking into the clayey soil, and is enveloped in dust blown off the infertile beds of what were once salt lakes. The lakes formerly acted as a moderating force on the climate, and their desiccation has led to a sharp change taking place. One has to bear this in mind if one is to understand the attraction which the valley had for immigrant peoples in ancient times.

The pressure of primitive warrior tribes from the north obliged the Toltecs to move southwards. Tula was abandoned in 1168, and it is only in our own day, nearly 800 years later, that it is re-emerging as a much-abused monument to the culture of a bygone age. In the Valley of Mexico, inhabited by the descendants of peoples of the Teotihuacán culture and Toltec colonists, a cultural upheaval resulted when the newcomers arrived. They settled in towns around the shores of Lake Texcoco such as Azcapotzalco, Cuautitlán, Colhuacán, Tlacopán and Texcoco itself. Some Toltecs moved on southwards to Cholula in the Puebla valley, and even reached Nicaragua in Central America. Already at an earlier date

Toltec migration to the south

85

other Toltecs had left Tula for the Yucatán peninsula, and as mentioned above had received Chichén Itzá as a reward for the aid they rendered the winning side in the civil war. They transformed this Maya city into a larger and more magnificent version of Tula — clear testimony to their vigour and adaptability.

In the footsteps of the Toltecs there followed the tribes who had been responsible for their southward trek. The one thing they all had in common was their language, Nahuatl, which is still the vernacular of about a million people for whom Spanish is the official language. Last of all to arrive were the Aztecs, who brought with them their steadfastness of will. Their leader, Huitzilopochtli, was deified after his death and became their favourite god. They appeared uninvited in the 13th century, at the very time fierce battles were raging between the city-states of the valley. According to various chroniclers it was only in 1318 or 1325 that they finally settled down to build towns. Several names have been given to this people: Tenocha, after a mythical ancestor, and Azteca after their primeval homeland of Aztlan. But already before they reached the valley they called themselves Mexica.

On the little islands where they settled the area under cultivation began to grow apace. The outcome of the internecine feuds between the tiny city-states proved favourable to the Aztec city of Tenochtitlán-Mexico. The history of the valley during the centuries that preceded the Spanish conquest is one of conflict, of battles and attempts at mutual extermination, in which success lay now with one combatant, now with another. The population was heterogeneous. It probably included descendants of the first peasant settlers and of the peoples of Teotihuacán culture, as well as some Toltecs and members of the primitive tribes that had driven them from Tula. The Aztecs had no forbears worthy of admiration, no noble kinsmen who cared to acknowledge their existence. By military prowess and sheer ebullience, by purposeful cunning and calculation, these parvenus rose to become rulers and succeeded in developing a civilization that was refined in externals but was largely rude and barbarous beneath the surface. They were, so to speak, the Romans of Mexico. They attained their aims by skilful diplomacy, making and breaking alliances as it suited them, and gradually expanded their sphere of influence until they were in a position to make conquests in far-flung territories. Tenochtitlán became the military and political centre of the valley, while Texcoco, on the eastern shore of the lake, was foremost in the intellectual sphere. Nezahualcóyotl, who ruled over Texcoco, is the first identifiable personage in the history of ancient Mexico. For the men mentioned in the Mixtec codices or in the various chronicles are no more than shadowy figures, genealogical ciphers or semi-legendary characters. Nezahualcóyotl was a universal genius, poet and philosopher in one, statesman, legislator and 'builder of roads and waterworks'. This most remarkable ruler, who erected a temple in honour of the Unknown God, claimed to be a descendant of the priest-kings of Teotihuacán — whether this claim was founded or not we shall never know. He helped the Aztecs to build two monuments that made Tenochtitlán chief among all the cities in the Valley of Mexico; he was also responsible for the construction of fine temples and palaces, for the beautiful gardens in his home town of Texcoco, and for a place of worship on Texcotzingo Hill. Water was carried there by an aqueduct, and since the remains of this have been preserved, as have flights of steps and recesses in the shape of elegant bath-tubs hewn into the mountain, we know that this was not legend but reality. What the chronicles have to record about this memorable man might easily be dismissed out of hand as pious exaggeration, but what we know of his great technical and administrative feats must fill us with admiration. Nezahualcóyotl died in 1472. The tales of his accomplishments as legislator, poet and philosopher, written by a relative after the Spanish conquest, have perhaps been embroidered. The 'Fasting Coyote', as he was called, has his niche in world history — not as a warrior or conqueror but as the builder of useful public works, as a poet and thinker. He belongs among the few heroes of ancient times who owe their fame to deeds of peace.

Achievements of the 'Fasting Coyote'

Nezahualcóyotl assisted his fellow-ruler Moctezuma the Elder in building a dam 10 miles long between Tenochtitlán and Lake Texcoco. Twenty thousand men are said to have been engaged in its construction — evidence of the power of organization that was feasible in those early days. Since very plentiful sources of fresh water were situated within the area enclosed by the dam, the water around Tenochtitlán, though not exactly fresh, did at least have a low salt content.

Nezahualcóyotl's second masterpiece was an aqueduct carrying drinking-water from sources near Chapultepec across the lake to the city. According to the chronicles it was built within a single year and was completed by 1466. During the siege of Tenochtitlán it was cut off by the Spaniards, on Sunday, 26th May — 'after mass', as we are told. But immediately after the town had been captured, on 13th August 1521, Cortés gave orders for it to be repaired at once. It was used for many years during the colonial era, and was abandoned only when the sources dried up. Originally the islands were small in extent, but with the growth of population they were enlarged by filling in the open stretches of water between them and by the use of rafts, which were covered with silt from the bottom of

FIG. 49 — *Aztec bowl with painted ornament. At the beginning of recorded history, about 900 A.D., a new ceramic style developed in the Valley of Mexico. Between that time and the arrival of the Spaniards four markedly different styles succeeded one another. After Covarrubias.*

FIG. 50 — *Aztec clay bowl with criss-cross incising on the floor: a 'molcajete' used for grinding 'chili', or red pepper. This bowl belongs to the fourth period, when naturalistic elements appear to have been added to the hitherto strictly geometric ornamentation. After Covarrubias.*

the lake; on the edges of these square rafts quick-growing trees were planted, whose roots, and those of plants grown on the rafts, soon reached down to the flat bottom of the shallow lake. By the constant application of silt the rafts were made into dry land, new ones continually being added. Even today Xochimilco, the 'floating gardens' south of the capital, conveys an impression of what the areas around Tenochtitlán must have been like at that time.

When the Spaniards entered the town on 8th November 1519 they found themselves marching along a well-constructed causeway. At first they passed a part of the town that had a great deal of greenery and huts built of light materials; then the ground became firmer and the houses were built of sun-dried bricks and reddish-brown volcanic rock. As they neared the centre the architecture became steadily more magnificent. Hernando Cortés, the dauntless commander of the Spanish expedition, wrote to Emperor Charles V: "Moctezuma's palace was so incomparably fair that it is almost impossible to describe its exceptional splendour. I must confine myself to saying that Spain has nothing to offer that can equal it."

As the Aztecs' power grew, emissaries were sent from the capital to conquered areas to ensure that taxes were paid promptly and that they tallied with the amounts entered in the main ledger kept in the state tax office at Tenochtitlán.

The island city was connected with the mainland by three great causeways that started from the walled temple area in the centre of the town and led north, west and south. At certain points there were gaps spanned by wooden bridges, which could easily be removed when attack threatened. Two smaller causeways enabled goods to be transported to the great market at Tlatelolco.

There is no picture extant showing Tenochtitlán in all its glory. But the earliest map of the city, which dates from 1550 and is in the University Library at Uppsala, gives one a fairly good idea of the town and its surroundings. The lay-out of the main streets, canals and causeways, the aqueduct of Chapultepec, Nezahualcóyotl's dam and much else are clearly indicated. Churches were later built on the sites of the ancient temples and on all sides of the large plaza (which still today extends over the same area that it did in pre-Spanish times), and palaces were built for the viceroy and his officials. But in the country-side the pattern of life remained essentially Indian: the people earned their livelihood by tilling the soil with primitive implements. It may be noted that the first Spanish town, built upon the ruins of Tenochtitlán, disappeared leaving even less trace than its predecessor.

Tenochtitlán was literally razed to the ground. Virtually all that remains of its buildings, so far as is known, are the foundations of two pyramids, one of which supported a double temple dedicated to the rain god Tlaloc and the tribal god Huitzilopochtli; it is the largest and most important sanctuary to be found in the extensive temple area at Tenochtitlán. The cathedral was erected at the south-western corner of the city, partly on the ruins of what had been the pyramid temple of the sun god. The other pyramid is said to have been the largest of all those in the eastern part of the city, and was situated on the small island of Tlatelolco. At Tenayuca a fairly well-preserved pyramid which has been enlarged six times and restored to perfection, gives an idea of the appearance and construction of the temple pyramids of Tenochtitlán and Tlatelolco.

FIG. 51 — *Ornament on a clay bowl of the second period, black on orange. These bowls are of the tripod type and are much more numerous than those of other kinds. After Covarrubias.*

Moctezuma himself took his uninvited guest Cortés to see the fine watchtower of the large pyramid. On 12th November 1519 it must have been difficult for strangers to enter the temple area at Tenochtitlán. We can gain a good impression of the capital from the account sent by Cortés to Emperor Charles V and from Bernal Díaz del Castillo, who wrote his memoirs in old age. From the temple pyramid at Tlatelolco they looked down upon a city of gleaming white pyramids, palaces, houses, gardens, canals, streets and markets.

Cortés then asked for permission to see the idols in the two temples crowning the pyramid. Bernal Díaz relates that in one of them an enormous stone figure was placed on an altar. The interpreters explained that this was the war god Huitzilopochtli, their supreme deity and protector. He had a broad face with monstrous repellent eyes; his whole body was covered with precious stones, gold and pearls, and round it were coiled great snakes, likewise of gold and gems; in one hand he held a bow, in the other arrows; he wore a necklace consisting of faces in gold and hearts in silver, all of them embellished with large numbers of blue stones.

The other figure was no less imposing than Huitzilopochtli. His face resembled that of a bear; his eyes glittered, for they were made of mirrors in polished stone; his body was covered with precious stones, and his girdle made up of figures like little devils with serpent tails. The name of this figure was Tezcatlipóca; he was lord of the realm of the dead. Inside there was also to be found a brazier with incense, called copal; in these braziers the priests were in the act of burning the hearts of eight men who had been sacrificed earlier in the day. The walls of the sanctuary were so bespattered with blood that they were as black as the floor, and the stench was overpowering.

In the other temple was an imposing idol, part human being and part lizard. Half the body was covered with precious stones and the other half covered with a cloak. The body of this figure was said to be filled with the seeds of all the plants of the earth, for this was the god of sowing and the harvest. Here, too, everything, both the altar and the walls, was covered in blood. And the odour was nauseating, worse than in slaughter-houses.

The Aztec Olympus included a number of other special and local deities, to our mind distinctly uncongenial. In order to be really beneficial to

FIG. 52 — *Incised ornament on a clay spindle-whorl. As late as 1932 I saw women spinning yarn on a spindle in small villages in the Valley of Mexico. The spindle-whorls were frequently of considerable antiquity. The women had a legend that the Blessed Virgin herself had placed them in their maize fields. Teotihuacán. Statens Etnografiska Museum, Stockholm.*

The Aztec god Xolotl, represented as a skeleton. He is an incarnation of the planet Venus as the evening-star. On his back he bears the image of the Sun, which shows that he was the god who guided the dead on their dangerous journey through the nether world. The symbols and hieroglyphs found on all six sides of this figure have yielded much information for the hieroglyphists — above all Eduard Seler, the eminent specialist in this field, who has made a detailed analysis of this idol, so difficult for us to comprehend. It has been worked with great skill in nephritic stone, the minutiae of the hieroglyphs being rendered with an astonishing sureness of hand. It is not known when, where and in what condition this figure was found, but it may have originated from the Valley of Mexico and no doubt dates from the Aztec period. *Lindenmuseum, Stuttgart: loaned by the Württembergisches Landesmuseum in the Museum für Länder- und Völkerkunde. Height 11¼ in.*

Limestone plaque from the ruined city of Chincultic in the state of Chiapas. The decoration, in relief, consists of a band of hieroglyphs representing, among other things, a certain day in the year 590 A.D. and a kneeling ball-player. The magnificent head-dress was certainly not worn during the game, as was the case with the corset-like girdle, from which appendages in a softer material hung down to the upper part of the thigh, the knee- and foot-pads on the right leg, and the pad on the right arm. The ball-game was probably performed as a rite; the ball may have represented the sun. But the Aztecs also showed a lively interest in the ball-game as a profane sport. The ball had to be put through stone rings affixed high up on the vertical longitudinal walls of the ball-court; the hard ball, the size of a child's head, could only be touched with one's back and knees. *Museo Nacional, Mexico City. 21¼ x 22 in.*

Cylindrical sacrificial receptacle of clay from the ruined Maya city of Palenque, with the face of the Sun ▶ God in relief and a square ornamented plaque to screen off the vessel. The eyes are enclosed within arcs resembling spectacles. The nose is aquiline and the front teeth of the upper jaw have been filed off to form a 'T'. This figure also forms the main element in the hieroglyph for the day *ik*, one of the 20 day signs, which together with the numerals 1 to 13 made up the ritual year of 260 days. But *ik* also means, among other things, air, wind, life and spirit. The Sun God and the T-shaped teeth are symbols of life, and may have other implications besides. The large pyramid at Palenque was erected over the sepulchral chamber of a powerful priest-king — the first exception from the rule that Mexican pyramids served exclusively as the bases for temples. *Museo Nacional, Mexico City. Height 45½ in.*

Clay figure from Jaina I., off the coast of the state of Campeche. It dates from the classic epoch of Maya art and is modelled in a style typical of Jaina — great art on a small scale; the human figures display an aristocratic air of superiority, refinement and restraint but are at the same time distinctly individualistic. They are thus very far removed from the rough and brutal beauty expressed in Aztec art. This plate depicts a woman, simply dressed, in a seated posture; the careful modelling makes the figure extraordinarily lifelike. Aztec art has rightly been called a triumph of inhumanity. In Maya art, on the other hand, we come across men and women who have come straight from their daily chores to act as models. They stand silently brooding, with a truly Indian taciturnity, keeping their message to themselves. Morley and other authorities assign Jaina art to approx. 600—950 A.D. *Museo Nacional, Mexico City. Height 8¾ in.*

The city-state of Mayapán held sway over Yucatăn from 1200 to 1450. The rule of the Toltecs in Chichén Itzá was now a thing of the past, and power shifted to this large walled city. The harsh military system of government was ruinous to the arts, and religion ceased to play the dominant role it had had hitherto. Mayapán has yielded a large number of incense-burners or funerary urns which, like the one shown above, were produced *en masse* of badly fired clay, and are thus porous and fragile. The figure is holding with both hands the symbol of maize and a vessel. It is a sad example of degeneration. *Museo Nacional, Mexico City. Height 21¾ in.*

'Jaguar vessel' from the Nicoya peninsula, on the western coast of Costa Rica. Black and red ornamentation on a brownish-red ground. This is an example of the negative painting particularly common in this area. The ornaments and decorative motifs were painted on with wax, and the vessel was then covered with paint; after firing the design was left in negative form on the painted ground. Such vessels also appear in Nicaragua, where there are several local variations, and there are some vessels bearing distant affinities to these in Honduras. This vessel is a fine example of the wealth of ancient ceramic ware in Costa Rica, which few lands can rival in the variety of shapes and decorative motifs, as well as of techniques. The imagination displayed is almost overwhelming. Both artist and craftsman show a masterly perfection of skill. *Koninklijk Instituut voor de Tropen, Amsterdam. Height 12½ in.*

Tripod vase from the Nicoya Peninsula. The tripod form was common in Mexico and Central America. In its more developed form the legs occur in the shape of birds' heads, snakes or grotesque animals.

Two pendants (pectorals) cast in gold, probably representing jaguar deities in human form. The jaguar god must have played an important role, since it is depicted more often than any other deity. But no traditions about it have been preserved. Costa Rican metal-workers were naturally in touch with their fellow-craftsmen in Veraguas and Chiriquí (western Panama). The ornament shown below on the left is executed in a marked Veraguas style. Of all the ancient American metal-workers the Mixtecs in Mexico attained the peak of perfection. Their refined gold ornaments were produced by artists who at the same time possessed prodigious skill as craftsmen. The next best are the goldsmiths of Colombia, followed by those of Panama and Costa Rica, whereas those from Peru, who could build upon a tradition of many centuries, outshone the more recent metal-workers of the north both from an aesthetic and a technical point of view. Gold from Coclé, Veraguas and even from Colombia reached northwards as far as northern Yucatán. Both these pendants originate from the San Isidro General region, Costa Rica. *Museum für Völkerkunde, Munich. The larger pendant measures 2¼ in. in height, the smaller one almost 2 in.*

98

man, their force had to be continually renewed. The power they required came from human blood, still more from human hearts. The Aztecs had to make one military campaign after another to take the prisoners for sacrifice to their insatiable idols. From a practical point of view their creed proved right until the Europeans arrived. It was, of course, not only religion that led them to engage in human sacrifice. It spread terror of the master race and ensured that taxes were paid promptly. It had political advantages, since the gods were particular and only the best sufficed; thus human sacrifice was a means of eliminating the best warriors of the subject peoples. But the Aztecs had gone too far. Cortés, for all his greatness as a statesman and soldier, could never have transformed Mexico into New Spain by skill and courage alone. He took advantage of the hatred for the Aztecs that existed among their subject peoples, and this turned the scales in his favour.

Had we been present when Moctezuma and Cortés climbed the pyramid we should perhaps have preferred not to make the acquaintance of these fearsome Aztec gods and the sacrificial routine of the priests — wholesale human slaughter — and should have gone instead to the market near the pyramid, the largest in the city. Goods for sale were brought here from far and near by porters or by canoe.

In one of his reports to the Emperor Cortés writes that the market at Tenochtitlán was twice the size of that at Salamanca. Bernal Díaz gives a detailed description of this market, its organization and all the varieties of merchandise that it had to offer. The order that was maintained in it was exemplary. Among the merchants were men who dealt in gold and silver jewellery and precious stones, in coats, plumes, fabrics, and clay vessels from many different districts and of many different kinds. There were also slaves, food-stuffs such as cocoa, fatted dogs, honey and sweets, leather, paper, colouring matter, flowers and much else besides. He concludes his account with the remark: "Many of our soldiers who had travelled extensively in the world, and had been to Constantinople, all over Italy and to Rome, said that never before had they seen a market of such size, so well arranged and with so many people and such a variety of wares." Specimens of some of the goods on sale have been found by archaeologists: for instance, clay vessels, stamps, spindle-whorls, spear- and arrow-heads, as well as knives made of obsidian (volcanic glass). But other crafts may

The great market at Tenochtitlán

FIGS. 49, 53

also have been represented at the market of Tlatelolco, though in a more simplified form. Among the presents which Moctezuma had despatched to Cortés was a mask and a magnificent plumed head-dress. This mask represented Quetzalcóatl, for Moctezuma believed that Cortés was this very god, who had now returned. He and his companions would now assume power, for this had been foretold in the prophecies. Cortés was also given two other masks and another plumed head-dress, in case he should wish to appear in the guise of Tlaloc or Tezcalipóca, as well as a second set of the insignia of Quetzalcóatl. Three of these masks may today be seen in the British Museum. The museum also houses, among other treasures, a magnificent sacrificial knife and a great skull of rock-crystal. These masks and a number of other items testifying to the curious objects which Spain's new subjects were able to fashion were sent by Cortés to the Emperor in 1519. Other collections also no doubt found their way to Europe at an early date. Much has been lost, including almost everything in gold, but nevertheless a great deal has been preserved. The collection in the Ethnographical Museum in Vienna, for instance, contains superb examples of feather-work, such as fans, feather shields and plumed head-dresses, as well as a turquoise shield in wood overlaid with mosaic. The masks are overlaid with mosaics of turquoise, mother-of-pearl, jet or red or white mussel-shells. Where the eyes have been preserved, they are of white shell and polished pyrite. It is almost miraculous that feather-work sent to Europe in 1519 should have survived up to the present time. The quality of perfection attained by Aztec goldsmiths is not known; the best Mexican artists in metal-working were the Mixtecs.

Aztec ceramic ware is characterized in particular by black designs on a yellow, brown and red ground; these are also to be found on cups and bowls of the ordinary and the tripod type. Every 52 years the Aztecs expected the end of the world to occur, and they would then destroy all their earthly possessions. Study of the various caches of pottery found in the Valley of Mexico, which had been deliberately smashed all at once, shows that Aztec ceramic ware can be divided into four periods (4 x 52 = 208 years). It was in 1507 that fires were lit for the last time on the summit of Mt. Iztapalapa in the Valley of Mexico, announcing the beginning of a new 52-year epoch. In broad outline the changing style of Aztec vase painting can be traced back to 1299.

The range of decoration on ceramic ware was gradually enlarged as black on a orange-coloured ground gave way to black on a lustrous red ground, with a smooth, almost glazed, polished finish, until finally there appeared black designs on a white ground, as well as stamps and spindle-whorls, FIGS. 52, 53 engraved with elaborate skill or reproduced by means of moulds.

FIG. 54 — *Obsidian skull. The eyes and teeth were fashioned with the aid of tubular bores. To the Aztecs there was nothing terrifying about death: their gods demanded human sacrifice and they used skulls to embellish their temples. After Bliss and Lothrop.*

As Tenochtitlán grew in glory and splendour, three social classes emerged. At the top were the chiefs, warriors, priests and merchants; the bulk of the population was formed by the middle classes; and at the very bottom came the slaves and unattached persons. As only some people were needed for the production of food the others were free to devote themselves to various specialized pursuits, which partly explains the rapidity with which the Aztecs were able to develop their material culture to such a pitch of refinement and technical perfection. The introduction of specialist craftsmen had the result that for the first time in the country's history the clearcut dividing-lines between the styles of the various peoples began to disappear. The Aztecs left their mark upon everything. The most important components of their style are the large dimensions, the dramatic quality of expression and the morbidity of the figures. A people that gave themselves up to the mass sacrifice of human beings must have been of a sombre, passive and fatalistic turn of mind. The fearful demands of the gods made people resigned to death. It was seen as something natural and not at all terrifying; and traces of this outlook still remain today. Aztec art often reflects a gloomy conception of life; it can be interpreted as the expression of an anguished people driven to the monstrous and the macabre. Our attitude to art and life differs radically from that of the Aztecs.

FIG. 54

FIG. 55 — *The gods of fire and water were the oldest in the Aztec pantheon. The god of fire, Huehuetéotl, who carries a bowl on his back for the flames, was known already in the pre-classic period, and the rain god Tlaloc played a leading part in all the Mexican civilizations. Every mountain had its Tlaloc, who gathered the rain clouds and scattered them over the sky. After Peterson.*

Like the Romans the Aztecs had a large pantheon. Their own deities played the most important part, but their far-reaching connections lead them to adopt those of other peoples as well. This pantheon was, however, not well ordered; some gods had different names, while others appeared in various guises and had functions that overlapped.

FIG. 55 — There was no supreme god, but the four most powerful ones were Huitzilopochtli, the tribal god, who was at the same time the sun and war god; Tlaloc, rain and water god as well as god of agriculture; Tezcatlipóca, the war god, who saw and knew everything (he appears in two forms, red and black, as the friend or enemy of man); and lastly Quetzalcóatl, 'the plumed serpent', a culture hero who had been active since the days of the Teotihuacán culture; his functions varied, but he was associated with water and wind.

The colossal statues of the great gods in the main temple area at Tenochtitlán, as well as those which Bernal Díaz describes, with more imagination than factual knowledge, in his account of his visit to the temple pyramid at Tlatelolco, were probably completely destroyed by the Spaniards. But new excavations in the centre of this ancient city are yielding fresh finds.

During the fierce battles of the conquistadors they threw everything into the canals to give themselves freedom of movement. After the capitulation on 13th August 1521 the ground was levelled for the new town, the first one built by the Spaniards, which has disappeared without trace.

In 1790 a colossal statue of Coatlicue, goddess of earth and death, was found at the south-eastern corner of the 'Zócalo', the main square. Already at that time the climate had changed; the figure was excavated and today it occupies a prominent place in the Museo Nacional. It measures 8 ft. 6 in. in height and weighs about 12 tons, but what strikes us most is not its large dimensions but its terrifyingly inhuman and morbid appearance. The attire of the goddess consists of plaited serpents, the pectoral is a skull, and the necklace is made up of human hearts and chopped-off hands. The head has been cut off, and in its place are two serpent heads joined together, giving it a hideous and fearsome countenance. From an artistic as well as from a psychological point of view Coatlicue is one of the masterpieces of Aztec art. She has several companion figures on a less pretentious scale: all of them are female, with skull-like heads and are clad in skirts of plaited serpents.

The plumed serpent motif lent itself very well to sculpture. Aztec art is characterized by its heaviness and extreme monumentality; the involute body is indicated summarily, while the head, on the other hand, suggests vigour and action. Xipe Totec, the god of sowing, originated from Oaxaca; the cult associated with him is to our eyes repellent in the extreme. His priests wore human skins flayed from the victims of the sacrifice. The force contained in the skin was transferred through the priest to the god. Not even a god had constantly at his disposal the power to make the maize sprout and grow to ripeness; he had to be supplied with fresh power, and it was thought better for a human being to be sacrificed than for a whole nation to perish. There are many sculptures of Xipe, but in most cases these are relatively tame versions, lacking in true Aztec vigour; it is as though the macabre guise acted as an impediment to artistic expression. But there were also exclusive gods, who must have had little relevance for ordinary folk. Of these less popular deities, the work of astronomer-priests, Xolotl, carved in the form of a skeleton, is a fine example. One of the popular gods is Xiuhtecutli, who is represented as a very old man. We encounter him already prior to the Teotihuacán period, seated with a brazier on his back, which is bent with age. It seems as if the energetic Aztecs had endeavoured, though with little success, to persuade the oldest and most distinguished of their culture heroes to perform various functions, following the example set by his fellows.

Although in Mexico, as elsewhere, the mystery of birth was and still is a recurrent problem, it can hardly be assumed that Tlazoltéotl, the goddess of pregnancy, concerned herself with the child-bearing of women from the common people. But in the hands of a highly-gifted artist this painful event in the lives of ordinary folk could serve as the motif for a work of art.

The plumed serpent

PLATE P. 71

PLATES PP. 68, 74

PLATE P. 91

PLATE P. 67

Some other gods stand out from the rest in the pantheon by reason of their comparative humanity. Ehecatl, the god of wind, bears a beak-shaped mask. He is depicted in a stiff and tense attitude, which may be connected with his function of bringing forth the winds. But there are suggestions of composure and harmony in Xochipilli, the god of love, flowers and music, the spouse of Xochiquetzal, a young goddess of growing vegetation and patroness of the domestic handicrafts of women. He is depicted seated with crossed legs, his completely human appearance distinguishing him from the other deities. He, too, is a stranger from Oaxaca and has not been imbued with the vigour of his fellow-deities. He is adorned with flowers; but in the hitherto best-known example, in which he is represented in natural size, he is unfortunately shown wearing a mask.

FIG. 56

It is strange that he should be the only Aztec god to be embellished with flowers, for they were a people with a fondness of flowers, and made abundant use of them both in their religious cults and in everyday life. The maize goddess Chicomecóatl is a dignified old lady. She was responsible for the household, and there was no need for her to follow the fashion. Her image is be seen on the front of a stone slab, with the head, face and attributes modelled in bas-relief. Particularly numerous, and almost always identical, are the figures of the maize goddess found in the Valley of Mexico and the area close by. She has a younger sister in Santa María de Guadalupe, one of whose functions is the difficult one of protecting motorists! It seems as though by the end of the 15th century Aztec art had reached its apogee, at least from the standpoint of attaining colossal proportions. Most remarkable perhaps is the famous 'Stone of Tizoc', a drum-shaped stone measuring 8 ft. 8 in. in diameter and lavishly decorated with sculptured figures. More imposing still is the colossal Aztec 'Calendar Stone', as it is called, which was excavated near the place where Coatlicue was found in the same year as the 'Stone of Tizoc'. The smoothly polished surface of the calendar stone bears a wealth of detail in relief, carved with admirable skill; the disk measures about 12 ft. in diameter and the weight has been estimated at 24 tons. Nothing was too difficult for Stone Age man. In the centre of the stone is the sun god, followed by the four 'epochs of the world', day-signs, symbols, etc. On the interpretation of this calendar stone whole treatises have been written.

One sculpture in the round of very great artistic merit is a recumbent jaguar which, like the 'Stone of Tizoc' and the calendar stone, formed part of the decoration of the walled temple area. The jaguar measures 7 ft. 4 in. in length and has a large depression in its broad back, in which were deposited the hearts of the victims of the sacrifice. It may have been used in the main temple dedicated to Huitzilopochtli, the tribal god, and

Tlaloc, the rain god. In 1487, when the temple was consecrated after reconstruction work during which further storeys were added, a fantastically large number of prisoners of war were sacrificed. The figures given by different reliable witnesses vary from the modest total of 19,600 to as many as 100,000.

Aztec culture drew inspiration from several sources: from neighbours whose culture was akin to that of Teotihuacán and also from the Toltecs. But Mixteca Puebla culture probably had an even more important influence upon the Aztecs. Artists from this area who were skilled in the technique of feather-work, mosaics and metal-working were brought to Azcapotzalco, where they formed colonies. Their great artistic period coincides with the zenith of the empire's power, i.e. between 1440 and 1519. The unravelling of the involved threads that lead to the sources of the high culture of the Aztecs would be a good subject for a specialist study. It would certainly be worth while examining how it was that noblemen who thought themselves so pure that, on meeting an unwashed Spaniard, they had to hold a bunch of flowers before their noses, at the same time allowed their priests to slaughter masses of worthy and innocent people. The Aztecs, with their realistic outlook, obtained from the Mixteca Puebla culture in Oaxaca and Puebla their symbolism and mythology, as well as the feeling that art had a function of its own to fulfil and not merely a religious one. It was in the pictorial writing which they adopted from these masterly artists that they derived the ideas which they translated into their great works of sculpture. The fine works of art and beautiful objects which they imported also inspired them to produce masterpieces of their own. Within a surprisingly short space of time these primitive immigrants, or at least the well-born among them, became civilized, and developed a fondness for luxury, for gold jewellery and precious stones, gorgeous fabrics and feathers, as well as for music, singing and flowers.

Mixteca Puebla culture

Aztec artists seem to have struck out along a path of their own to a greater extent than the other peoples of ancient Mexico. Aztec monumental art has its own individuality; it possesses masculine vigour; it combines realistic figures of animals, human beings and men in divine form with sublime religious ideas beyond the grasp of ordinary mortals. They were attracted by mass and volume. The primitive cubism of a not so distant past, geometric block-shaped syntheses, are still alive with them. Ungainly lines and forms are imbued with an elemental untrammelled force. Only in rare instances were their figures fashioned as works of art — indeed, there is no word for 'art' in Nahuatl, the Aztec language — but it is in this light that they are interpreted by modern man, who sees them

Uniqueness of Aztec monumental art

as dramatic and monstrous gods of terror, charged with a fearsome expressiveness.

It was not until later that the works of these ancient masters aroused general interest. However, modern artists have profited from an acquaintanceship with the art of ancient Mexico. The great English sculptor Henry Moore, who has made a close study of Aztec art, has testified as follows: "Mexican sculpture seems to me to be true and right. Its 'stoniness', by which I mean its truth to material, its tremendous power without loss of sensitiveness, its astonishing variety and fertility of form-invention and its approach to a full three-dimensional conception of form, make it unsurpassed in my opinion by any other period of stone sculpture".

But already in 1520 Mexican artists earned unusually high praise from another European artist: Albrecht Dürer, the greatest figure in the history of German art, who journeyed from his native city of Nuremberg to the Netherlands and in August or September of that year visited Brussels, where what one may call the first European exhibition of Mexican art was being held. His diary is written in a dry and matter-of-fact style, but he makes use of his stock of superlatives when he describes the treasures from the legendary land of the Occident, gifts from the Aztec chief Moctezuma through the agency of Cortés to Emperor Charles V. At this point Dürer is not sparing with praise; he is both astonished and fascinated. The gold naturally makes a great impression on him, but as an artist he appreciates other values far more:

"I have also seen objects", he writes, "brought to the King from the new Land of Gold: a sun all in gold, as much as 6 feet in diameter, and a moon all in silver, likewise of considerable size; there were two chambers full of the armour used by those people, and all kinds of weapons, cuirasses, wondrous shields, strange clothing, bed-clothes, and all manner of curious objects for various purposes, more exquisite than any marvels. All these things were so costly that they are estimated at 100,000 guilders in value. And all my life long I have never seen anything that gave me such delight as did these objects. For among them I have seen wondrous and artistic things, and was amazed at the great ingenuity of this people in a foreign land. And I cannot describe all the things that have been displayed before me there."

IX. MAYA CULTURE

The Maya Indians have been called an enigmatic people, and rightly so Although many distinguished scholars have grappled with the problems of Maya civilization over the course of a century, the results of their work have been astonishingly meagre. How, where and when did this, the world's most important Stone Age culture, evolve? Why were all their cities, magnificently embellished by the most talented sculptors, abandoned? What is the message contained in their hieroglyphic script, the finest and most intricate of its kind known to us, engraved with stone tools and with an incomparable sureness of hand? How was it possible for the Maya astronomers, the most outstanding of their time, to measure without the aid of any instruments the rhythmic movements of the heavenly bodies with an accuracy that amazes all the experts of our own day? Where were their skilled architects trained, and where did their sculptors learn the arts of carving? These and many other questions have as yet remained unanswered.

The evolution of culture is usually seen as a relay-race, onward and up- THE CULTURAL
wards: one phase follows another, and each one registers further progress SEQUENCE
towards the final goal. In ancient America, however, there are frequent instances where the sequence is reversed or follows a completely different course from the one we might expect. The evolution of Maya culture can be traced, and in part also dated, from the time of their most ancient city right up to the Spanish conquest. But it is not possible to trace it back to its primitive first fumblings. The earliest stage known to us appears already fully-fledged. The chronology usually applied nowadays to the 'classic period', when Maya culture first appeared and reached its first flowering, is the work of three scholars who have given their names to it: Thompson — Martínez — Goodman. A long time ago H. J. Spinden, an expert on the Maya who happily is still pursuing his researches, drew up a chronology which sets all the datings back by 260 years. This hypothesis has been substantiated by C-14 tests. The material analysed originates from the colossal city of Tikal, which is now being explored and restored. The data hitherto published coincide almost completely with Spinden's estimates, based on the date signs on door-lintels. This is remarkable in the extreme. But we do not know what these dates refer to — present, past, or future — and this dating is thus of no conclusive value. Dr. J. Eric Thompson, the only survivor of the triumvirs, still adheres to his former opinion. There is a hiatus in the process of evolution if we follow Spinden's correlation, and more than goodwill is required if the threads are to be linked to produce a coherent pattern. We shall therefore here follow the chronology adopted by Thompson and most Maya scholars.

Expansion of culture

Prior to 300 B.C. there occurred in this region, as at Teotihuacán (Teotihuacán II-III) and in the Zapotec country (Monte Albán III), a great cultural expansion of explosive force. It resulted from the strangest culture ever developed by a people unfamiliar with metal, the wheel or any other mechanical appliance. This development came about in northern Guatemala and the adjacent parts of Mexico, Honduras and El Salvador. It seems absolutely incredible that a high culture should have been able to evolve all of a sudden in a country such as this, where the humid unhealthy tropical jungle is poor in natural resources and inhospitable to man.

We cannot answer or explain this fact. We can only say that large cities — or, to be more accurate, religious, cultural and administrative centres of small agricultural city-states, developed in an area which today is the least attractive of all. This culture, which mysteriously enough appears fully-fledged from its very beginnings, may be compared to a plant imported from an unknown country when already in full bloom. Everything points to the fact that in this isolated Maya realm peace and concord generally prevailed. The cities have no walls or defence works; and the number of weapons depicted or actually found is strikingly small. The people lived off the soil, and probably paid taxes in kind; they will have frequently gone to the cities for religious ceremonies, which probably reached their climax on the platforms of the pyramids before the temples which housed their gods. The humbler folk will hardly have taken any interest in the intellectual problems that absorbed the ruling priesthood.

The Maya were entranced by the passage of time: the mystery of eternity, of the eternal flow of time from past to future. We regard time as a thread on which to string events, the thread serving to ensure consecutive order. The length of an epoch is measured subconsciously according to its wealth of content, as it is in a man's memory. But for the Maya time was a path paved with milestones — milestones that probably had nothing to do with indicating the way. Such milestones, in the form of stelae (stone columns), were erected during the golden age, which lasted for six centuries from the end of the 3rd century A.D. The inscriptions on them belong to a realm beyond that of mankind, a realm of astronomy and chronology. Less esoteric knowledge was no doubt written down on paper made of bark such as is still produced nowadays for clothing by the Lacandones, a small and primitive Maya tribe who have survived in this

area. The tallest of these stelae is 39 ft. 4 in. high and weighs about 65 tons. Before the stelae were erected a similar function may have been performed by wooden totem-poles like those found among Indians on the north-western coast of Canada — although these are of later date. Maya sculptures in the round and reliefs are otherwise only rarely notable for their large proportions. If they seem fascinating to us, it is because of their refinement, natural vigour, air of solemn mystery, strict adherence to form, and the patience and composure that emanates from them — as well as the humility and superior skill evident in the touch of master-craftsmen. Everything that transpires within their field of vision, so far as anything transpires at all, does so without haste. It is anything but an everyday product designed for popular use.

Fig. 59 — *In the Maya 'cities' the priest-kings obtained the provisions for their courts from their peasant subjects. This painting, showing such a delivery of food-stuffs, is on a clay vessel from Nebaj, Alta Verapaz, Guatemala. After Morley.*

pop

uo

xul

yaxkin

zac

ceh

pax

Kayab

imix

ik

cimi

manik

chuen

eb

cib

caban

FIG. 60 — *For the last century a number of scholars have been trying to solve the riddles of Maya hieroglyphs, but hitherto in vain. About one hundred signs are known. Eight of the 18 month signs and eight of the 20 day signs are given here. After Covarrubias.*

The events of the day, or the days themselves, were borne along the streets by divine bearers, who from time immemorial alternated in carrying their burdens. If the bearer was well-disposed towards mankind the omens for the day were favourable. But some of the bearers were by no means well-disposed, and then the situation was critical. This gave the priest, who was at the same time both astronomer and astrologer, and who knew the days and the bearers, great opportunities to strengthen his position, and that of the priestly caste as a whole, *vis-à-vis* ordinary folk. That everything had its price of course goes without saying.

The Maya have been called the Greeks of America on account of their temperate and intellectual approach to life. Their hieroglyphic script, of which only a fraction has as yet been deciphered, consists for the most part of completely abstract characters; despite its complexity it shows a surprising uniformity over the years and in different places. There can hardly be any other script surpassing that of the Maya in beauty. Those who wrote it faced a tremendous task. Not only did they have to know the value of each of the characters in the script, and how they had to be combined to form the names of persons or things, or abstract concepts; but they also had to be competent artists and skilled craftsmen. For when carving on stone no mistakes were permissible.

Even if scholars should one day be able to read all the inscriptions, and the three books that have survived — for many thousands were burnt by fanatical Spanish missionaries — it still seems unlikely that anything sensationally novel would emerge. They probably contain notions expressed in the form of symbols, mainly concerning the results of studies made by the astronomer-priests, their application in practice by astrologers, and information about gods and religious ceremonies. The codices are partly in the nature of calendars of prophecies about divine inter-

vention in human affairs, and partly of statements about illnesses inflict-
ed by the gods as penalties for offences committed against them, and
about the penance appropriate to each such sin — esoteric matters which
only the priests could understand.

In their talent as astronomers these Stone Age people surpassed their
contemporaries the world over. The passionate interest shown in astronomy, astrology and mathematics was so general that it took on a religious
character. By continual observations carried out over long periods of time,
without the aid of precision instruments, the Maya astronomers obtained
results so striking that their modern colleagues are filled with amazement
that such feats should have been possible. In solving mathematical problems the Maya used the vigesimal system, i.e. each unit was progressively
twenty times larger than the one inferior to it. In using a sign for zero
they were a thousand years ahead of their time. Their calendar is made
up of a combination of numbers and names. Only after 52 years does a day
recur with the same number and name. The calendar takes its origin from
a certain mythical date in the distant past, in the year 3113 B.C. It is a
veritable triumph of abstract thinking. There are some students of the
Maya who have maintained that this calendar, and possibly the script as
well, were devised by a single individual, a superlative astronomer- and
mathematician-priest, an almost superhuman genius who systematized
observations made over the course of many generations.

The cities produced not only educated administrators, hieroglyphists,
astronomers and astrologers — who were able to turn their knowledge of
the stars to good account — but also architects and artists of every kind.
Exquisite clay vessels were made and decorated with consummate skill.
Fine objects of various kinds, many of them splendid accomplishments of
Stone Age man, were made of wood, bone, mussel-shell or stone. With the
achievements of their weavers we are only indirectly acquainted, through
reproductions of priest-kings and their courtiers, whom we find depicted,
magnificently attired and wearing feather ornaments, on stelae, reliefs,
murals and clay vessels. Their robes and jewellery are reproduced accurately down to the last detail; they are without question splendid examples
of exquisite craftsmanship.

Maya monumental architecture comprises both pyramids surmounted by
temples and buildings that have been termed palaces. The latter are often
embellished with fine stone-masonry, but are palaces in external appearance only. The true arch was not known. By 'corbelling' something resembling an arch was obtained, but the rooms that resulted were small and narrow, and the walls disproportionately thick in order to support the weight
of the roof, which was formed of superimposed slabs, each jutting out fur-

Astronomy

FIG. 60

FIG. 61 — *Reverse of a schist looking-glass with mosaic of polished pieces of pyrite. It was probably worn as a pectoral. Kaminaljuyú, Guatemala. After Bliss and Lothrop.*

ther than the one below until they met at the top. The result was that the rooms were exiguous in relation to the total size of the building, and it was thought satisfactory if they amounted to one-third of the volume of the block-shaped structure as a whole. These dark and dismal rooms must no doubt have been regarded by the Maya as unfit for dwellings, and with a few exceptions must have been used only as storage-places, in which were kept all manner of objects used in rites and ceremonies. Probably everyone, including men of highest rank, lived in airy open dwelling-houses thatched with palm leaves.

Most of the cities had ball-courts.

FIG. 63 — *Scene on a tripod which may originate from* **Teotihuacán**. *A spokesman of the priest-k holding a discussion with four men armed with javelins and spear-throwers. After 'Expedition', No. 2, 1960.*

The ball was made of rubber and was large and durable. For more than a thousand years, as has been mentioned, right up to the time of the Spanish conquest, this game was part of religious ritual; it was played in an endeavour to determine the will of the gods. In the Aztec period it also assumed a secular character, and was played by professionals in a strongly competitive spirit. But the arts of the ballgame do not properly belong to the history of art, and it may only be remarked in passing that the ancient Mexican game was too strenuous for it to be revived in our own day and introduced into the Olympic Games.

FIG. 62 — *Central part of a polychrome tripod from Campeche, probably from the late classic Maya period. After Bliss and Lothrop.*

FIG. 64 — *Central figure on a polychrome clay bowl from Yucatán. The Maya potters were often only of mediocre skill, but the men who decorated their vessels sometimes showed real artistic talent. This figure is not so much naturalistic as expressive. Former Staatliches Museum für Völkerkunde, Berlin.*

Apparently the cities vied with one another in building pyramids, ceremonial flights of steps and palaces arranged around a central court; it was to these plazas that the rural population would come in order to watch the processions and other ritual spectacles. All the high cultures of ancient America display an abnormally keen interest in architecture. The construction of flights of steps simply for their own sake is something typical of the Maya. A spirit of friendly rivalry must have prevailed. Though each city was a chapter into itself in regard to layout, architecture and decoration, the culture of all of them was to a certain extent homogeneous. This must be attributed to the ease with which ideas, astronomical observations, inventions and discoveries could circulate between one city-state and another. "Civilization means communication", it is true, but how was it possible to maintain such close links between cultural centres in tropical jungle country? In 1946 a town which had not hitherto been known to exist was discovered buried in the jungle in the state of Chiapas. It was called Bonampak. Twelve centuries ago the rooms in one of the buildings in this town were decorated with murals covering an enormous area 172 square yards in extent. They give us an unexpected opportunity to look behind the scenes of Maya civilization, so to speak.

The paintings are very dramatic, yet exquisitely refined in form. Battle scenes, musical bands at full blast, processions with the participants bearing masks of terrifying demons, and warriors in magnificent attire sentencing near-naked prisoners to barbarous tortures — all this is depicted with scrupulous accuracy, the brutal and ugly

FIG. 65 — *Schematic transverse sections of Maya buildings showing different types of vault-like roofs. The true arch was unknown in ancient America, but the Maya made solid stone roofs with the aid of 'corbelled arches', i.e. by carrying both walls inward slightly by*

elements being treated in a manner that can almost be termed beautiful. From this we can see that not everything was so classical and refined as the elaborately carved reliefs seem to suggest. These paintings reveal the truth: the Maya city-states were indeed exceptionally well-organized, but violence and tyranny were not unknown. If this had not been so, the Maya would not have been human.

Palenque, in south-east Mexico, is famous for its elegant temples and its PLATE P. 104 palace, which has a three-storeyed tower and exquisite stucco reliefs. In the temple on the largest pyramid one of the flagstones in the floor was found to be larger than the others. When it was raised in 1949 it was discovered that it hid the entrance to a stairway blocked with earth and rubble, which led down into the heart of the pyramid. It was not until 1952 that archaeologists succeeded in reaching a colossal stone door. When this was pushed aside it revealed a capacious sepulchral chamber. Along its walls nine priests of high rank were depicted walking in procession; the figures are executed in stucco and are larger than life-size. The priests are arrayed in magnificent robes and wear fantastic head-dresses; in their hands they carry sceptres bearing images of the rain and sun god. The bur- ial-chamber is dominated by a colossal stone slab completely covered with sculptured figures, the 'tree of the world direction', certain deities, as- tronomical symbols and so on. The chronological hieroglyphs give the years 603 and 633. This stone not only tells of the innermost mysteries of the Maya religion, but is also unquestionably one of their finest artistic achievements. This slab, which lay upon a massive rectangular block, was raised by means of a winch — it weighed about 5 tons — and all the ex- cavators' expectations were fulfilled. Cleverly concealed beneath a rock ledge was a tomb hewn out of the block, containing the remains of the man in whose honour the sepulchre and pyramid had been built. The skeleton alone had stood the test of time; of the clothing nothing at all remained. The dead priest- king wore hundreds of beads of light-green jadeite, rings on each finger, ear-plugs and other ornaments of the same material, the costliest to be had and the one with the most effective magic properties. It has been suggested that the existence of pyramids in ancient America indicates

means of overlapping courses until the gap could be bridged. In order to keep the stones in place the walls had to be very thick. As a result of this method of construction the amount of room in the interior was only a fraction of the total volume of the building. After Peterson.

that there were links between this part of the world and Egypt. But the Egyptian pyramids are three thousand years older than the American ones which, apart from this single exception, never contained tombs but were the bases of temples.

The classic epoch of Maya art began at the end of the third century A.D. and lasted for 600 years. The cause of its collapse has been, and still is, a matter for conjecture and further study. The new land of Yucatán can hardly have been particularly enticing to an agricultural people such as the Maya. Epidemics, exhaustion of the soil by clearing with fire, and even (in all seriousness) moral decline, or rebellion against the excessive demands made by the priesthood — these are some of the reasons usually given for the migration that took place. But why should the morals decline suddenly, or epidemics ravage this particular area? Eric Thompson, at present the most distinguished expert on Maya civilization, stakes everything on a single theory: that the people grew tired of the increasing demands made by their ruling priestly caste for labour in the building of temples and for dues of all kinds; that they had had enough of theocratic tyranny, reasoning that the gods of fertility had been neglected in favour of astronomical abstractions utterly beyond the comprehension of ordinary mortals. Since the priests were neglecting their duties to establish contact with the gods, the source of rain, growth and harvest, emigration was the only way out. No battles were fought; nothing was destroyed; the population simply abandoned the cities, leaving the priests to their fate, and gave up their fields and homes to seek their fortune in the north.

But I should like to put forward a different hypothesis. Emigration may have been the result of sudden growth of lush vegetation, stifling everything, which commenced in the south. Originally the Maya territory can hardly have been jungle. It was possible for them to cut down the jungle with their stone-axes and turn it into poor-quality arable land, which was soon exhausted. But if they were constantly engaged in a struggle against the giant trees and fast-growing undergrowth of the jungle they probably did not have the time to build cities, make new tracks, or keep open those that already existed. There were priests, scholars, artists, merchants and warriors to be kept, stone to be quarried, carved and transported, limestone to be burnt, and beams to be hewn from tree-trunks. There are still some Maya people, the Lacandones already mentioned, living in the old territory. Although they possessed all manner of useful tools such as axes and knives, as well as medicine, etc., they have given no sign of progress and have retained nothing of the high culture of their ancestors. American scholars have calculated that a Yucatec peasant only needed to work for 48 days a year to obtain sufficient maize for himself and his family. It seems to me most likely that this figure is too low, as could be proved if these scholars were to leave their desks, go to Yucatán and equip some peasants with stone-axes and see how much they could manage to do with them.

The causes of the migration will certainly always be a matter of dispute. In any case it is certain that by the 10th century the old area had been evacuated except for a few stragglers such as the modern Lacandones. The golden age of the Maya had come to an end; they continued to survive, but they had played their role in world history — and a great era it certainly had been. Most of them went to the Yucatán peninsula; here there was an ancient Maya settlement with large cities, the most important of them being Uxmal, which had some exquisite architectural monuments. The epoch of classic cultures, in which peace had prevailed, gave place to an age of unrest, wars and migrations. The route taken by the Maya was only a short one, but towards the end of the 10th century a strange warrior people arrived in Yucatán from distant parts: the Toltecs, coming from Tula, north of the Valley of Mexico. According to tradition, as we know, they received Chichén Itzá as a reward for their part in the civil war and transformed it into a new Tula, but larger and more magnificent. The old Maya buildings remained in being, and indeed they are still standing today, but the victors left a lasting imprint upon the city.

Yucatán is a flat limestone tableland. The rain-water percolates into the rock and is drained off by subterranean rivers. Here and there the top stratum has collapsed and small lakes, known as *cenotes*, have formed. In the area of Chichén Itzá there are two such *cenotes*, one of which was used as a place of sacrifice. On this site a large number of objects were found, including jewellery of jadeite and gold. Up

Fig. 66 — *Conjectural reconstruction of a temple pyramid at Tikal, Guatemala, by Tatiana Proskouriakoff, elaborated by Miguel Covarrubias. A small sanctuary is reached by a steep flight of steps; the steps are narrow, but Indians have broad feet and went unshod. The temple has a screen façade.*

FIG. 67 — *A priest-king on a journey: a schematic drawing of part of a scene painted around a clay vessel. The party seem to have stopped for a rest, since the dog is stretching itself in the shade in a very realistic manner. Ratininul, Guatemala. After Morley.*

to this time metals were unknown: it is a remarkable fact that spectroscopic tests have shown that the gold was imported from Colombia — the concentration of impurities in the metal is the same in each case.

From the top of the high main pyramid one can gain a fine view over the surrounding country-side, which is so flat that one would think one were at sea. In the west monuments dating from the Maya period rise above the tree-tops, but it is those of the Toltecs that attract one's attention most. The central temple, with serpent columns supporting the lintels, is situated on top of the high symmetrical pyramid. This monument is rigid, clear and logical in structure, the equivalent in stone of a mathematical calendar system. This is evident from the number of superimposed platforms, stairways, niches and so on. Hidden in this pyramid is an older pyramid crowned by a temple, completely intact, around and upon which the more recent one was built. The enormous ball-court, measuring 524 ft. x 131 ft., has a temple also provided with serpent columns. These Toltec elements occur once more in the so-called Temple of Warriors, one of the finest monuments in ancient America. The name given to this temple is derived from the warrior figures featured on the square columns of the façade, which are life-size and were originally lavishly painted. The same kind of columns and warrior figures occur in Tula, and they bear so great a resemblance to each other that one is inclined to think they may have been the work of the same artists. The temple on the lower pyramid was encompassed by a colonnade. On the entrance side the roof was supported by four, and on the north side by five, rows of columns. This was one of the several remarkable innovations which the Maya architects now set eyes upon for the first time. A reclining figure, the 'Chac Mool' of Tula, apparently formed part of each sacred building. Standing figures — of colossal size at Tula, but small at Chichén Itzá — supported the roof-beams of the entrance and the large stone altar slabs. The entrance was framed by serpent columns, giving a very dramatic effect. The head of the rattlesnake rested on the floor, its fearsome jaws wide open. Its body, decked out with feathers of the sacred *quetzal* bird carved in bas-relief, formed the actual column; its tail supported and in part encircled the horizontal beam of the lintel.

Strange gods were now venerated in Chichén Itzá, but they were not re- *New gods* cognized by the Maya; nor did the latter have any affection for Toltec art. The Maya deities were not excessively prodigal with benevolence. For a good maize harvest they required incense, food and drink, but also blood. Human blood was the most precious sacrifice a man could make. The gods needed blood of high quality to obtain the power that enabled them to fulfil their functions each year; it was therefore the duty of a god-fearing people to supply them with what they needed. Very fine reliefs show devotees pulling knotted cords through holes cut into their tongues. Such self-sacrifice for the general good recalls the deeds of the Christian martyrs. Evidently the Maya felt an urge for sacrifice. By constantly increasing the size and number of their temples and other monuments they devoted the fruits of their labours to the gods. This gave them the sense of participation essential if a religion is to endure.

But the new gods at Chichén Itzá had greater pretensions. The sun god was degraded, becoming the god of war, whose appetite had to be assuaged with the hearts and blood of human victims. If he did not have his fill he had no power and was unable to perform his functions. It became necessary to wage continual campaigns to procure prisoners for sacrifice. Young men were trained and organized into two military orders of knighthood, the eagles and the jaguars. The priests, who had brought about the constant man-hunts, were brushed aside and the warriors took charge. But in 1200 Chichén Itzá lost its political power. The reason for this development has never really been clarified. The town remained a place of pilgrimage (in our own day more intensively so than ever before, but the pilgrims are now tourists!). But the centre of political power in northern Yucatán was now transferred to Mayapán. For the first time a militaristic city-state had emerged in Maya territory.

Mayapán, like Teotihuacán, was a genuine city, and not merely the residence of chiefs, priests, soldiers and officials. A wall some five miles long afforded protection to its 4500 houses and twenty pyramids. Quality had been the characteristic feature of Maya art during the classic era, and the Toltecs in Chichén Itzá, too, were not niggling where it was a matter either of a temple or of some object for everyday use. But the story that emerges from the ruins of Mayapán is a disheartening one. The Mexican and Toltec influence exhausted itself and the religion and language of the population again became Maya. But for some mysterious reason, apart from clay figures which served as incense-burner, a catastrophic artistic PLATE P. 95

decline now set in. Even the incense-burners, the best objects that were produced, would not have satisfied the standards of the classic period. They were produced mechanically one after the other and in moulds — one is tempted to say, by a conveyor-belt method that owed nothing to Henry Ford. There was only a superficial and conventional interest in religion, and materialism was triumphant. Of the culture that had once been so brilliant little remained. The warrior city exhausted the resources of the country. Towards the middle of the 15th century a revolt broke out; Mayapán was taken by storm and burnt to the ground. However, little was achieved thereby, for now everything collapsed and a time of confusion and internecine struggle began. Thus in 1541 Yucatán easily fell into the hands of the Spaniards.

Dzibilchaltun In 1941 the American archaeologist E. Wyllys Andrews established that only a few miles north of Mérida, the capital of Yucatán, there lay the remains of an enormous ancient city. Excavation work was begun in 1956, but only brief accounts are as yet available. Dzibilchaltun seems likely to have the effect of an atomic explosion on Maya studies: it is the largest city of ancient America, one of the oldest Maya towns and certainly the last that they inhabited. It contains many hundreds of ruined houses, processional routes, numerous huge temples, enormous buildings in the nature of palaces, and twelve *cenotes,* the whole covering an area of at least 19 square miles The first buildings appeared at least a thousand years before the birth of Christ; the city flourished during the classic period (A.D. 300—600) and survived crises and wars right into the colonial period. Then for four hundred years Dzibilchaltun served as a quarry for Mérida and many haciendas; and today its ruins still furnish material for the highways of Yucatán.

Kinsfolk of the people who lived in this jungle area in ancient times, and their descendants, may be found in the highlands of Guatemala and the adjacent districts of El Salvador. These are areas suitable for agriculture, with a pleasant climate and an abundance of minerals, including the priceless jadeite. In spite of all their material advantages, however, the Maya who lived in this area reached a level far inferior to that of the inhabitants of the lowlands and their descendants. Their architecture and sculpture were undistinguished; they had no knowledge of the corbelled

FIG. 65 arch or dated stone columns, or of the calendar or the philosophy based upon it. They owed their cultural progress solely to extraneous influences. Kaminaljuyú is the name given to an ancient town near Guatemala City. Its history dates back to a period long before the classic era, but remarkable finds do not occur until it fell under the influence of Teotihuacán. Tripods with conical lids, thin yellowish-red ceramic ware and other elements typical of Teotihuacán during the classic epoch are present in identical form at Kaminaljuyú. It can scarcely be a question of trade, for this Teotihuacán-type pottery sometimes has elements unknown elsewhere in Mexican art. Teotihuacán influence is shown still more conclusively by the fact that Tlaloc, the Mexican rain god, is still venerated in the highlands of Guatemala.

Eric Thompson, who has dedicated a lifetime of study to the Maya, past and present, and has compared his views with those of other scholars, sums up as follows: The Maya are unusually honest, good-natured and patient; they are clean and moderate in their habits and value staying-power above brute force. They are deeply religious and have a strong community sense. No one may strive after more than his fair share, for whatever exceeds this limit can only be obtained at someone else's expense, and regard for one's neighbour is more important than anything else. This most favourable résumé is endorsed by other experienced scholars. The four million pure-blooded Maya of our own day are just as puzzled as we are by the achievements of their forbears. Their passion for learning, their artistic accomplishments, their zeal for building are all things of the past. It is astonishing that this same people, living in the same milieu under the same conditions, show no affinities with their ancestors, those pillars of a civilization that attained the highest peak of intellectual achievement in ancient America.

The Maya made no practical discoveries that increased the well-being of the people or reduced the heavy burden of toil that was their lot. We may say that they excelled in unpractical matters, but failed in the practical sphere. However, the Maya held different views from ourselves about what is useful and what is not. The study and comprehension of the divine order that governs the world, and control over their own fate, were to them intellectual attainments that by no means lay beyond the realms of practicability.

X. CENTRAL AMERICA:
BRIDGE BETWEEN TWO CONTINENTS

Central America, the isthmus that connects Mexico with Colombia, is a bridge between two continents, and not merely in the geographical sense. Already the earliest discoverers of South America chose this route, and since those prehistoric days it has been taken by many other peoples as well. Some of them settled in the area, which helped to make the cultural picture very heterogeneous.

The lush rain forests of the eastern seabord are directly connected with those of South America, and the population, which is fairly closely connected with the inhabitants of the jungles east of the Andes, penetrated as far as the area of the Maya. The Maya may perhaps have obtained fruitful stimuli from these peoples; indeed some authorities believe that they themselves may have immigrated from South America during very early times.

On the Pacific coast the arid savannah and the highlands covered with oak and pine forests encouraged active commercial relations, and in this area rich cultures were able to evolve. From the south the Chibcha tribes advanced as far as Lake Nicaragua, where they came upon alien tribes from the north and the Chorotega of Nicaragua itself. Both the Nicarao, who formed a ruling class, and the Aztec merchants and gold prospectors thus gradually fused with the indigenous population. At the time of the Spanish conquest they were still distinct from the peoples of the surrounding area.

THE LANGUAGES OF CENTRAL AMERICA

A map showing the distribution of the various languages spoken in the area gives a picture of the cultural conditions prevailing when the conquistadors arrived. This linguistic map is unusually simple by American Indian standards; one might have expected greater complexity. From the relatively straightforward situation that existed in the early 16th century archaeologists have endeavoured to establish, by undertaking systematic studies, a clear picture of the variegated background, although so far this has unfortunately only proved possible in a limited number of areas.

The Chorotega, an advanced people who live in Nicaragua, had a language of their own which was also spoken in some areas of southern Mexico, western Nicaragua and northern Costa Rica. Honduras and eastern Nicaragua could boast of several independent languages. Chibcha was spoken over the greater part of Costa Rica and everywhere in Panama. Chibcha tribes controlled western Colombia, except in the area along the Pacific seabord. The Nicarao, who had emigrated from Tula in or before 1168, settled on the shores of the great lake that has been named after

FIG. 68 — *Carl Bovallius, the Swedish zoologist and naturalist, was one of the first to study the prehistory of Nicaragua. On his journey of exploration in 1881–3 he collected archaeological material from Zapatera I. in Lake Nicaragua. The figures served as caryatids. After Bovallius.*

them: Nicaragua, 'the water of the Nicarao'. A small band of Nahuatl-speaking merchants sent out from Tenochtitlán-Mexico, who heard of the Aztecs' surrender while they were in this area, settled along the banks of Chiriquí Lagoon, on the Atlantic coast of northern Panama.

Broadly speaking, this was the picture when the Spaniards arrived at the beginning of the 16th century, and these cultures — and the native languages as well — were quickly destroyed. But remains of Indian cultures and languages have been preserved in the areas that had nothing to offer Europeans and where they did not wish to settle.

Boundaries were no obstacle to trade. Gold from the Peruvian coast found its way to Guatemala, perhaps as far as Monte Albán. And gold figures from Panama and Colombia reached Chichén Itzá. Maya ceramics were imported by the Chorotega, who in turn supplied clay vessels produced in Costa Rica.

The people of Panama engaged in trade as far south as Ecuador. In 1526, in an attempt to reach the Inca empire by sea, the Spaniards came across a large fleet of sailing vessels off the coast of Ecuador on their way north. On board were all manner of goods for barter; they were supposed to be exchanged for a cargo of a certain kind of sea-shell which the Peruvians used in making jewellery.

In spite of their many varied languages and the influences exerted upon them from north and south, the more advanced peoples of Central America definitely possessed certain cultural and artistic affinities among themselves. They had in common a lively interest in pottery. They displayed

FIG. 69 — *Stone club-head from Costa Rica. Although the inlays in the eyes and teeth have been lost, this jaguar head gives a vivid impression of the ferocious cruelty of this beast of prey; it is a work of monumental sculpture in miniature. S. Linné Collection, Stockholm.*

skill in modelling, had a sure command of technique and a rich imagination in matters of decoration. Their output was enormous, particularly of fine clay vessels which served a purely decorative purpose and had hardly any practical worth.

The Chorotega had close links with the Maya already in their classic period, but by and large they followed a path of their own. If the designs on Maya ceramic ware are realistic, those of the Chorotega are symbolic, for the figures of the ornamentation, particularly the snakes (which even include plumed serpents, introduced by the Nicarao), and also the jaguars, alligators and apes are boldly reduced to their basic essentials or stylized beyond recognition. The potters of the Nicoya peninsula incontestably surpass all others. Their tripods, hemispherical vessels, bowls and PLATE P. 96 zoomorphic urns, with multi-coloured decoration, are among the most outstanding works of pottery produced at the time. Although these craftsmen borrowed ideas from various sources they were themselves true creative artists. This no doubt accounts for the high quality of their pottery, as well as for the many different styles that exist.

The tripod is a type of vessel characteristic of Mexico and Central America. If the base is solid, the tripod may serve some practical purpose. But whatever its function it was developed further. In its boldest form the legs become almost more important than the vessel itself and are fashioned with particular devotion: they occur in the shape of birds' heads, snakes or monsters, held in place by a rudimentary bowl. If the idea of such tripod vessels did not emerge independently, it must have been introduced from Mexico, for in South America this type of vessel is very rare.

FIG. 70 — *Stone implements for grinding maize are the oldest of Indian kitchen utensils. This 'metate' may have served a ceremonial purpose. Nicoya, Costa Rica. After Joyce.*

It is strange, however, that Chorotega customs and deities resemble those of South America rather than those of Mexico. The decoration of their ceramic ware is in many cases purely polychrome, but Chorotega potters also produced massive pieces with conical lids. The lids themselves are not painted, but are crowned by an alligator with its tail hanging down. The animal is effectively stylized, typical parts of the body, such as the scales of its armour, being used as independent decorative elements. The Chorotega were no doubt influenced by Maya culture to some extent, but they did not adopt any of their great achievements. Like all the other primitive Central American peoples they had no stone monuments or temples. The contrast with Mexico is only too apparent, for there the interest in architecture was so great as to be almost abnormal.

In the archaeological exploration of Central America several Swedish scholars have done pioneer work. As early as 1882—3, for instance, Dr. Carl Bovallius carried out some fruitful investigations, among other places on an island in Lake Nicaragua, where he studied the remains of a primitive settlement and took photographs of a number of stone statues which had survived in part as constructional details on a building of considerable size. Some of these were already known, but it was only through Bovallius' illustrations that accurate reproductions of them became available. These

FIG. 71 — *The National Ethnographical Museum in Stockholm possesses two giant stone figures from Costa Rica, about 6 ft. 6 in. high. By comparison with them the man shown here looks like a tiny dwarf, since he measures a mere 9½ in. in height. S. Linné Collection, Stockholm.*

statues were ascribed to the Chorotega; however, they do not exhibit any influence of the great Maya sculptures, and on the contrary have certain Mexican features. The Mexican colony situated close by has left few immediate traces of its existence, but these strangers from afar enriched the art of this area by introducing the plumed serpent and other demons that recalled their distant homeland. Curiously enough, some of these statues are akin to others that occur in Colombia, near the sources of the River Magdalena.

Between 1896 and 1899 Prof. C.V. Hartman carried out extensive archaeological excavations in the highlands of Costa Rica, as well as archaeological and ethnographical studies along the Pacific seabord. In 1903 he made another fruitful journey to Costa Rica. He was the first scholar to work in that country on scientific lines. He published the results of his field-work in the highland area inhabited by the Guetar in a lavish edition which greatly advanced our knowledge of Costa Rican prehistory and is still unsurpassed after a lapse of almost fifty years.

Hartman summarizes his findings as follows: "The culture to which the remains described belongs is apparently that of an advanced Stone Age people who possessed gold and copper ornaments but no metal weapons or implements. We have no data enabling us to establish at what point in the past it originated, but the occurrence of beads in the graves shows that it still continued to exist after the arrival of the Spaniards."

FIG. 69   In their sculpture interest concentrates on their artistically-shaped club-heads, particularly those in the form of jaguar heads, which give an impression of composure and dynamic energy. They are as full of vigour as the animals themselves. These club-heads, which were only used for ceremonial purposes, are among the finest achievements of Central American sculpture. If they were ten to twenty times larger they would not merely vie with, but would by far surpass, the fearsome serpent heads of the Toltecs and Aztecs. An arresting effect is also produced by their elabor-
FIG. 70   ately carved stools, cylindrical tables, and magnificently decorated grind-stones, which were probably used for ceremonial purposes. The latter have
FIG. 71   three or four legs and are frequently made in the form of jaguars, animals or human beings. The human figures are massive, with crude facial features and a morose expression. They vary in height between a few inches and about six feet. All of them are naked, usually asexual, and most of them are furnished with head-trophies.

Head-trophies are still worn today by the Jivaro in Ecuador. They have been discovered in graves on the coast of southern Peru; and demons embellished with the same macabre feature on clay vessels and textiles were made by the earliest cultures of the Peruvian seabord. There must be

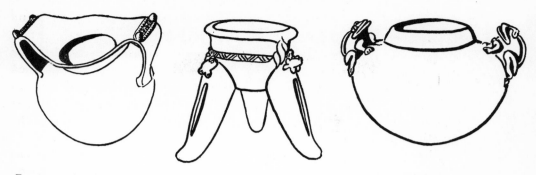

Fɪɢ. 72 — *Clay vessels from Chiriqui province, western Panama. America has abundant ceramic ware of archaeological interest, but few areas rival this in the large numbers of clay vessels of different shapes and varying styles of decoration that were found here by professional grave-plunderers.*

some connection between them, but it is not possible to point to any stylistic affinities. On the other hand there are close parallels with western Mexico in the way in which the trophies are worn, and in much else besides.

The Guetar of Costa Rica spoke the Chibcha language. But the South American tribes who conversed in this tongue stood at very different levels of culture. Some of them were quite primitive, while others were developing an advanced culture. Many of them have now disappeared, but the Cuna-Cuna on the coast and the islands off-shore to the east of the Panama Canal are still today the bearers of a rich and fascinating culture. The Cuna-Cuna are a healthy people, full of vitality; their great chief, or 'priest-king', dictates fables, historical legends and sagas to his scribes, who take them down on a typewriter. The menfolk frequently hire themselves out as crew on trading vessels and sail all over the globe; when they return home they rejoin their tribe and revert to tilling the soil, fishing and trading with the population of the Canal Zone. The womenfolk still make unique gaily-coloured blouses in appliqué work; they wear large ear ornaments and gold nose-rings. Although the scribes have learnt modern techniques the medicine-men still have their own individual hieroglyphic script.

Early Costa Rican pottery is characterized by lavish decoration in colour, the elements consisting of demons in animal and human guise and mythical creatures reduced to enigmatic signs and symbols. One popular motif was a pair of faces, one of which was upside down over the other, as on a playing-card. No attempt was made to give the impression of illusion, but the peculiar vividness of form testifies to their inexhaustible wealth of ideas.

At Chiriqui in western Panama a culture developed which, judging by its

FIG. 72

FIG. 73 — *Polychrome ornament on a fairly shallow bowl resting on a tall elegant conical base with slightly flaring sides. The figure is of a 'dancing crocodile god', a strange combination of various elements of alligator, ape and human being. Probably from Coclé, Panama. After Holmes.*

art, was akin to that of the Guetar. Their graves are so rich in gold that they seemed to be veritable gold-mines. Professional grave-robbers successfully pursued their quest for buried treasure here, as they are still doing today; it has been said that there are families in Panama who owe their fortunes to gold dug out of these graves.

But it was not until the beginning of the 1930s that a find was made which entirely justifies the name coined for this country by the Spanish conquistadors: Castilla del Oro, or 'the Golden Castile'. At Coclé the American archaeologist Dr. S. K. Lothrop had the good fortune to excavate an exceptionally rich gold treasure-trove. It had been known to Erland Nordenskiöld when he undertook his expedition to these parts in 1927, but he had not been able to examine it then. This find originated from a most artistic people. It comprised magnificent pieces of gold jewellery, helmets and ornaments of all kinds, large amounts of pottery, finely-worked gems with stones mounted in gold, as well as other proofs of the virtuosity displayed by these artists, who lived and worked in a veritable golden age. The discovery was one such as archaeologists dream of but rarely have the opportunity to make.

In his studies of the large quantities of pottery found in the graves of powerful chiefs and princelings Dr. Lothrop succeeded in classifying the material and even identifying certain anonymous artists. During Nordenskiöld's expedition in 1927 archaeological explorations the first ones of their kind, were also carried out in western Panama. On the Pearl Islands in the Gulf of Panama offshoots were encountered of the lavishly painted clay vessels of the Coclé culture.

PLATE P. 140

It is an open question whether the mining and working of metal was discovered and developed independently in America. There is evidence pointing to contact across the Pacific: not so much the fact that in the Old World metallurgy dates from an earlier period, or that similar decorative elements occur on both sides of the Pacific, but that all the complexities of metal-working appear both on the eastern and western shores of that ocean. It would no doubt have been possible for one invention or

FIG. 74 — *Clay vessel from a grave in Veraguas, Panama. The polychrome ornament shows a serpent demon, perhaps distantly related to the Mexican Quetzalcóatl. This vessel was discovered by Dr. Lothrop, together with other finds of gold, ceramic ware and similar objects, during excavations in the provinces of Coclé and Veraguas. After Lothrop.*

another to be made independently, but where whole complexes are found to be the same this suggests borrowing. However this may be, the working of metal commenced in Peru and then spread slowly northwards. In Mexico metal-working was not introduced until the late 10th century. In Peru alloys of gold and silver were used, but in Mexico and Central America gold was only alloyed with copper.

In Colombia alloys contained all three metals. Bronze, an alloy of copper and tin, found in Peru and Mexico, was only used for weapons and tools. The alloy of gold and copper was the easiest to work, for in their pure state these metals melt at temperatures of 1945° F. and 1981° F. (1063° C. and 1083° C.), whereas the ideal alloy (18% copper and 82% gold) melts already at 1612° F. (878° C.).

A very popular method of bronze-casting was *à cire perdue* (lost wax process). The object was modelled in wax; if it was to be hollow, the wax was placed around a core of clay. This was then covered with an envelope of clay; the wax melted away when the molten metal was poured in, and then the outer envelope was broken away.

Of all the metal-workers in ancient America the Mixtecs attained the highest level of achievement. The creators of the finds in 'Grave 7' on Monte Alban were craftsmen of unrivalled skill. But they could also boast of a rare artistic sensibility that placed them in the front rank of the artists of the classic period.

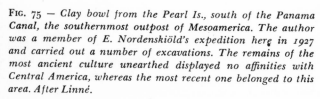

FIG. 75 — *Clay bowl from the Pearl Is., south of the Panama Canal, the southernmost outpost of Mesoamerica. The author was a member of E. Nordenskiöld's expedition here in 1927 and carried out a number of excavations. The remains of the most ancient culture unearthed displayed no affinities with Central America, whereas the most recent one belonged to this area. After Linné.*

129

The existence of the Inca empire had already been known for a long time on the Pacific coast of Panama, for when Vasco Núñez de Balboa crossed the isthmus of Panama in 1513 and discovered the Pacific he was astonished to learn on good authority that to the south there lay a mighty empire. It is by no means impossible that the Aztecs and Inca had vague notions of each other's existence. Had development continued along normal lines these two countries, which were close to one another from a cultural point of view, would no doubt have established contact with one another, and in that case the Spanish conquistadors would have been unable to subdue these two empires and so earn a place in history as legendary conquerors; the leading civilizations of the time in America would not have suffered so rapid a decline, and would have been able to give the West the benefit of their centuries-old experience in learning and the arts.

PART II: THE ART OF THE ANDEAN LANDS
by Hans-Dietrich Disselhoff

I. THE SETTING

There can be no doubt that the peoples of Mexico and South America were in contact with one another in ancient times, long after the two continents had been slowly settled by people from the north and south of Asia. What form these connections took no one will ever know for certain. Nevertheless the fact that they existed can be deduced from the presence of pyramids (i.e. the bases of temples in the shape of truncated pyramids) both in Mexico and along the Peruvian coast. Other pointers are the parallels between certain myths and rituals, the obvious affinity between the ancient centres of La Venta in Mesoamerica (p. 65) and Chavín in Peru (p. 156), and lastly the clear resemblance between certain clay figurines from Ecuador and others from the area inhabited by the Maya. It must have been a question of cross-fertilization rather than simple parallels between kindred peoples. We now know that metal-working occurred first in South America; this, together with certain other evidence, suggests that the movement was one from south to north, at least in certain periods. The most reliable testimony, from a relatively late date, of trading contacts between the two continents of the western hemisphere has been handed down to us in the story of the discovery of Peru. I have in mind the oft-cited account of the astonishing encounter between a Spanish caravel and a Peruvian merchant vessel bound for the north. In 1526, about five years before Francisco Pizarro conquered the Inca empire, his helmsman came across a raft with sails, bound for northern shores with a cargo of Peruvian goods, consisting of pottery and metal ware.

Finds in Peruvian graves show that red shells (*spondylus pictorum*) were imported from Central America for ritual purposes and as raw material for use in various crafts. Mexican graves of late date have yielded gold jewellery, such as imitation feather diadems, which look exactly like those from Peru. Gold vessels from Ecuador and northern Peru are found encrusted with turquoise imported from the north, and the raw material of the few pieces of jewellery made of jadeite or jade unearthed in Peru probably originate from Mesoamerica. No doubt all these objects made of more impermanent materials that found their way from Peru to Mesoamerica fell prey to the ravages of the humid subtropical climate, whereas the exceptionally dry climate on the Peruvian coast contributed in large measure to the preservation over the course of many centuries of such impermanent articles as fine fabrics in llama and vicuña wool and all objects made of bone and wood.

In this respect the coastal belt of Peru may be compared to Egypt. Just as the flood-waters of the mighty Nile fertilized the land of the Pharaohs every year, thus making the great achievements of Egyptian culture possible, so more than twenty small Niles, so to speak, flowed across the deserts of the Peruvian coastlands from the Cordillera to the Pacific. Rain fell in the mountains every year, and already in ancient times alluvial floods transformed the desert into a land of fertile oases. With the introduction of artificial irrigation great civilizations were able to arise in Peru. But how did all this begin?

As in the case of ancient Mexico and the Maya lands, the art of ancient Peru can by no means be regarded as primitive. At the time of the Spanish conquest there existed in Peru and in areas that now form part of neighbouring countries a mighty empire, possibly the only genuine empire in the New World. It was an amalgam of several Indian peoples speaking many different languages. We do not know for certain whether other Indian empires may not have existed before the rise of the realm of the Inca, which constituted the climax of ancient Peruvian civilization, but there are many indications that support such a hypothesis.

Mesoamerica and Greater Peru are the principal centres of high culture in the New World prior to the Spanish conquest. For this reason in the second part of this volume attention will be focused upon ancient Peruvian culture and art. The Spaniards invaded these two areas (Mexico and Peru) armed with the Christian cross, with iron swords, cross-bows and muskets. They found there a princely splendour and a developed state organization that was unknown in the adjacent territories. It seems that outside the main centres architecture, pottery and weaving did not attain such a high level, although gold-working flourished in the southern part of Central America and the northern part of South America.

After some experience it is easy for an observer to recognize the special features common to American art objects that distinguish them from those found in other parts of the world. At the same time it is also possible, by and large, to distinguish between the style peculiar to Greater Peru and that of Central America. It is obvious that this Greater Peruvian style embraces variants that differ according to their location in space and time. But is it at all possible to speak of art in ancient America in our sense of the term? Probably only in the sense in which we speak of the art of Africa and Oceania. Perhaps to an even greater extent than in these areas almost all the works of art produced by the ancient Indians — sculpture, painting, and even textiles and jewellery — are imbued with religious concepts and aspirations. The artist, unconscious of his own talent, fashions a figure in order to confine within it certain demonic forces which he believes to exist. Magic holds sway over matter. It is only in modern times, when man is reaching the culminating point of rational thought, yet at the same time seems to be threatened more than ever before by uncontrollable cosmic forces, that the European mind has become more susceptible to the charms of ancient American art. It is easier for us to understand the work of these Indian artists — whose names will always be unknown to us, as are those of the artists of the early Middle Ages, when religious belief was still paramount — than it was for the discoverers and conquerors of the New World, bound as they were by the limitations of dogmatic creeds. The way in which the accent on form is sometimes carried to the point of abstraction, however, has only an apparent relationship to our own modern art. There is a fundamental difference here. The connecting link with the world of gods and spirits, with a religion rooted in the community, is an essential characteristic of ancient Indian art, which makes it altogether different from the individualistic self-glorification that marks the art of our own era.

GREATER PERU AND
ECUADOR

II. GREATER PERU

During the past two decades archaeologists have come to use the term
'Central Andes' for the coastlands and mountainous areas of modern Peru,
including the Bolivian highlands, as distinct from the northern Andes
(Ecuador and Colombia) and southern Andes (north-western Argentina
and northern Chile). The term 'Greater Peru' also covers part of these
two border areas, which at the time of the Spanish conquest formed part
of the great Inca empire. Long before the days of the divine emperors who
ruled over this realm for almost two centuries the whole area of Greater
Peru was the scene of cultural movements of which each had something of
its own to add that enriched the whole.

The area where most archaeological exploration has been done is Peru
itself. But even here much more excavation work has to be carried out if
the wide gaps in our knowledge that remain are to be closed and the
numerous blank patches on the archaeological map filled in. Note that
I say an *archaeological* map. For, apart from a few exceptions, we are
indebted to archaeology for our information about ancient Peruvian art.
For we have not even the beginnings of a written script to assist us in dating, as we have in Mesoamerica — unless we may consider as a sort of
pictographic writing the great number of painted vases that have been
preserved from certain periods and the figures woven into garments,
fabrics and covers by the ancient weavers. But pictures of this kind are
only an inadequate substitute for the hieroglyphs of the Maya and the
pictographic signs of the Mexicans.

The greater part of the cultural history of ancient Peru can be understood
only with the aid of archaeology. The German scholar Max Uhle must be
regarded as the pioneer in this field so far as the Andes are concerned. His
first systematic excavations — the first ever made in Peru — were carried
out before the turn of the century. Among the Peruvian scholars who
followed in his wake pride of place is taken by Julio C. Tello. French
archaeologists, too, as well as others from Germany, have worked in Peru;
among the latter H. Ubbelohde-Doering may be singled out for particular
mention.

It would be impossible to write a history of ancient Peruvian art and
culture without taking into account the results of the excavations that
have been carried out — not, unfortunately, in all areas. But by far the
greater part of the art objects in museums and private collections are

the product, not of proper excavations, but of the efforts of zealous and unscrupulous treasure-hunters, who have been active ever since the earliest days of the colonial period. In later times, when remunerative prices came to be paid for pottery, this too became an object of interest to treasure-hunters; and at an even later stage grave-robbers also took a fancy to textiles, which they had formerly been content to leave lying in the desert sand. And these fabrics are frequently of unique beauty. They are probably the most precious articles bequeathed to us by the inhabitants of the oases in the Peruvian river valleys. These lace-like gauzes, tapestries and velours are not to be found in any other part of ancient America. Peru can boast of almost every kind of fabric known to the Old World. Intricate dyeing techniques, such as the *ikat* and *plangue* methods, were familiar to the Peruvians, as were cotton fabrics in a plain weave that were subsequently painted. Some weaving techniques are thought to occur only in ancient Peru.

Almost all the textiles that have been preserved up to our own day originate from the dry sands of the coastal strip. But we can probably assume that fabrics of equal beauty were also produced in the mountainous areas, and no doubt textiles, being less easily destroyed than pottery, must have contributed more to the dissemination of certain styles than is commonly supposed. The highlands provided important raw materials for weaving: the wool of the llama and alpaca, as well as the finest quality wool, that of the graceful vicuña. Particular importance attaches to weaving for two reasons: firstly because it is a specifically Peruvian art, and secondly because of the role it plays in the dissemination of certain styles. Although several scholars have studied ancient weaving techniques, the progress made towards establishing the exact localities of production, and the chronological sequence of various styles, has been much less significant than in the case of ceramics, the most instructive material in Peruvian archaeology.

We have an incredibly large quantity of ceramic ware from many areas and epochs, mostly found in graves. Just as the weavers only made use of the most simple implements for the manufacture of even the best fabrics, so the potters worked without using a potter's wheel. They could make the finest circular objects by hand. Later moulds were used as well. They had no knowledge whatever of any kind of glazing, such as often lends the pottery of eastern Asia its particular aesthetic charm.

THE NATURAL SETTING When one approaches the coast of Peru after passing through the Panama Canal, the lunar landscape might make one think that one were about to land upon another planet. The dark green of the wooded coastlands of

Colombia and Ecuador gives place to the yellow of the Peruvian desert shimmering under the noonday sun — or, more frequently, when the sun disappears behind clouds, taking on a greyish colour. Sand-dunes of varying height alternate with precipitous cliffs. Here and there brown or blackish rocks rise up directly out of the sea, tinged with red by the setting sun. In the distance one can dimly make out the bluish outline of the Cordillera.

If one arrives from the east by air, one catches fleeting glimpses of a strange landscape. Passing rapidly over the vast forests of the Amazon basin, much of which belong to the republics of Ecuador, Peru and Bolivia, one's eye is caught by the High Cordillera ranges, running almost parallel, above which tower several gigantic snow-capped peaks, rugged mountain massifs without trees or vegetation. Here and there lie a few green upland pastures. Then, far below the wings of the plane, one sees at last the dazzling desert, traversed by arid valleys. If one flies on in a northerly direction narrow strips of green appear at infrequent intervals, becoming wider towards the north, as the rivers here carry more water. These mountain streams flow from east to west, from the Andes to the Pacific. The harm they do is outweighed by the blessings they bring: their water is the life-giving force in this desert country. In the north of Peru the desert abuts almost directly upon the more humid bush country near what is today the border of Ecuador. To the south it extends as far as the north of Chile. This is one of the most arid parts of the earth.

In olden times these mountain streams seem to have carried more water than they do today. Around their estuaries were large areas overgrown with reeds and brushwood, a refuge for game, waterfowl and deer. Nowadays, even during the rainy season in the mountains, the rivers often fail to reach the coast, since their water is already drawn off to irrigate fields of rice, cotton and sugar-cane. What the inhabitants of the coastal region call rain is generally no more than a dense mist that falls in the form of drizzle. Only at irregular intervals of many years is there proper rainfall, which may have a catastrophic effect, since the houses in the villages are built of clay and straw, and are far from solid. This was the case already in ancient times, and still today it sometimes happens that, even without any rain falling, large areas of fertile land are swept away by raging torrents or buried under masses of stones and debris. The tropical lowlands in the east lie outside our scope; from an archaeological point of view they are as yet virtually unexplored territory. The same division into coastland and sierra holds good here. We are best informed about the coastal zone. But in olden times contact may have been closer between the inhabitants of the mountainous areas and the coastal strip than between the inhabitants of the various valleys, which were separated from one another by great stretches of barren desert. Many fertile highland valleys still invite excavation. According to Julio C. Tello, the Nestor of Peruvian archaeology, a higher civilization developed here earlier than on the coast; only later, as improved irrigation methods came to be mastered, djd it extend down the valleys to the coast. Much work remains to be done before we know the whole truth.

THE PEOPLE Like most Indian peoples, the ancient Peruvians were not great seafarers; this is the view prevalent among scholars, and it is a well-founded one. One cannot sail far in boats made of rushes, such as are still used nowadays at some places along the west coast and on Lake Titicaca, for the rushes absorb the water and after a certain time lose their buoyancy. Rafts were apparently not used before the late Inca period. The Andes were undoubtedly settled in the very remote past by people who came overland from the north.

The great variety of human types in the Andes, even within a limited area, is clearly illustrated by the well-known portrait heads of fired clay found in graves in the northern coastal province (cf. p. 145). Among them are faces almost European in type, comparable to the faces one finds on medieval sculptured figures. Others have somewhat Mongolian features. Both types can be seen even today among Indians living in one and the same village. This resemblance to peoples of the Old World has led some imaginative writers to advance the oft-reputed hypothesis that Peruvian man originated from Phoenicia, the sunken continent of Atlantis, or even from Egypt or Palestine.

In actual fact it has been proved scientifically that the first immigrants were nomadic hunters who came from the north of the continent ten or twelve millennia ago, or even earlier still. They already brought with them from Asia different racial characteristics. Now and again in the course of centuries vessels from South-east Asia, and later also from the Pacific islands, may have landed on South American shores. There are some scholars who ascribe all the metal-working in South America directly to influences from Asia. In any case the view prevalent until recently that all ancient American culture was autochthonous has now been challenged. Our knowledge about the distant past is still far from precise. But one thing we are able to trace is the development of definite individual features in the culture and art of the New World.

It is no longer possible to ascertain the exact number of the many languages that were still spoken in the Andes when the Spaniards appeared

Large figure of a shark with its tail raised high, in very fine gold. It is massive, but the ventral side is hollow. Its weight is considerable: approx. 3 oz. Apart from a few exceptions the cultural centres of ancient America showed no interest in depicting fish. Of course the Colombian and Mexican peoples dwelt in the interior, but all of them must have known of the existence of fish. The peoples of the Peruvian coastlands and of Central America must have had unusual possibilities for studying oceanic animals, which must have stimulated their imagination. In the Peruvian coastlands fish were very often represented on fabrics and clay vessels. This figure was found in the San Isidro General region, Costa Rica. *Museum für Völkerkunde, Munich.*

Clay bowl from Coclé, Panama. The abstract or consciously non-naturalistic style of painting in ancient America reaches its zenith in the ceramic ware from Coclé. During the drought years 1930, 1931 and 1933 two sites at Coclé were excavated by archaeologists from the Peabody Museum, Harvard University. Amazing finds were made: exquisite clay vessels, gold ornaments, magnificently shaped stones mounted in gold, etc. On the Pearl Islands, off the Pacific coast near the entrance to the Panama Canal, Erland Nordenskiöld's expedition of 1927 discovered in the course of archaeological excavations the remains of two cultures superimposed upon one another. The ceramic ware from the more recent one belongs stylistically to that of western Panama, the archaeology of which was at that time still virtually unknown. Petrographic analyses have shown that this ware was produced on the island. *Private collection; Munich.*

Painted hands on a cotton fabric (fragment). **Enviro**ns of Ica, southern Peru. Paracas Cavernas culture Dating approx. from the time of Christ. *Museum für Völkerkunde, Berlin. Length approx. 21¼ in.*

Embroidery on a shroud from the Paracas peninsula. Hovering mythical beings, half man and half fish. Paracas Necropolis culture. 1st century. A.D. *Museum für Völkerkunde, Munich. Much reduced in size.*

Clay jar with the characteristic Chavín spout. Northern coastlands of Peru. Dating from approx. the time of Christ. *Bernouilli Collection, Basle. Height 6½ in.*

Clay vessel in negative painting with composition of sculptured figures. Upper Santa valley. Recuay style. Approx. 500 A.D. *Museum für Völkerkunde, Berlin. Height 8¾ in.*

Painted clay vessel: portrait of a prince or priest. Moche culture. Middle of the 1st millennium A.D. *Museum für Völkerkunde, Berlin. Height 11 in.*

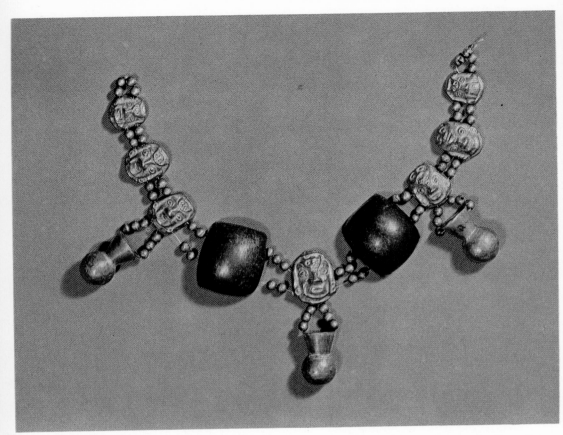

Necklace with hollow gold beads. The colour of the large square beads points to the use of a silver alloy. The faces and jar-shaped beads enable this necklace to be assigned to the Moche culture. Etén, near Chiclayo. After 500 A.D. *Museum für Völkerkunde, Berlin. Length 11 in.*

on the scene. Of some only the name has been handed down to us, and it is often impossible to discover whether this name refers to a proper language or merely to a dialect. Under Inca rule, as we know, an official language was introduced, which led to the partial or complete disappearance of the languages spoken by the peoples subject to them. There was undoubtedly a great variety of languages, which shows that the population was divided into many different groups.

Higher cultures arose quite gradually with the first cultivation of crops. Millennia elapsed between these early beginnings and the arrival of the subjects of the Emperor Charles V, with their horses, iron helmets and superior weapons. The Spaniards were struck by the golden splendour of the Inca nobles. Their magnificent tunics of vicuña wool, with bright designs in beautifully harmonized colours, seemed to Spanish eyes as though spun from the finest silk. They also had reason to admire the exquisite workmanship of Inca ceramic ware, their carvings in wood and bone, and their inlaid work of red shell and green turquoise. Most of the Spaniards, however, themselves little more than barbarians, only noticed the absence of things they took for granted: first and foremost the Christian religion, but also horses, carts and iron implements; for the few bronze weapons and implements the Peruvians possessed were of course technically far inferior to those of the Spaniards. The Bronze Age had only begun in earnest with the advent of Inca rule, and tools of wood and stone still played an important role. If Spanish agriculturalists and craftsmen would have been given Peruvian implements for ploughing, weaving or chiselling stone, they would in all probability have been able to make little profitable use of them. Primitive tools are, of course, no criterion of artistic quality. But one cannot help being astonished at the works of craftsmanship produced by the peoples of the Andes despite the simplicity of their weaving devices, their lack of iron and their ignorance of the potter's wheel. Sometimes it actually seems as though the very technical imperfection of their instruments encouraged these Indian artists to make the most of their manual skill. Some craftsmen became real artists in the course of their efforts to honour their gods and semi-divine princes.

Not even an approximate date can be assigned to the stone blades, pro- jectile points, scrapers, fishing-hooks, hammer-stones and crude stone vessels found in Greater Peru — the scattered evidence of their existence left behind them by primitive hunters and fishermen. Some scholars reckon with a date between 7000 and 3000 B.C. No doubt millennia went by before the first crops were sown: ultimately there were over thirty different kinds of domesticated plants in the Andean area, more than were known in any other part of ancient America.

As has already been mentioned, the initial stages of a higher culture coincide with the beginning of the cultivation of plants. The American Junius Bird was the first to study plant chronology, in his exemplary excavations at the mouth of the River Chicama in northern Peru. He made a cross-section from top to bottom of the vast refuse heap known as Huaca Prieta,[1] which rises to a height of nearly 40 feet. From the thickness of the individual strata it is possible to tell their antiquity, and thus reconstruct in outline the mode of life of the inhabitants of the coastland in early times. Mussel-shells are the remains of consumed crustaceans; parts of nets with perforated stones used as weights provide evidence that fishermen lived here, while bones of mammals testify to the fact that they hunted animals. At various sites the inventory differs in detail. Even cotton is to be found at this stage among the remains of plants. It may be assumed that it was cultivated, too, as were gourds, beans and capsicum pepper, which still plays a very important part in the diet of Peruvians at the present day; whereas maize, or Indian corn, one of the staple food-stuffs in later periods, was still unknown. Men also gathered various kinds of roots, tuberous plants and seeds.

In contrast to the caves in southern Chile, Peru did not yield any remains of a pure hunter culture — hewn stone blades in association with the bones of long-extinct animals. These hunters of wild horses, gigantic sloths and guanacos are estimated to have lived in the 7th millennium B.C. — earlier still in the northern regions.

Primitive plants It is surprising that all the early settlements on the coast of Peru, of which thirty have been discovered in the course of the last ten years by the French archaeologist Frédéric Engel, already show remains of domesticated plants and garments knotted from fibres of cotton-plants and wild plants. It has not been possible to establish for certain the existence of any settlements of fishermen and hunters proper. On the surface some ancient stone blades have been found, isolated from other traces of human activity. Engel has made C-14 tests on samples of organic matter obtained from his excavations of several ancient settlements on the coast. All these indicate the period 4000—3000 B.C., most of them the first half of this millennium. Common to all these sites is the complete absence of pottery in the earliest layers. For this reason the whole lengthy period of primitive hunters and agriculturalists has been called the pre-ceramic period. Cooking was done on heated stones in vessels made of gourds or from similar substances. But in addition to stone implements and weapons, the arid soil also yielded shells, bone and wood, as well as spindle-whorls of stone, wood and fruit-stones, wooden needles and bone for making knotted fabrics and for sewing. Of their work naturally only fragments have survived, for in the course of millennia garments in close contact with the bodies of deceased persons disintegrated. These men were by no means primitive savages, as was once almost universally thought; this is shown by the mere fact that they appreciated fine clothing. Engel found that the dead were buried in their houses of stone or clay, in association with very fine fabrics knotted in various techniques. We are indebted to him for all we know about the technique and ornamentation of these textiles. Such fabrics and bags were produced without the aid of any instrumental device. Engel was also able to find lace-like gauzes, open-work, primitive embroidery, multi-coloured ribbons, feather-work and even *kelim* tapestry. Not only do simple geometric designs occur, in zig-zag, striped and rectangular patterns, but also parts of animals and even whole bodies of animals, reptiles, fish and felidae. For the cultural histor- FIG. I ian it is interesting to note that all these articles must have been produced without the simple loom that came into general use later; and it is no doubt even more interesting and important that after the invention of the bobbin, i.e. with an improvement in technique, the textiles at first lost some of their artistic quality. J. Bird, too, found only a few genuine fabrics in the Huaca Prieta, all unusually narrow and devoid of ornamen-tation. At the end of the pre-ceramic period the loom must therefore already have been in existence.

It goes without saying that among the early finds there also occur engraved ornaments of bone, mussel-shell and stone. To satisfy their human vanity these primitive agriculturalists wore wooden ear-plugs, occasionally painted red. They adorned themselves with bead necklaces of bone, shell and perforated fruit-stones. They even made mirrors of polished lava.

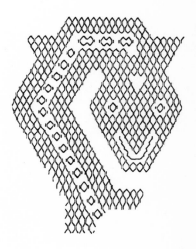

FIG. 1 — *Fish or serpent. Detail of knotted cotton threads found in the pre-ceramic cemetery of Asia, south of Lima. After Fr. Engel.*

It is of course not always possible to distinguish between amulets and jewellery.

If the dates obtained by the radio-carbon method are reliable, there is a gap between the time when plants were first cultivated and the first visible signs of the emergence of a high culture. About this period we are still so much in the dark that we cannot define its limits exactly. There is no bridge, no direct transition from the early beginnings described above to a period of cultural history that embraces the whole of Peru. This era seems to appear quite suddenly; and it was one in which, more than in any later period, works of art were produced that were inspired by profound religious feeling. I have in mind the art of Chavín in the north and Paracas in the south of Peru: in both cases the accent was wholly upon religion. This has been referred to as a cultist period. It has still been assigned to the pre-classic period, following the division of Peruvian art into pre-classic, classic and post-classic, on an analogy with the classification made in Mesoamerica. But in my view there was at no time in the history of Greater Peru an age more brilliant than this, and therefore I do not readily subscribe to the term 'pre-classic' as applied to Chavín.

'Chavín horizon' is an expression that seems to me more appropriate, for all its ambiguity. For from a chronological point of view this period is not sharply defined. Greater Peru, in all its expanse, suddenly opens up before us. Although most of the characteristic features usually associated with a high culture are lacking, yet this is an early apogee of civilization; it is now that in many man-made objects a religious intensity comes to be expressed such as was rarely attained in subsequent epochs. Can this culture have been introduced from other lands?

The beginning of maize cultivation and decorated ceramics occurred almost simultaneously. In the first part of this volume mention has already been made of the striking affinities and obvious resemblances between unique forms of the late archaic epoch in Mesoamerica and the Chavín horizon in Peru. As in the case of Olmec art, that of Chavín seems strange in many of its aspects; it appears to be distributed over a fairly wide area and to have been introduced from foreign parts. In short, it abounds in riddles. No answer can as yet be given to a number of questions: Where did this complex style come from? Was Greater Peru influenced from the north? Or did both these great areas borrow from some unknown common source, the identity of which can only be guessed at? Let us rather keep to the tangible evidence. Since mention was made above of the art of weaving, of products which we are able to see and touch, let us turn first of all to the south of Peru, where conditions for the preservation of impermanent material were far more favourable than they were in the north, and in the first place examine the province were the finest textiles were produced: Paracas.

Today the Paracas peninsula, situated to the south of the seaport of Pisco, is a windswept desert entirely covered with sand-dunes, and is regarded purely as wasteland. Excavations carried out very recently support the view of the late Carrión Cachot, the Peruvian archaeologist, who maintained firmly that in ancient times some of the desert of Paracas was transformed into fertile land by removing the sand down to a certain depth, thus exposing the moist soil below. The moisture was derived from underground watercourses. Previous Peruvian excavations carried out on the peninsula had already brought to light subterranean dwelling-chambers. But the most recent excavations led to the discovery of complete houses, the roofs of which were thatched with straw. Remains of settlements were found as well as burial-places.

After Tello, on his frequent visits to the peninsula between 1923 and 1925, discovered four hundred 'mummy packs' containing valuable shrouds, the authorities took pains to ensure that no unauthorized person should purloin any of this precious national property. Until recently it was not possible for any archaeologist, whatever his qualifications, to obtain a licence to carry out excavations here. But no one could prevent vandals from digging up rare ceramics and mummies interred with costly

FIG. 2 — *Design on the cotton swathing of a mummy, painted in yellow, brown and red. Deity with serpents as its hair and girdle. Early Paracas. After Bird and Bellinger.*

Fig. 3 — *Hovering demon, from a large shroud (manto). Polychrome embroidery on a dark green ground. The colours used were mainly various shades of blue and green, olive, pink and dark red. Paracas Necropolis. After Bird and Bellinger.*

embroidered fabrics, and from selling them at high prices in other countries. Paracas textiles hardly ever appear on the open art market, and their prices continue to soar upwards. Before the name Paracas meant anything outside Peru, some Paracas fabrics of fine quality had already come into the possession of museums or private collectors. A few years ago it became known that the so-called Paracas style originates not only from the peninsula itself but also from the Nazca and Ica valleys situated some distance to the south-east.

It has always been the practice to distinguish between two phases of the Paracas culture: Paracas Cavernas and Paracas Necropolis. Necropolis is regarded as the later phase, and rightly so. The term is derived from the various burial-sites discovered by Tello. The embroidery on the large shrouds, or mantles (*mantos*) as they are called, is unsurpassed in its soft harmonious polychrome tones — this, at least, is the opinion of Junius Bird, one of the most distinguished authorities on the technical aspects of Andean archaeology.

The chronological sequence of Cavernas and Necropolis can scarcely be called in question any longer. It is curious that Cavernas cannot boast of such splendid achievements in textile art, but instead has produced particularly attractive polychrome pottery, whereas the monochrome ceramic ware of the Necropolis phase pales in comparison with the unique splendour of its textiles.

A great number of different kinds of textiles were already known in the Cavernas phase, including lace-like gauzes and embroidery in a stem stitch in which wool yarn was employed on cotton fabric. In addition to white and brown, the natural colours of the wool and cotton, there existed two different shades of red and a greenish blue. A sort of cotton swathing in a simple weave, used for mummies, is invariably found painted, in various shades of brown and yellow, some red and a very small amount of blue. There are figures of deities with serpents depicted FIG. 2 by means of angular jagged lines.

The most important preliminary process in weaving consists of spinning the raw fibre into yarn, and here it seems that the Paracas spinners were able to produce astonishingly fine threads with the aid of a simple hand-spindle. On occasion llama wool was already used as well as cotton, and this practice increased with time — a sign of growing commercial links with the mountainous areas, for it is only there that various kinds of woolly-haired camel thrive. The llama and alpaca, the only large domestic animals in America, must have been reared in the sierra at a relatively early date; the vicuña, which produces the finest wool, is a dainty animal that can only live in freedom. During the Inca period battues of vicuña were organized annually for the ruling élite. The animals were driven into pens, shorn and then released again. Their fine wool was reserved for the clothing of men of rank.

The articles of clothing worn by the Cavernas people consisted of short shirt-like tunics, loin-cloths, turbans and waist-bands. We have here the first evidence of the standard clothing of the ancient Peruvians, most of which was still worn in the days of Inca rule. Their tombs, the so-called *cavernas*, are shafts hewn — with a considerable amount of effort — into the rock: the upper part is sometimes lined with masonry. They may be over twenty feet deep. At the bottom these shafts broaden out into spacious circular sepulchral chambers. The basic type of these shaft tombs was also common in western Mexico, Colombia and in parts of the highlands of Ecuador. The 'Paracas' *cavernas* discovered by William Duncan Strong near Ocucaje in the Ica valley in 1953 each contained only a single body and were much simpler narrower tombs, covered with round pebbles or clods of clay. On the Paracas peninsula, on the other hand, up to fifty-five packs wrapped in simple cotton material have been found in one single bottle-shaped shaft. A large number of skulls — probably for purposes of magic medicine — were trephined, a process well-known to us from the primitive civilizations of antiquity. In Paracas some perforations in the skulls were covered with gold-plating. There were also found obsidian knives — the surgical instruments used by the priest-doctors to perform major operations.

The well-known Necropolis situated on the peninsula itself has rectangular subterranean chambers from which, already in the 1920s, Tello recovered over four hundred mummy packs containing the most gorgeous fabrics. Such sumptuous expenditure on the cult of the dead was hardly ever rivalled in later Peruvian history. The living seem to have

FIG. 4 — *Double-spouted ivory-coloured clay vessel with plastically rendered beans. Late Paracas (Paracas Necropolis). After Bennett.*

spent almost their whole lives thinking of death, as they wove these fine garments and large shrouds, the latter embroidered with figures in harmonious colours. Hardly any of the articles of clothing have been worn. These garments were woven specially for the dead, two or more of the same kind sometimes being made for the same person. The body, placed naked in a seated position, is wrapped in several layers of coarse cotton fabric like the coats of an onion. The mouth and eyes are often covered over with thin gold-plating and the toes and fingers tied together with cords. The brown faces are powdered with pulverized ferric oxide to give the colour of fresh blood. The heads were moulded artificially in early childhood and seem very narrow.

It is possible that in former times the Paracas peninsula itself, now no more than a desert, could boast of extensive fields of cotton-plants — we can imagine their red and yellow blossoms swaying in the wind — and the downy seeds yielded the raw material for these numerous shrouds.

FIG. 3

On the hem of the shrouds (*mantos*) figures are embroidered; sometimes they are almost completely covered with embroidery. It is not only their religious content that entitles them to be classed among the world's finest works of art. They feature mythical beings, monstrous deities, warriors and dancers with trophy heads, birds drawn in a more or less naturalistic manner, fish, batrachia, and bizarre products of a mystical imagination. There are demons who float up and down, spew snakes out of their mouths, sometimes wear crowns on their heads, and hold in their talons feather fans, clubs, sheaves of arrows and sacrificial knives. There are ubiquitous cut-off human heads, with grinning expressions on their faces; these are often reduced to symbols, as the magic-working trophies of fearsome deities. But what delights our eyes, as it must have delighted those of the gods, is the wealth of harmonious colour. A careful count has revealed no less than 190 shades, and as many as 22 on a single fabric.

The mineral paints and pigments have been surprisingly well preserved. On one and the same fabric identical figures in a series are coloured in a certain rhythmical sequence, no doubt in accordance with the specifications of some ritual; this has been interpreted by Tello as the symbolism of a lunar calendar. What to us seems to be simply ornamentation was undoubtedly imbued with a religious significance. None can match these artists in their sure sense for harmonious colour or for the arrangement of figures within a given framework. It has been estimated that several years' work went into the making of a single large shroud. Modern artists complete their work much more rapidly, for their paintings are but an expression of personal feeling — not works designed to honour the dead or divine beings.

It appears that all the mummies found in the well-known Paracas Necropolis are male. Were these sacerdotal dignitaries, who interceded for the living with the gods in the world beyond? Ubbelohde-Doering was the first to put forward specifically the idea that the painted and woven figures and objects were prayers in pictorial form. We shall see how plausible this idea is. Incidentally, some of the mummy packs recovered did not contain the bodies of deceased persons but were completely filled with beans. Beans were an important article of food, and their rapid rate of growth made them a symbol of fertility. They may also be seen on one of the few painted cotton fabrics from the Paracas Necropolis that features a feline demon, or a priest disguised as one, drawn in a curiously realistic manner. Paintings on fabrics also recur in later periods. The pottery of Necropolis is technically superior to that from the *cavernas;* the walls are thinner and the firing superior. One connoisseur (Kroeber) says of the plain ivory-coloured ceramic ware of this period that it is "of a refined specialized elegance, the final point in the development of style." We shall discuss this relativistic approach later. Kroeber was not aware at the time that painted pottery would also be found in association with this ivory ware. Stratigraphic excavations carried out by W. D. Strong have established the chronological priority of Paracas

FIG. 4

FIG. 5 — *Clay bowl, painted after firing. The contour lines are engraved. The feline demon with a tongue like a whip is represented on both sides: here it bears obsidian knives, while on the opposite side it wears a trophy head. The colours include green, ochre and a little red on a sandy yellow ground. Museum für Völkerkunde, Berlin.*

Cavernas ceramic ware, called by this scholar 'Early Paracas'. It foreshadows the polychrome ceramic ware that was to become characteristic of southern Peru. There are flasks with narrow necks (with and without handles), deep bowls, jars with two spouts connected by a bridge in the form of a band, and others in which a plastic animal or human head takes the place of a spout. There are a few clumsy engraved clay figures, flat and unwieldy. Common to all is the decoration with incised contour lines, enclosing areas of colour, all applied after firing — this being a kind of cloisonné. The drab colours giving the impression of paste were probably applied after firing in pulverized form without sufficient binder; this is why they smudge easily. Nevertheless their soft lustre gives them a peculiar charm. The colours are dark red, above all dark yellow, olive green or bluish-green. Black jars devoid of any decoration also occur. The frequent representation of mythical beings with features of beasts of prey ranges Early Paracas in the Chavín horizon. In addition to cloisonné there also appear designs of purely geometric character in 'negative painting'. Occasionally the design took the form of simple figures of fish or birds; in negative painting these designs are covered over so that the light colour of the surface of the vessel stands out against a dark brown background. Negative painting often appears in Early Paracas ceramic ware on the same vessel as positive painting in paste, which is applied to incised contour lines, whereas in Late Paracas pottery negative painting only occurs on a few pieces, and then always on its own. The delight in curvilinear forms and spirals, a very typical feature of Chavín style, is absent in the angular ornaments on Paracas painted vessels.

CHAVÍN Chavín art proper gives in many ways an impression of such maturity that, owing to its almost contrived stylization, until twenty years ago it was assigned to a much later period than it is today, when we have the results of excavations to guide us. Radio-carbon analysis shows that it goes back as far as the beginning of the first millennium A.D. The terms 'Chavín horizon', 'Chavín culture' and 'Chavín style' are derived from the name of a small place called Chavín de Huántar in the north Peruvian highlands. Already in the middle of the last century travellers noted the ruins of a very ancient fort in the narrow valley of the River Mozna, which issues forth from the Cordillera Nevada. This building was certainly neither a fort nor a castle *(castillo)*, but a colossal temple. In 1873 the discovery was made of a strange relief on one of the stone slabs of this temple, which was called after its discoverer the Raimondi Stele. On it is carved a monstrous deity holding a sceptre in each hand and crowned by the jaws of beasts of prey, surmounted one upon another; between abstract volutes are rearing and writhing serpents, forming, as it were, the halo of the deity.

The wealth of curved lines found in this style is a characteristic feature of Chavín. No other style of Greater Peru has such vigorous curvilinear forms. It seems to suggest distinct affinities with the Olmec style in Mesoamerica. As in the case of that strange style, Chavín does not possess any absolutely uniform features, either as regards stylistic phases or various localities. It is surprising that so far no major systematic excavations have been made at Chavín de Huántar as they have been on an extensive scale in the temple cities of Mesoamerica. The little we know about the life of man in that distant time we owe to excavations carried out at several places on the coast, in particular at the edges of the oases in the beds of the northern rivers.

As regards the type-site itself we may agree with the late Wendell C. Bennett, the American archaeologist, that the temple complexes were probably erected by pilgrims who made their way to this high-lying

FIG. 7 — *Stone plaque in relief. It depicts a god in the guise of a beast of prey, holding in one hand a sceptre decorated with the head of a serpent and an eagle, and in the other hand a heart; the feet are shown differently. He is accompanied by serpents. Environs of Chavín de Huántar. Private collection, Lima.*

Fig. 8 — *Plaque in relief, of hard stone. Mythical condor, bearing on its back elements of the head of a beast of prey, and with serpents writhing in its claws. Chavín de Huántar. After a photo by Rojas Ponce.*

valley on certain festival days to make sacrifice to the gods who lived there. Bennett refers in this connection to the customs that can still be observed among pilgrims today: "During one or more weeks in the year many people made the pilgrimage to a centre like Chavín de Huántar for religious celebration. While great numbers were assembled, the building materials would be brought in, stones dressed, and some of the larger slabs put in place. When the ceremony ended and the pilgrims returned to their distant homes, specialized architects carried on the construction with a few local labourers." The valley of Chavín is much too narrow to have offered sufficient room for the fields of permanent settlers. Today there are several places of pilgrimage in the Andean lands where Christian churches and chapels have superseded pagan temples.

Adjoining the three-storeyed main temple at Chavín are several smaller buildings; in the centre is a sunken courtyard with stepped terraces leading out of it. In the dark inner rooms, which are reminiscent of Maya ritual chambers in their small size, one finds stairways and subterranean galleries. The exterior masonry, made of roughly-hewn stones, is in part faced with polished slabs. Here and there we see human heads of stone inserted into the masonry by means of tenons. The old wrinkled faces have serpents coiled around them. Is there some affinity here with the ancient Mexican rain god?

On stone reliefs in the round the image of the supreme deity of Chavín occurs again and again, either in the guise of a human being in jaguar

FIG. 7

form, wearing a serpent girdle, or of a condor, the great vulture of the Andes; this bird is regarded still today in some areas as the ancestor of man, but in Chavín it generally bears the features of a jaguar. These elements often appear separately — rendered by curves and symbols so abstract as to be scarcely recognizable.

Looking at the flat reliefs carved in stone, one is automatically reminded of metal engravings; and a small number of embossed gold ornaments in the inimitable Chavín style have in fact come on to the market. Most of them originate from the Lambayeque area further north, where this style may have survived for longer. It is a fact — at least, according to the present state of our knowledge — that metal-working began in Peru at least five hundred years earlier than in Mesoamerica. But we still do not know exactly where it originated, or the routes by which it spread from one part of America to another.

It is almost unbelievable that so far no exact plan has been compiled of such an important site as Chavín de Huántar. Basically the whole complex is oriented from west to east. The architecture can by no means be regarded wholly as primitive: there must have been a long process of development, the various phases of which are, however, not known. When details are published of the recently-discovered ruins of three-storeyed temples in the upper valley of the River Marañón, this will give us some means of comparison. A second and larger complex of ruins from the Chavín horizon, situated on the upper course of the River Jequetepeque, has been known for some time. Peruvian scholars have given it the name of 'Kuntur Wasi', or the Condor House. There are said to be extensive mountain cemeteries in the vicinity, but they have not yet been explored. In 1946 American archaeologists discovered thick layers of refuse from the Chavín horizon in the Virú valley further to the south. Several buildings of rubble and clay with rectangular ground-plans belong to the same period. Cone-shaped clay tiles, a characteristic feature of this epoch, were also found. The larger buildings may have served as temples. If potsherds from the Chavín horizon should be found there, this may indicate that the smaller buildings on isolated hills were some kind of mountain shrine from the same phase. Already in the 1930s the interest of specialists was aroused by Tello's discovery of Chavín buildings in the upper part of the coastal valleys of Nepeña and Casma.

FIG. 9 — *Mythical personage with club. Singular decoration of curved lines with human faces in profile. Bas-relief on one of the numerous stelae near the ruined temple at Sechin, Casma valley. Chavinoid style. After Julio C. Tello.*

FIG. 10 — *Recumbent god in the guise of a beast of prey, engraved on a bone spatula Found by Fr. Engel near an ancient stepped building on the steep rocky coast at Las Aldas, central Peru. After a photo.*

The bas-reliefs on the clay walls of temple complexes executed in Chavín style were painted in several colours. Unfortunately all the mural decorations on clay walls, and all the large clay sculptures, that are known only from these two valleys have been destroyed in the course of time.

Stone is much more resistant to deterioration. The engravings on stone stelae found at Cerro Sechín in the Casma valley are in an archaic style FIG. 9 recalling that of Chavín, but with some divergencies. The figures represented here have often been compared to the 'Danzantes' on Monte Albán in southern Mexico. If there is any close affinity here it will probably be coincidental.

The fact that no traces of the Chavín horizon have so far been discovered on the southern Peruvian plateau does not necessarily mean that it did not exist here; there is, however, no doubt that related features occur in the art of Tiahuanaco (cf. p.p. 200 f.).

We are best informed about the appearance of the Chavín horizon in the northern coastal area through the excavations carried out by Larco Hoyle in the Chicama valley, although we are fully justified in rejecting Larco's suggestion that the Chavín horizon originated in the coastal area. Larco has called this whole culture period 'Cupiznique', after a valley in the desert which branches off from the Chicama valley and is said to be the main site of Chavín graves. The pottery is monochrome, either an earthy brown or black; where it has a more reddish hue, this is due to an improved firing technique. The ornamentation gives the impression of being engraved in stone, or else of being fashioned in bas-relief. In part it consists of abstract circles and volutes, in part of thorn-like projections, in which case the circles may correspond to the spots of the jaguar and the volutes to the animal's tail; in other parts one can make out the whole body or the head of the god, portrayed as a beast of prey, stylized to a varying degree. Less frequent are fully-modelled animals and fruit, or even houses and human beings. It is only in a later phase that bichrome painting appears; as in the case of Early Paracas the outlines are engraved. The colouring — a metallic black and a dark red — was, of course, applied before firing.

The climate of the northern part of the coast is not quite so arid as that of the south. For this reason, probably, only occasional shreds of textiles were found — apart from a few exceptions. But the dress worn by the figures indicates that, in contrast to Paracas, the people of the south wore only loin-cloths and turbans.

The vessels here already occur in quite a variety of shapes; their massiveness and colour are suggestive of stone. The elegant and vigorous stirrup-shaped spout appears for the first time in this area; the tradition survived in the north until the colonial period. It may be noted that at present Chavín ware fetches the highest prices of all Peruvian ceramics on the art market. Its verve, it is true, also lends it a particular charm. The massive spout alone necessitates great skill on the part of the potter, and can hardly have been produced when technique was still in its infancy. Other articles much sought after by potential buyers are flasks with wide necks and pots engraved in Chavín style.

FIG. 11

Some bone amulets and spatulas also bear engraved ornamentation in Chavín style. Larco's team of excavators recovered from a grave in stony soil on the upper reaches of the River Chicama the remains of a body buried lying on one side, wearing a ring of bone on each finger. Life-like little apes were modelled on these rings. Thus a distinct realism may exist side by side with abstract stylization.

FIG. 10

A few miles north of the modern Peruvian capital of Lima, not very far from the bathing-resort of Ancón, the discovery was made during building work of deep refuse deposits containing Chavín potsherds. This is now a barren area of sand-dunes; but in the lower strata large reservoirs were found — evidence that the Chavín people were already able to organize a regular water-supply. Naturally they had not as yet developed a system of superb irrigation works such as was constructed later in the

FIG. 11 — *Dark-coloured clay jar with enormous stirrup spout. The engraved decoration represents the stylized head of a beast of prey. The singular stirrup spout occurs for the first time in coastal Chavin ware. Chicama valley. After Larco Hoyle.*

FIGS. 12, 13 — *Clay flasks of various shapes with hatched and punched decoration, typical of Chavín ceramic ware, from the Chicama valley. Chavín ware is the most costly and is only rarely to be found in European museums. Most of it is in the private museum of the Larco family, at present at Lima. After Larco Hoyle.*

river-bed oases when they became densely populated and when the cultivation of maize increased.

Just as we should not imagine pre-classic Mexico to have been a centralized empire, we ought not to think that there existed a great political empire at the time of the Chavín horizon, as some nationalist-minded Peruvian scholars have held. On the other hand, we may agree with Trimborn that it is doubtful whether "the people who brought about such a radical change in religion and aesthetics were really no more than planters of crops living in small settlements." This author believes that social stratification took place once the chiefs had strengthened their position, as is always the case before the stage of high culture is reached. Without such preparation it would have been difficult for the new *Weltanschauung* to have found acceptance over a wide area — an outlook expressed in fixed symbols and in the veneration of a deity manifested as an animal of prey. Whether this unity was forged by means of armed force remains conjectural, although it seems unlikely that this was a golden age of peace and plenty. The gods portrayed do not by any means seem meek and mild. They were equipped with fangs, paws and talons and demanded trophy heads and human blood if they were to bring the life-force to the plantations (which were comparable to gardens rather than fields). We cannot entirely exclude the view that the country was conquered and subjected to the rule of an alien élite, who introduced new crafts, such as gold-working, and proper weaving techniques, as well as fearsome new deities. There was doubtless a certain amount of feuding over land and hunting rights. But the rational manner in which agriculture was carried on, and in particular the cultivation of maize, afforded a fair degree of prosperity and sufficient leisure to build temples and fashion stone idols, made in a laborious process with stone tools and sand.

We can only guess at the place of origin of this ruling élite, which seems to have appeared on the scene simultaneously with the cultivation of

Figure vessel of painted clay, showing a man asleep, wearing a patterned garment and large ear-plugs. Moche culture. Middle of the 1st millennium A.D. *Bernouilli Collection, Basle.*

Head of fox. Embossed work, consisting of several parts. Gold, copper and silver alloy; teeth of shell. Moon Pyramid, Moche. *Lindenmuseum, Stuttgart. Height 6 in.*

Death mask from the Moon Pyramid, Moche. Gold and copper alloy with silver-plate; eyes of shell. The movable ears originally bore ornamental plugs. *Lindenmuseum, Stuttgart. Height 10¼ in.*

Magic fish. Double-spouted clay vessel from the temple city of Pachacamac. Approx. 800 A.D. Transitional style between Early Lima and expansionist Tiahuanaco. *Museum für Völkerkunde, Berlin. Length 7 in.*

◀Clay vase with a figure carrying a spear-thrower and club painted on either side. Parrots and arrows in the form of birds over a frieze of trophy heads. Late Nazca culture. After 500 A.D. *Museum für Völkerkunde, Berlin. Height 8¼ in.*

Polychrome incense vessel with plastic head of animal in clay. Classic Tiahuanaco style. First half of the 1st millennium A.D. *Fritz Buck Collection, La Paz. Height 11¾ in.*

Incense vessel with engraved ornamentation in the form of a mythical being, half llama and half beast of prey. Classic Tiahuanaco style. First half of the 1st millennium A.D. *Fritz Buck Collection, La Paz. Height 15 in.*

Ornamental plaque of *tridacna* shell, encrusted with gold and precious stones. The winged figure is carrying missiles (*bolas*) in one hand and a club in the other. Expansionist Tiahuanaco, between 800 and 1000 A.D. Coastlands of Peru. *Private Collection, Zurich.*

Fig. 14 — *So-called stirrup-spouted vessel, painted in red and white. Only the eyes, mouth, nose and ears are rendered plastically. Head vessels such as these, rather primitive and rare, are direct precursors of the portrait heads of the Moche culture. Salinar, Chicama valley. After Larco Hoyle.*

maize, the production of ritual vessels to honour deities in animal guise, and, so far as we are aware. the first attempts at gold-working. There is much to support the hypothesis put forward by Tello and his school that the fertile upland valleys were the womb of the first higher cultures in Peru. The only conclusive evidence is the sudden appearance in the coastal area of maize cultivation in association with ritual vessels executed in Chavín style. The genesis of advanced culture therefore seems to be connected with the origin of maize — something that is still a puzzle to botanists. In any case maize·is a very highly-developed kind of grain, and it takes some time before the techniques of cultivating it are mastered.

The Chavín horizon disappeared as quickly as it had appeared, but of course left behind clearly discernible influences both in the religious and the artistic sphere.

TECHNICAL
PROGRESS

Stratigraphic excavations, particularly in northern Peru, have, however, shown that before regional cultures began to flourish there was an intermediary epoch called by American scholars the 'experimental' or 'formative' period. The experiments referred to are technical improvements.

It may be stated as a fact that with technical progress the veneration of deities in animal guise receded into the background.

In this connection it is of interest that, as religion lost its substance, so the quality of artistic achievement deteriorated as well.

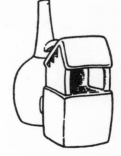

Fig. 15 — *Double-bodied vessel in reddish clay, with a house Gallinazo or Virú style. The conical spout is typical of Virú ware. Gallinazo, Virú valley. After Willey.*

It seems that the priests ceased to supervise the craftsmen's work, and that men became more conscious of their own power, less deeply moved by fear of these monstrous deities than they had been formerly. If this were not so, one could hardly account for the fact that ceramic ware lost a good deal of its artistic expressiveness. Figures of animals of prey now come to display a naive realism, and anthropomorphic clay sculpture often borders upon caricature. The eyes, shaped like coffee-beans and affixed to the head, or rendered by incised lines, involuntarily remind one of early Mexican clay figurines.

The Chavín style was undoubtedly one that extended over the whole of Peru. But it would probably be going too far to conclude that the entire country was governed by priests, and that their rule was finally brought to an end by successful rebellions. This is the accepted picture with regard to Mesoamerican civilization. But in that case we are dealing with a period that is better documented.

Once again it is the northern coastal valleys that have yielded most archaeological information about the formative period. The first phase is associated with Salinar, the name of a hacienda in the Chicama valley, and the second with Gallinazo, a site in the Virú valley.

The technique of firing ceramic ware in the white-on-red or Salinar style is superior.

The expression 'white-on-red style' is also used with reference to the simple painting on Salinar ware, and also 'negative style' with reference to the second, or Gallinazo, phase.

FIG. 14

White painting on a reddish ground appears in the central coastlands, both south and north of Lima, as well as in the highlands and coastal areas of the north of Peru. The main centre of negative painting is in the northern plateau, i.e. in the upper part of the Santa valley. The style of ceramic ware in that area is usually referred to in specialist literature as Recuay. It is also called 'Callejón de Huaylas' after the mountainous valley of that name in which the village of Recuay is situated, PLATE P 144 near which this ceramic ware first came on to the market. Already in the south (Paracas) we came across painted vessels in negative technique, in which — as in the case of the *batik* method in weaving — a covering material, such as wax or resin, is used.

The technique of firing the ceramic ware in the white-on-red or Salinar style is superior to that of the preceding epoch, but despite the use of brush and paint it is less attractive. The decoration consists only of simple geometric signs. A striking feature of the Gallinazo or Virú ware FIG. 15 is the long cone-shaped spout; for a short time it entirely superseded the stirrup spout which Salinar had adopted from Chavín.

There are of course overlaps in time. As the name implies, the Virú or Gallinazo style was at first located in the relatively narrow valley of the River Virú, which empties into the ocean south of the two larger valleys of the Moche and Chicama (the home of the Moche culture). Eventually Moche (Mochica) culture penetrates into the Virú valley, where the negative style and other manifestations of the local Gallinazo culture date from an earlier period than they do in the neighbouring valleys to the north. Salinar is the direct fore-runner of the Moche style. Salinar pottery adopted the stirrup spout from the Chavín of the coastal area, but it lost some of the latter's massiveness and refinement. The spouts of the jars modelled in clay became narrower and were furnished with a band-shaped handle. The vessels feature modelled quadrupeds, birds, houses and human beings. The figure of a medicine-man treating a sick person lying before him, modelled in relief on a hemispherical vessel with a band-shaped handle, anticipates similar representations met with on Moche pottery. The houses of this period are light and airy, well-adapted to the climate. Moche ceramic ware can boast of a fair number of architectonic variations, which have had a stimulating effect on architectural design in modern Peru. FIGS. 16, 17

Only a few hammered-out gold ornaments are known from Salinar, but Lothrop speaks of a 'renaissance of metal-working' in the Gallinazo period: "New metals and new techniques of working them came into use." Previously nothing but pure gold had been used, but now an alloy of gold and copper was employed. Primitive copper-casting in moulds now appears for the first time. The oldest copper bells in America originate from this period and locality. But despite the technical improvements made the achievements of the goldsmiths were not of such a high aesthetic order as they were in the Chavín era. Here, too, this was a stage of experimentation prior to the efflorescent period that was to follow. A distinct style derived its name from Recuay, a village situated on the upper reaches of the Santa, the greatest of all the rivers flowing into the Pacific, and the only one that first travels a considerable distance from north to south, watering a broad mountain valley, before turning towards the coast. Negative painting is one of the characteristic features of this style, as it is of the Virú style. The ceramic ware is much more varied in form: among twelve different shapes we meet, for the first time in Peru, tripod vessels. There are also animal and human figures in clay. One favourite product is a composition of figures remotely resembling those of Colima in Mexico. The colours range from white, red and orange to black; occasionally a modelled head projects from a painted figure, as in European baroque. A favourite motif in painting is a kind ot dragon or feline animal from whose head there radiates a comb-like ornament. There are also angular schematized snakes and fish. The stone figures of this district on the upper reaches of the Santa seem rather primitive when compared to those of Chavín. Most of them are human figures, with their feet turned inwards, carved only partly free from the block. They sometimes appear in association with animals of prey, and are frequently furnished with trophy heads. Dress ornaments executed in flat relief on stone often have the same motifs as those of painted clay vessels. The jaguar figures remain rigid and static.

Incidentally, some genuine Recuay vessels have been found in the Virú valley, showing clearly that trade relations existed in early times between the two centres where negative painting was practised. From a chronological point of view Recuay pottery survived right up to the flourishing period of the Moche culture — the evidence of this will be considered below. The more primitive Virú ceramic ware, too, has been found in remoter places long after the Moche craftsmen developed to perfection their realistic figured vessels. The Moche painted vessels are directly based on the white-on-red tradition of Salinar ware, which also served them as a model for their clay sculpture and various stylistic elements in their pottery.

MOCHE CULTURE — In speaking of Moche we are not referring merely to the site of the pyramids and the present-day village of that name, situated at the issue of the Moche valley, but to a whole culture which flourished for some centuries in several northern valleys.

In the Chavín culture the human face was rarely represented, being overshadowed by terrifying deities. But as techniques progressed, before the beginning of the classic period of regional cultures in north and south Peru, fumbling attempts were made to fashion human beings; however, they did not get beyond the stage of schematization. The peak of achievement was reached with the Moche people, who produced genuine portraits in ceramic ware. There can be no doubt that their vessels in the form of human heads were genuinely intended to be portraits. A variety of ethnic types were represented, for at the beginning of our era many different races inhabited the most fertile river-bed oases, from Nepeña in the south to Jequetepeque in the north; by means of impressive irrigation systems they succeeded. in transforming arid desert into plantations of maize and various other crops. At that time all the edible plants which the Spaniards came across 1500 years later were probably already known. There were as many as thirty native varieties; in addition to these there were plants grown as luxuries, especially the tobacco and coca plant.

The River Moche is one of the mountain streams that flow from the Western Cordillera to the Pacific Ocean — 'the South Sea', as the Spaniards called it. Where the river issues forth from the mountains there stand the weathered ruins of two famous monuments built of rectangular sun-

FIG. 18 — *River scene with reeds, fish, aquatic birds and water-lilies, painted on a stirrup-spouted vessel of the Moche culture. Environs of Trujillo. Museum für Völkerkunde, Berlin.*

FIG. 19 — *Large clay bowl, painted in brownish red on an ivory-coloured slip. The central register on the inside of the bowl probably represents a ceremonial head-dress in the form of a fan. Private collection, Switzerland. After a photo by Ferdinand Anton.*

dried bricks. The stepped pyramid, which in Spanish times (but not before) was named 'Huaca del Sol', 'the Sanctuary of the Sun', is one of the largest ancient Peruvian monuments. The pyramidal structure proper is built on a long stepped terrace about 750 ft. in length and the whole edifice measures 134 ft. in height. Treasure-hunters tried to burrow beneath it by diverting water from one of the canals, but their efforts made no impression upon this solid mass of rectangular clay brick.

At first glance it is even more difficult to reconstruct the original appearance of the Moon Pyramid, which was built on a rocky spur opposite the Sun Pyramid, than in the latter case. The names given them are certainly misleading, for Spanish chronicles record that the coastal population venerated the moon, nor the sun, as their supreme deity.

These great monuments in the Moche valley have given their name to the very advanced Moche culture, formerly erroneously termed Early Chimú. It has yielded a whole gallery of vases bearing painted scenes, FIGS. 18, 22–23 which give us some idea of the way of life of the Moche people, their religious practices, deities, and so on. We have a veritable library of information on the cultural history of ancient Peru. Of course, it is not easy reading, for there are no hieroglyphs to help us as in the case of Greek painted vases.

A large number of effigy vessels are still hidden in the soil. The many examples of Moche ceramic ware to be found in the great museums of the world come almost exclusively from plunder; in many cases the

FIG. 20 — *Stirrup-spouted jar with abstract decoration, painted in brownish red on a cream-coloured ground. On the top is a sheaf of weapons in heraldic style; a club-head and the ends of four spears can just be made out. Moche culture. Site of discovery not known. Museum für Völkerkunde, Berlin.*

layout of the grave furniture, a valuable source of information, was disregarded or even destroyed. No more than a handful of vessels and figures have been excavated systematically.

The home and centre of the Moche culture was probably the broad valley of the River Chicama, which is particularly rich in large isolated pyramids; new graves are constantly being discovered there by treasure-hunters. Some of the sacred buildings were demolished quite recently because they interfered with the cultivation of sugar-cane. But even today one can still see, rising above the green fields, dozens of ancient monuments — mute witnesses to the glories of ancient Indian civilization. In the surroundings of these temples we can be sure to find cemeteries. Some distance from the coast, where the valleys become narrower, the trained eye can make out, high up on the dark rock, patches of yellow masonry; these are remains of the forts which once guarded the entrances to the valleys, clinging to the rock like medieval castles. Here, too, Moche graves have been discovered among the rocks. Generally speaking, all Moche graves are much more lavishly furnished than those of the preceding period. The dead are always buried lying on their backs. Deceased persons of noble rank were buried in association with vessels of various shapes, globular jars and jugs with stirrup spouts, bowls flaring out widely and painted on both the inner and other surfaces, vessels decorated in relief, and mould-made clay sculpture in the form of fruit, animals, human beings and deities.

The dead wore costly ear-disks, mosaics of turquoise encrusted upon gold, necklaces of hollow beads and medallion beads with faces (cf. Plate on p. 146). Goldsmiths learnt the art of casting in gold by the *à-cire-perdue* process and of gilding copper objects. They mastered the technique of producing an alloy of copper and gold and of soldering trinkets of gold and silver. In addition to these they had implements of copper, bronze only being discovered later.

Fig. 21 — *Clay jar. According to Ubbelohde-Doering the painted decoration represents a dead warrior in his transfiguration as a bird demon. He is bearing the club-head typical of Moche warriors and a round shield. Upper Chicama valley. Private collection, Peru.*

In later times, right up to the present, the platforms on ancient sacred buildings, as well as the terrain in front of them, were favourite places of burial, being considered holy ground. Max Uhle, the doyen of German authorities on Peruvian archaeology, was the first to establish for certain the relative antiquity of Moche culture when he discovered, buried in upper strata near the Moon Pyramid at Moche, ceramic ware in Tiahuanaco style (cf. p. 200) and other later styles. At that time he still believed that Moche culture had been introduced from Mesoamerica, since he had no knowledge of the preceding cultures and regarded the products of this advanced culture as the oldest testimony of a higher civilization on Peruvian soil.

PLATE P. 163

Moche ceramic ware is characterized both by realistic modelling of the

FIG. 23 — *Warrior with prisoner. The desert landscape is suggested by dunes, cacti and tillandsia. The richly-accoutred victor carries on his club the arms and clothing of his naked prisoner. Detail of painting on the inside of a large clay vessel. Museum für Völkerkunde, Berlin.*

FIG. 24 — *Colibri in the guise of a man running a race. Races between various mythical creatures are featured very frequently on Moche painted vases. After a vessel owned by the Museum für Völkerkunde, Berlin.*

figures and talented draughtsmanship. Objects are always painted in two colours only. Reddish-brown figures are painted with a fine brush on an ivory-coloured slip. The differences in brush-work would probably make it easy to identify certain workshops. The names of the artists themselves will of course never be ascertained; we do not even know the language they spoke.

Clay sculpture reaches its apogee in the portrait heads already mentioned. Although most of the Moche ceramic ware housed in museums originates from graves plundered at random, we do know that portraits of the very same person have been found in graves situated in various valleys. As the prevailing custom was to place portraits of princes in the graves, it would be inapt to think in this connection of the principle of the 'living corpse', i.e. that these could be portraits of the owner of the grave, on similar lines to Late Egyptian mummy portraits or the portrait statues of ancient Egypt. The same face was copied in the same clay mould in different ways, and we shall not go far wrong if we imagine these to have been portraits of venerated dignitaries, who were to continue to afford the deceased their magic protection in the nether world. It has been suggested that they were local or chief princes who ruled simultaneously over several valleys. This would tally with the fact that the finest and most naturalistic portrait vessels seem to belong to a later Moche period.

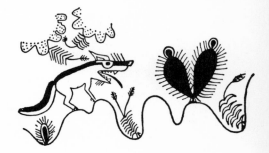

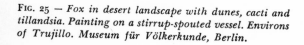

FIG. 25 — *Fox in desert landscape with dunes, cacti and tillandsia. Painting on a stirrup-spouted vessel. Environs of Trujillo. Museum für Völkerkunde, Berlin.*

FIG. 26 — *Dancing warriors: detail of a scene on a stirrup-spouted vessel in the Museo Nacional, Lima. Each man has a strikingly different head-dress, although the rest of their attire is standardized. The chief item is a sleeveless tunic which covers the loin-cloth and is held in place over the hips by a belt, so that the lower part resembles a kilt. The objects like axes hanging down from the belt are large copper bells, such as were found by the author in natura. On their legs the dancers wear something resembling gaiters, also with bells. Ear-disks were presumably the insignia of men of rank, as was the case later in the Inca period. After a drawing by A. Jiménez Borja..*

One of the elements employed in attempting to establish a chronological sequence is the shape of the stirrup spout, and the technique whereby it was made; the earlier spouts were modelled more elaborately.

The course of events may be reconstructed as follows: the individual Moche valleys, which at first may have been under the dominion of local princes or high priests, later came to be unified under a single ruler. The Chicama valley may have been the starting-point of this unifying process.

The Moche were a warrior people; if this had not been so, we should not find so frequently depicted on their vases battle scenes, heraldic fasces of clubs and shields, and figures in relief of individual warriors equipped with cone-shaped helmets, shields and clubs. In battle scenes the enemy is usually depicted wearing the same garb, suggesting that these were feuds between different groups of Moche over land and water rights. But there are also some painted vases in which Moche warriors are depicted fighting scantily-clad enemies. In the Museum of Ethnography in Berlin is a vessel bearing painted figures which indicate that it was the Recuay people from the mountainous hinterland with whom the inhabitants of the fertile coastal valleys engaged in combat.

FIG. 27 — *A deity with gloriole being carried in a sedan-chair by men with bird-like features. Moche painting. After Rebeca Carrión Cachot.*

FIG. 28 — *Sea-shell demon with desert plants. Painting on a clay vessel. Museum für Völkerkunde, Berlin.*

Human sacrifice was apparently as common here as it was in Mesoamerica, and trophies of heads and limbs were valued for their supposed magical properties.

The construction of the massive pyramids of the Moche period was only feasible through the use of communal labour, either on the part of prisoners of war or the subject masses who owed allegiance to the ruling priest-kings. Many hands must also have been engaged in the difficult task of building the long canals that supplied the plantations with the all-important water on which the crops depended. One aqueduct in the Chicama valley, believed to have been built in the Moche period, is nearly a mile long and fifty feet high. The old main irrigation canal in the same valley measures some eight miles in length. These painted vases give a clear impression of the sort of clothing worn and implements used. We have scenes of stag-hunting, with nets and spear-throwers; this was apparently a pastime reserved for men of high

FIG. 29 — *Female weavers at work in a house thatched with reeds. Noteworthy are the simple weaving device, still used in Peru today, the bobbins, the tablets with textile designs, and the clay vessels in Moche style. Detail of the painted decoration on the inside of a large clay vessel. British Museum. After a copy by G. Kutscher.*

FIG. 30 — *Animal in the crescent moon against a starry sky. From a stirrup-spouted vessel owned by the Museum für Völkerkunde, Berlin.*

rank — or so at least the attire of the participants suggests. The articles of clothing worn by men include head-bands, skirts, girdles and loin-cloths, and those by women long coats; they have not been preserved so well in the more humid soil of this area as they have been in the more arid south. A pictorial vase now in the British Museum illustrates the method of manufacturing textiles: a whole row of women are working under the supervision of overseers. Other crafts may have been carried out in the same organized fashion.

Among these realistic representations of everyday life are scenes, still more common, that depict the realm of the gods. The whole of nature seems to be alive with demonic forces. The nooses around the prisoners' necks are shown in the form of hissing serpents, and weapons and tools have human limbs. But the hybrid figures, part human and part animal, that appear never possess the frightfulness of the stylized Chavín deities. There are a fair number of representations in which the dead are shown drinking, dancing and making music, reminding one rather of the medieval Dance of Death motif. Even landscapes are suggested in these pictorial vases: hills are indicated by irregular wavy lines and the sea by symmetrical ones. Different species of desert and aquatic plants, as well as animals, are depicted, each of them readily identifiable. The blind,

FIG. 25

FIG. 31 — *Dance of the dead beneath the stars. The dead are depicted fully dressed, dancing, drinking and making music, with their faces mutilated in a curious manner. The two jugs no doubt contained 'chicha', the drink of the dead. Moche culture. After a scene on a vase in the Museum für Völkerkunde, Berlin.*

FIG. 32 — *Sea-eagle in front of (according to G. Kut-scher) a sacrificial bowl filled with human blood. After a scene on a vase in the Museum für Völkerkunde, Berlin.*

sick and crippled are also frequently portrayed. It is very curious to find, on mortuary
offerings, contrived erotic scenes. One explanation for this may be that it was desired to
let the dead partake in the pleasures of this
world. But what benefit can they possibly have derived from the pictures
of illness and infirmity? It is striking that the subject-matter in works
of sculpture differs from that in painting. The figures in relief usually
depict heads of demons. There is no stone sculpture whatever, and
sculpture in wood is rare. Figures of prisoners in wood and clay have
been found on the islands off the coast where sea-fowl nest and deposit
guano. Agriculture must have been developed to such a pitch that the
fertilizing properties of guano were known and turned to good account.
The number of murals on clay or stucco walls no doubt exceeds by far
those known to us. Every now and then a new mural is discovered in
some brick ruin; but once it is brought to light it unfortunately very
soon vanishes, since insufficient protection can be given to it in this vast
thinly-populated country. In contrast to painted vases the murals are
polychrome, but they are painted in the same style and feature ceremonial
and ritual scenes. The contour-lines of the demons and human figures were
apparently engraved into the stucco before being filled in with paint.
By the 9th century, if not before, the florescent Moche culture must have
come to a sudden end with the introduction of a new religion — a process
probably accompanied by violence and warfare. Perhaps it had already
begun to 'wane', in Spengler's sense of the word, for in its last phase it
clearly shows signs of decadence. Incidentally, the existence of the five

FIG. 33 — *The 'god with the serpent belt' fishing.
This deity occurs frequently in Moche vase painting. The decoration is in an ivory colour on a
dark ground, or rather in a sort of negative technique. After a clay vessel in the Museum für
Völkerkunde, Hamburg.*

different phases referred to by some writers cannot yet be proved stratigraphically. But from a purely stylistic point of view it is not difficult to discern — in vase-painting, for example — a process of development from simple and sparing draughtsmanship, with only a small part of the surface of the vessel filled in, to a tendency to fill in the entire surface, even the spout forming part of the picture. In sculpture there are more erotic representations, but these continue to be rare. In the very last stage hybrid forms also appear, together with a new stratum that was later to be superimposed on everything else: the Tiahuanaco horizon, which apparently developed at the same time as a religious revival, and spread its influence over the whole of Peru. It is characterized by an individual style which appears in a number of variants, and for several centuries overshadows the local styles. In the south, it is true, this invasion seems to have been a peaceful one, without the violent conquest and political subjugation that took place in the northern valleys.

NAZCA   Almost simultaneously with the efflorescence of the Moche culture there lived in the valleys of southern Peru a people whose ceramic ware can at once be distinguished from the products of their contemporaries. This southern culture, and the style associated with it, have been named after the country town of Nazca, not far from Ica and a few hundred miles south-east of the Paracas peninsula — where the same deities and hybrid figures (part human and part animal) held sway as in the valleys of Nazca. We have come across them embroidered on magnificent shrouds in rich colours; and the same wealth of colour is also characteristic of the painted vases from Nazca.

Nazca culture was unknown before the turn of the century. Soon after the first graves in the Nazca valley had been rifled, Nazca vessels began to reach European museums, where their brilliant colouring earned them the admiration of expert and layman alike; no one had seen anything to equal them. But no scenes have survived in Nazca painting which throw as much light on the circumstances of everyday life as those that existed in Moche art, with the result that we know even less about the people who lived there than we do about the ancient inhabitants of the valleys in the north. Their natural environment must have been similar, but perhaps they did not enjoy the same relatively lavish degree of prosperity, since the southern valleys are narrower and the rivers carry less water than those of the north.

Only a few rivers convey their life-giving waters as far as the Pacific, and most of the old settlements are to be found in the upper parts of the valleys. The cemeteries are usually situated on the edge of irrigated fertile land; the dead are buried in a squatting posture, fully clad, in round or

FIG. 34 — *Tendrils with fruit and blossoms, painted in black, violet and dark crimson on a white ground. Detail of a double-spouted vessel. Classic Nazca style. Gaffron Collection, now in the Museum of Natural History, Chicago.*

angular chambers at the bottom of shaft graves. These graves are often covered over with beams or bamboo-canes.

In defining the Nazca style, it is best to start with their ceramic ware, for this is better-known and better-preserved than any other branch of their art. However, as already noted, far more textiles have been preserved in the more arid areas of the south than in the north. The Nazca fabrics are rich and varied, but are not so precious as those from Paracas.

It is Nazca pottery, rather than textiles, that deserves to be compared with that of Paracas. If we go by technical and typological principles it seems more likely that the rounded figures embroidered on Late Paracas shrouds were copied from the painted demons of Nazca ceramic ware than *vice versa*. For rounded lines are more easily painted than woven. But it transpires that this hypothesis is not valid. Here, too, then it must probably be a question of an overlap in time. But it is a fact that in 1953 W.D. Strong, in the course of careful excavation work in the area of Ica, succeeded in establishing distinct chronological starta. He discovered a 'proto-Nazca' style in ceramic ware, painted in a style similar to that of Early Paracas, but before firing; in both cases the outlines of the painted figures are engraved.

Out of the method of painting after firing, in which the paint is applied in pulverized form without an effective binder, so that it can be washed off with ease, there developed a technique whereby the paint is also applied before firing but with a resinous binder. Strong also supplies radio-carbon datings of the epoch he has termed 'proto Nazca'. In most cases the tests were carried out on charcoal, and only in a few instances on human hair and shreds of cotton fabrics. Whereas the beginning of Late Paracas dates from the 2nd century B.C. and reaches into the 3rd century A.D., 'proto-Nazca' dates from the 4th century A.D. and terminates at the beginning of the 5th century A.D.

This period is followed (although there is a certain amount of overlap-

ping) by the classic Nazca, called by Strong 'Middle Nazca'; according to radio-carbon datings this style lasted from the beginning of the 4th century to the end of the 6th century A.D. Finally, Late Nazca continues until after 1000 A.D.

In passing one may mention the interesting point that in early times a red-on-white 'style', if one may use the term, was sandwiched in, prior to proto-Nazca and simultaneously with Late Paracas. According to Strong: "The type is theoretically important as a possible southern representation of the white-on-red horizon style and/or tradition of the central and northern (Salinar) coastal area." Black ware decorated with polished fine-line incisions also still belongs to the Late Paracas. But all this ware is less characteristic of the south than polychrome, which can boast of a continuous tradition from the cloisonné ware of Early Paracas through the classic and Late Nazca periods right up to the time of the Inca empire. When polychrome Nazca ceramic ware first reached European museums in the 1880s it aroused admiration but no one was able to specify its exact locality of origin. It was some years later that museum curators and connoisseurs came to take a keen interest in the exquisite collection built up by a German oculist by the name of Gaffron, who lived in Lima. Some items from his famous collection are still to be found in German provincial museums, but most of it went to the United States a few years ago, when Gaffron's heirs sold it to an art museum in Chicago. Max Uhle was again the first person to carry out excavation work in the Nazca valleys on scientific lines. His significance as the father of Peruvian archaeology cannot be overestimated. In 1926 Heinrich Ubbelohde-Doering published his work *Altperuanische Gefässmalereien,* in which pride of place is taken by the polychrome Nazca pottery. But at that time nothing was known about the chronological development of this style. Six years later Doering went to Peru for the first time to carry out excavations near Cahuachi and other sites in the Nazca region; the results of his work are due to be published shortly. In the meantime American universities had begun to undertake field-work at Nazca. We have already mentioned W.D. Strong, who carried out excavations in conjunction with the museum at Ica;

FIGS. 34, 37

Polychrome clay bowl. Demon in guise of an animal of prey with trophy heads and stylized puma. Expansionist Tiahuanaco. Southern coastal region of Peru. *Private Collection, Zurich. Height 15½ in.*

False head of painted wood, placed on top of a mummy pack. The eyes are of shell and silver, the hair of vegetable fibre. From a grave in the temple city of Pachacamac. Expansionist Tiahuanaco. Approx. 1000 A.D. *Museum für Völkerkunde, Berlin. Height 11½ in.*

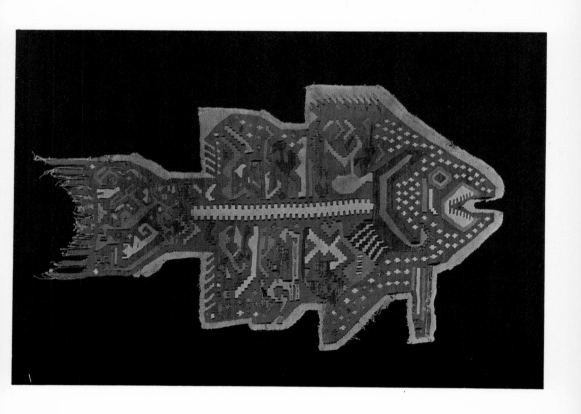

Fish with symbols of plants and trees. *Kelim* fabric, with cotton. After 1000 A.D. Pachacamac. *Museum für Völkerkunde, Munich. Length 19¼ in.*

Detail of a *kelim* fabric with mythological figures in the form of picture writing. Pachacamac. After 1000 A.D. *Museum für Völkerkunde, Munich. Actual size.*

Mythical bird or butterfly. Fabric woven in tapestry technique. Late Tiahuanaco, from the coastal area. ▶ After 1000 A.D. Place of discovery unknown. *Museum für Völkerkunde, Berlin. 19¼ in. x 14 in.*

Foxes dancing. Bronze top of a ceremonial staff. The rings bore small bells, only one of which has survived. Found at Chanchán, capital of the Chimú kingdom. Approx. 1200 A.D. *Norbert Mayrock Collection, Museum für Völkerkunde Munich.*

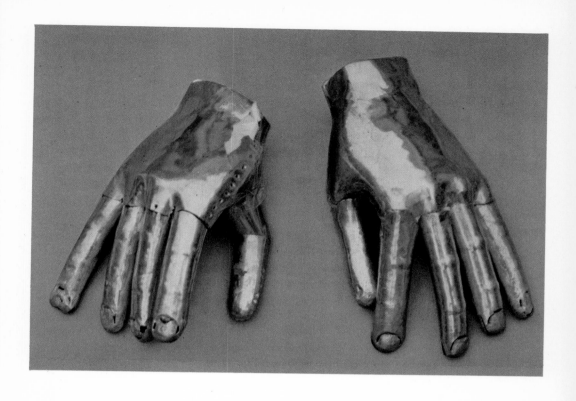

Funerary gloves in 18-carat gold. Each glove consists of seven parts and weighs 6 2/3 oz. The place of discovery is not known, but was probably somewhere in northern Peru. *Private collection, Peru.*

Clay jar painted with ornaments in imitation of textile designs. Typical Ica style. Between 1200 and 1500 A.D. *Museum für Völkerkunde, Berlin. Height 7¼ in.*

FIG. 36 — *Double-spouted clay vessel, typical of the Nazca culture. Polychrome on a light ground. A demon in the guise of a beast of prey is holding a twig with pepper-pods; he represents the god of vegetation. Classic Nazca style. Museum für Völkerkunde, Berlin.*

another scholar was John Howland Rowe of the University of California, who brought with him a team of assistants. The posthumous work of the Peruvian Tello on his studies in the Nazca area has not yet been published. Much still needs to be done to enlarge our knowledge of the southern peoples, whose love of colour stands in sharp contrast to its sparing use by the inhabitants of the northern valleys.

On the other hand it is a conspicuous fact that clay sculpture hardly developed at all in the south, whereas the north boasts of a wealth of sculptured figures. The little work in relief that exists is, as Doering has stated on one occasion, "not really sculpture but merely a complement to painting in the form of modelling." If they were not painted these figures would lose their very essence. It is their colour that gives them life. The range of colour in Nazca ceramic ware is exceedingly rich, at least as rich as on the shrouds from Paracas. It is strange that there should be no green, which we met already in Early Paracas and in proto-Nazca ware.

This brief occurrence of green has a remarkable parallel in Mexico, where it appears at the time of Teotihuacán only to disappear afterwards for ever. Despite their brilliance all the colours are softened to pastel tints, producing a harmonious impression and modifying to some extent the frightfulness of the supernatural beings represented. The main colours used are: brown, in shades ranging from light ochre and orange to a faded yellowish grey; red, in shades ranging from ruby and crimson to light brick and brownish purple; and various hues of ivory, which provide a most effective ground. The vessels on which white serves as a ground are often the finest and lightest in weight, with the thinnest walls. Outlines that formerly were engraved are now superseded by fine brush-work in black and dark brown, the effect of the contour line depending on the colour of the ground.

Naturally the figures are set off best against a white ground; on a dark one they are blurred, giving a mysterious effect. Black grounds are rare. One such painting has been interpreted by Doering as a mythical nocturnal landscape. More frequent is a red ground. The various shades of red were probably produced from pigment obtained from ferric oxide. Purple may have been obtained from organic colouring-matter; in one particular mixture it appears as lilac.

Almost all the vessels from the classic Nazca period are polished smooth, the slip and design appearing through what seems to be the finest glaze. Perhaps some kind of varnish was used. Nowhere in ancient America were potters familiar with a proper glazing technique; this was first introduced by the Spaniards, when it led to a deterioration in artistic quality.

Judged as works of craftsmanship the Nazca vessels are the *ne plus ultra* of pottery. Moche ceramic ware includes, in addition to exquisite pieces, a large quantity that is average or slightly above average in quality, whereas the Nazca vessels are of a more uniform standard. The clay is always finely tempered and the thin walls of the vessels are well fired; the colours shimmer forth like velvet from the smooth surface. Incidentally, it seems as though the Nazca potters used moulds less frequently than did their fellow-craftsmen in the north. Most of their vessels seem to have been produced by the primitive coiling technique, i.e. the damp clay was coiled upon itself in concentric rings and then burnished with simple polishing tools of wood or stone. Perfect roundness was obtained by hand without the aid of any mechanical device. Even without its distinctive colour Nazca pottery can easily be picked out from other Peruvian styles. Some vessels

FIG. 36 are more or less spheroidal and have two spouts connected by a bridge in the form of a band. The bases are always rounded, and never flat as in Moche and other ware. In addition to the double-spouted vessels there are tall beaker-shaped vases painted on the outside, shallow bowls painted on the inside, deep vessels with flaring sides, and jars with and without

FIG. 37 — *Hovering deity with human limbs, feather drapery and trophy heads, painted in ruby, pale lilac, brown, yellow, pink and cream on a double-spouted vessel. Classic Nazca style. Gaffron Collection. After a copy in colour by Ubbelohde-Doering.*

196

handles. As regards the so-called head vessels, almost their sole distinguishing characteristic is that they bear painted human heads in relief. They are not by any means portraits, such as we found in advanced Moche art, but typified faces devoid of any naturalism. The eyes are either semi-circular like the crescent moon, or almond-shaped; the mouth is suggested by horizontal strokes. The heads are mostly of deceased persons, frequently captured enemies. Such head vessels belong for the most part to the late phase of Nazca culture (approx. 5th–8th centuries A.D.), in which modelling in relief appears more frequently; but this always remains of secondary importance.

Already many years ago Kroeber, an American archaeologist and art historian, endeavoured to draw up a chronology of stylistic development in the Nazca area, which has apparently been corroborated stratigraphically by Strong's excavations. For once typological classification was proved right, although as a rule this is by no means a reliable guide!

So far as subject-matter is concerned, the painting of the classic and Late Nazca periods can be distinguished fairly clearly. Typical of the first phase is a decorative arrangement of various animals, fish and birds, as well as plant motifs. Among the birds the humming-bird and goatsucker are particular favourites: they are messengers of spring, bringing with them FIG. 35 water from the mountains. Of plant motifs the most popular are maize, beans and red and yellow pepper-pods. Everything is to a certain extent stylized and not close to life; inanimate objects, too, such as slings and arrows, tend to become ornamental or symbolic ciphers, such as footprints and hand imprints, or geometric signs.

Nor are demons absent from the painted vases of classic Nazca. They bear a great resemblance to the creatures embroidered on Paracas fabrics. In the earliest phase they are simple, as they are at Paracas; they appear on globular vessels with double spouts repeated symmetrically on either side, but in reverse. In this case they do not cover the entire rounded surface and have less anatomical detail than in the later phases, although sometimes features of the most diverse animals are combined. Trophy heads are nearly always present as attributes. In an exemplary study Eduard Seler has endeavoured to distinguish between the various demonic figures that existed in the Nazca people's imagination: between the spotted wild cat, still without any human attributes, as the provider of food, and the cat-demon, with human hands and feet, often with an abundance of trophy heads and vegetable attributes, and appearing in many varying guises — wearing a serpent on its head and trailing another behind it,

FIG. 38 — The 'cactus-spine' demon, floating downwards. Polychrome painting on a clay vessel. Late Nazca style. Museum für Völkerkunde, Berlin.

FIG. 39 — *Polychrome clay goblet. Simplified stylization of demons and heads. Late Nazca style. Museum für Völkerkunde, Berlin.*

with or without birds' wings, encompassed about by tadpoles (associated with moisture and fertility), amphibia, goatsuckers or humming-birds. Another mythical creature that occasionally appears is a god of vegetation in human form, wearing a peaked cap on his head like a dwarf in one of our own fairy-tales, and carrying tendrils and fruit in his hands. Trophy heads seem to have been the veritable alpha and omega of magical remedies; they are nearly always present in one form or another in Nazca art, in the final stage as abbreviated signs, or hieroglyphs. Some of these demonic mythical creatures seem to have sprung straight from hell itself. At times one can imagine the priest of some mystery cult tying a mask with cat's whiskers over his mouth and then appearing before the credulous throng as some god in the guise of an animal of prey, and thereby making them fear and obey him.

In painted vessels of the Late Nazca phase magical beings appear in an ever greater variety of manifestations and fill the entire rounded surface of the vessel. Whole mythical scenes are painted in the form of pictographic writing. In this connection we may recall the famous vessel at Munich, which depicts the rain god and the 'rain boys' carrying jugs of water; this may be ascribed to a late Nazca period. To this era also belong the head beakers which, according to Doering, have the eyes of dead persons affixed to them, and whose sewn-up mouths often represent actual trophy heads, and the female heads arranged in a row like a frieze. Most of the few figure vessels that we know of in the form of goddesses may also be ascribed to this period. In painting there frequently appears a deity in human guise holding pronged sceptres in his hands. Related to this figure is a creature called by American scholars the 'cactus-spine' demon. In its most recent form it consists almost entirely of spiral rays and hooks.

FIGS. 37, 38 The tall vases bear dancers and warriors. W.D. Strong calls this Late Nazca phase "an important and fascinating period, which lasted longer than classic Nazca," and links it with the giant furrows one can see as one travels by air over the *pampas* of the Nazca region, etched into the sand (which has a viscous quality owing to the presence of saltpetre). Maria Reiche has described them and endeavoured to interpret them as astronomical signs. With some justification Strong also correlates this period to the 'wooden Stonehenge' of Cahuachi, which is in fact a great agglomeration of remains of posts of houses from a fairly large town.

Finally, the last stylistic phase, continuing until after 1000 A.D., is even more distinctly marked off from its predecessor. One can detect a baroque resolution of draughtsmanship and to some extent a fading of the colour as well. The 'cactus-spine' demon is to be found in a large number of these representations. Trophy heads, hardly any longer recognizable as such, take on the form of symbolic ciphers, and are surrounded by a profusion of large and small rays terminating in hooks. Strong named this stylistic phase after a place called Huaca del Loro, 'sanctuary dedicated to parrots' where he found this ware in almost pure form.

About 1000 A.D. the old Nazca tradition collapses, as does that of the north, with the rise of the Tiahuanaco horizon, which comes to overshadow everything else — although the colours remain. In the south the victory of Tiahuanaco, expressed in art by new symbols and emblems, probably resulted from peaceful penetration by new religious ideas rather than from military conquest. But it is true that the importance attached to trophy heads in the preceding period points to the belligerency of the Nazca peoples. They may perhaps have engaged in tribal feuding and head-hunting, just as the Late Aztec 'flower wars' were fought to procure prisoners for sacrifice. Heads of enemies were, after all, thought a most valuable aid in ensuring that gardens and fields should prosper.

That so much space has been devoted here to Nazca ceramic ware, and so little to the equally magnificent Nazca textiles, is simply due to the fact that the ceramic ware has been defined much more clearly by stratigraphic analysis. Textiles, moreover, came on to the market from a much wider area. The reason for this lies in the very nature of the material. The classic phase is typified by a piece of fabric painted in polychrome, now in the Museum of Ethnology in Munich, which features a number of birds and produce of the fields. We have already come across painted textiles at Paracas. It was from this centre that Nazca adopted various textile techniques, including three-dimensional needlework and embroidery. But the Nazca people also invented some new techniques themselves. Apparently wool was now used more frequently than cotton, which points to increased trade with the highlands. More than one hundred different shades of colour have been counted on Nazca textiles. Some of these may be due to fading, but most of the dyes used were surprisingly resistant to the effects of light.

So far as metal-working is concerned, the south was retrograde by comparison with the north, although it was from the southern highlands that bronze was disseminated about the year 1000 A.D. Casting in metal was apparently not known in the classic period; gold alone was beaten out and embossed.

An extensive building complex from the classic Nazca period was discovered by Strong in the valley of the River Grande de Nazca at a site not far from where the river issues forth from the mountains. These structures were built of sun-dried brick; among them are some pyramids worthy of note. From earlier times we have only some small artificial mounds and ruins of houses built of clay and reeds. The shape of the sun-dried bricks develops in the course of time, from simple lumps of clay to cone-shaped, and finally rectangular bricks similar to those of the north. In later times the centres of settlement seem to have shifted to the lower reaches of the rivers. In general the history of this area differs little from that of the north.

Strange as this may sound, the coastal plain of central Peru (by which we understand the area immediately to the south and north of the modern capital of Lima) has only been explored very recently. To the classic period belong the foundations of Pachacamac, a famous place of worship a few miles south of Lima. It retained its importance until the Inca epoch, when the Temple of the Sun and other places of worship were erected there. The large pyramids built of rectangular clay bricks may also be ascribed to the classic period. The dead were interred in a recumbent position, as they were in the same epoch in the north; this contrasted with the custom adopted in the south.

FIG. 40 The classic period is characterized in several valleys of the central coastal area by painted vessels in the so-called 'interlocking' style. This seems to be an imitation of the designs on textiles. It is preceded in time by two style horizons which we have already come across in northern Peru. The first of these is a Chavinoid ceramic style with engraved ornamentation, authenticated by finds from Ancón (cf. p. 161) and elsewhere, and the second a ceramic ware with simple white painting on a red ground. A favourite design consists of rows of fish or angular ornaments overlapping one another in a purely decorative manner.

Finally, Early Lima ware, to which that of Tiahuanaco forms in some respects an appendage, shows a certain predilection for modelling. It is polychrome, a characteristic feature being the use of a light ochre colour. Some Nazca beakers are also decorated in a manner resembling the 'interlocking' style of the central coastal area. This is not the only evidence that

TIAHUANACO in ancient times connections existed between the southern part of the coast and the central part, which in turn, as has been mentioned, was already subjected at an early date to influences from the north.

Tiahuanaco is the name of a village on the Altiplano in Bolivia, inhabited nowadays by Aymara Indians and Mestizos. It is situated at approx-

FIG. 40 — *Polychrome beaker from the Nazca area, in the 'interlocking' style which serves as a link between Nazca and the central coastlands. Museum für Völkerkunde, Berlin.*

imately the same altitude as Lake Titicaca, from the southern shores of which it is only a few miles distant. On each side of the portal of the stately church, dating from the colonial period, is a stone figure of a kneeling deity, resembling one another as closely as two twins. They are carved in a strangely realistic style, with prominent cheek-bones and sharply defined ribs. But this style is at the same time hieratic, although these kneeling figures stand out from the block in which they are carved much more freely than do most of the standing figures known to us from Tiahuanaco. The word Tiahuanaco has never been explained really satisfactorily. In Bolivia the simplified spelling of Tiwanaku is often used. The village itself is unimportant, and owes its fame to the nearby ruins, which extend over several square miles of the plateau; around them on all sides are chains of hills. Aerial photographs would no doubt help to give a clear idea of its actual proportions.

There is very little to see on the surface today, and most visitors to this oft-mentioned and much-praised site — which for Bolivians has become almost a sort of national shrine — at first experience a sense of disappointment. What remains is the grandeur of the landscape, with its thin mountain air, warmed on a fine day by the bright tropical sun; a few stone statues, more or less archaic in appearance; and above all else the Gateway of the Sun, carved from a single block of andesite, Tiahuanaco's great landmark. It has been described many times, and has been said by imaginative writers to be the work of some prehistoric race of giants.

This monolithic gateway was only erected at its present site as recently as 1903, and may have had to change its whereabouts several times in the course of its history. It probably formed the main portal of a large temple that fell into ruin long ago. In the broad projecting part above the narrow low doorway runs a frieze, cut in relief, reminiscent of the pattern in a carpet, in the centre of which is a deity standing on a throne with steps, and holding a sceptre in each hand; the hem of his garment is embellished with trophy heads. This central figure has been identified as the sun god, since from his motionless countenance there radiate in all direction rays terminating in animal heads. The frieze has three rows of winged mythical creatures, wearing crenellated crowns on their heads, who are shown hastening towards the main deity with one knee bent; they, too, hold a kind of sceptre in their hands. The figures in the top and bottom rows have human heads with large round eyes, while those in the centre row raise their condor or eagle heads towards the sun; their hands and feet are fashioned like those of human beings.

Here and there, in the isolation of this vast plateau, are some smaller monolithic gateways, devoid of any decoration. The so-called Gateway of the

FIG. 41

FIG. 41 — *One of the flanking figures from the frieze, in relief, on the Gateway of the Sun. Condor deity with crown and sceptre. As though paying homage, these figures are hastening towards the figure in the centre, which probably represents the sun god. Classic Tiahuanaco style. After Max Uhle.*

Sun is by far the most imposing one and occupies a most important place in the history of art. Elements of the iconography found in its bas-relief spread over almost the whole of Peru and large parts of Bolivia as well. The relief of the gateway no doubt contained a symbolic representation of cosmic phenomena, and innumerable attempts have been made to interpret the system of calendar reckoning involved.

FIG. 42

Painted vessels and textiles of the expansionist Tiahuanaco period that followed in Bolivia and Peru bear representations of individual figures depicted on this gateway, or even mere parts of them, often very difficult to identify; moreover, they are subject to local modifications. The ruins of Tiahuanaco, situated on the Altiplano in Bolivia not far from the great lake and the present border of Peru, today hardly seem fit to have been the cradle of the whole pan-Peruvian culture. Nevertheless it was here that the elements of a basic style were most clearly formulated — a style which exercised a decisive influence upon later variants both in the hinterland and along the coast.

Bennett was probably the first to point to the three main phases of style in Tiahuanaco pottery. But a definite sequence of stylistic phases can only be established by the stratigraphic evidence obtained from large-scale excavations, such as are now being carried out by the Bolivian Government. Bennett, an American, was only given a licence for ten test-pits. Rydén, a Swedish archaeologist, was also given permission to carry out excavation work in only a very limited number of test-pits within the area of this complex of ruins. Prior to this no systematic excavations were made at Tiahuanaco, but in lieu of these vandals have been active ever since early Spanish times. Even today gold ornaments are occasionally found there.

Bennett included in 'Early Tiahuanaco' both incense-vessels with an in-

FIG. 42 — *Detail of a tapestry from the expansionist Tiahuanaco period. With some imagination one can make out the principal features of the condor deity in Fig. 41. The design contains almost every detail in an abstract or reduced form. I am obliged to Dr. G. Kutscher for drawing my attention to this phenomenon. Tiahuanaco style from the coastal area. Private collection, Switzerland. After a photo by Ferdinand Anton.*

cised monochrome decoration and also bichrome incense-bowls with stepped and zigzag designs. They have fretted rims and are decorated in relief with the angular head of a beast of prey. On the whole neither the form nor colours give the impression of being primitive. They could with good reason be regarded as decadent forms of some early phase that has not yet been discovered.

The so-called classic Tiahuanaco period includes incense-bowls similar to those described above, but with a much smoother finish. The colours, too, are more vivid and varied: yellow, brown and light grey on a yellow- PLATE P. 168 ish or light reddish-brown slip. The painted figures, mainly of sacred animals such as the puma and condor, or their heads, but sometimes of human heads, are outlined in white or dark contours. The accentuated contour line is a feature common both to Tiahuanaco and Nazca, the only difference being that the figures of the former are more rigid and simple. Symbols reduced to essentials, which become more frequent in the later phase, occasionally appear already in the classic Tiahuanaco style, as do sacred glyphs. The Tiahuanaco artist's palette is less varied than that of the Nazca artist, but they have a distant resemblance to one an- other. The clay sculpture is reminiscent of that in stone. Frequently in- cense-vessels take the shape of animals — not real animals, but mythical PLATE P. 169 creatures, which combine characteristics of the llama and an animal of prey. Painted puma figures are often depicted with bells round their necks and festooned with garlands; they have symbolic signs painted on their bodies. Stepped and other geometrical designs also occur on their own. Highly burnished black pottery is less common.

Along the whole Peruvian coastal area the post-classic period is characterized by flaring-sided beakers and drinking-cups.

The strict and simple lines in all the ornamentation are subordinated to a dogmatic symbolism which sought to exclude the slightest individualism.

Apart from kneeling figures of deities, such as now embellish the portal of the village church at Tiahuanaco, stone figures in an archaic style are never carved free from the block. And yet there was perhaps no other Andean people so accomplished as sculptors as these stonemasons of the highlands. This is illustrated by their miniature carvings, almost like architectural models, which show detail such as niches small steps and platforms, and even small round pillars. But there are also monoliths weighing several tons which are carved with equal elegance. An incalculable amount of material has been taken from this site to build village churches and houses; some even found an unworthy end when the railway line was laid linking the lake to the Bolivian capital of La Paz.

Most of the statues that have remained intact have a bas-relief, often with the shallowest of engravings, which in the case of some of the large

FIG. 42 figures envelops them like a cloak. There is no reason to doubt that, as has often been noted, the designs, even in the relief on the Gateway of

the Sun, are derived from the patterns of textiles. Unfortunately no old textiles have survived from the plateau region, with its heavy rainfall. The gorgeous Tiahuanaco tapestries and painted fabrics found in graves in the coastal areas probably belong for the most part to a late phase of Tiahuanaco culture. I know only of a single shred of fabric in the pure classic style of Tiahuanaco vase-painting; the site where it was discovered has unfortunately not been recorded. The figures on the Gateway of the Sun may indeed be identified on other textiles, but in most cases they are resolved into their several parts and stylized — only partly, no doubt, owing to the exigencies of weaving technique, but in the main as a result of deliberate abstraction.

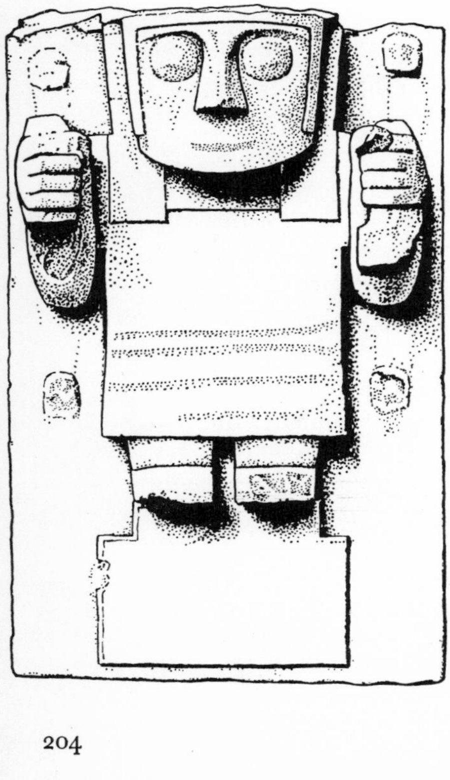

FIG. 43 — *Sandstone sculpture from a building in the ruins of Tiahuanaco. Classic Tiahuanaco style. Museum für Völkerkunde, Berlin.*

In 1533 the first Spanish soldiers arrived on the Bolivian plateau. On inquiry they were told by the local inhabitants: "Who erected these monuments no one can tell."

Hardly a century had passed at that time since the Inca armies had conquered the Bolivian highlands. According to Inca legend it was here that man was created, and sun and moon as well; but already in their day the temples had fallen into ruin and were covered with earth.

But this by no means entitles over-imaginative authors who have investigated the riddle of Tiahuanaco to claim for this ruined city, built on a plateau over 12,000 feet above sea-level, a legendary age of 15,000 years or more, to link it with the myth of the sunken continent of Atlantis, or to say that it was built by giants. The bold explorer Heyerdahl has even peopled the islands of Polynesia with fugitives from Tiahuanaco. But the colossal stone statues of Easter Island have nothing whatsoever in common with those of Tiahuanaco.

Was Tiahuanaco then the capital of a Megalithic Empire, as has also been suggested? This can hardly have been the case. The excavations which began two years ago have made it ever more probable that this was a city of pyramids like Teotihuacán in Mexico. On one of the smaller grass-covered mounds steps were unearthed. We may therefore suppose that the other hills, too, where sheep and llamas now graze, are in fact pyramids. Also the large hill known by the name of the Acapana was no doubt the work of human hands, an abode of the gods once crowned by an altar or temple. Some of the stone slabs, remains of stone girdled walls, are there to confirm this supposition.

Not very far to the north-east of the Acapana there extends from east to west a quadrilateral of which the sides measure some 420 ft. in length, the so-called Calasasaya. Today all we can see are a few crudely-hewn upright slabs, surrounding this square at irregular intervals. They once served as supporting pillars and were connected by masonry. Now the remains lie under the soil in a chaotic jumble, so that we can hardly avoid the impression that some enemy has been at work here, as is also the case at Teotihuacán, the city of temples in central Mexico. If history did indeed repeat itself at Tiahuanaco, we do not yet have any clues that might indicate when it was destroyed. I know only of one radio-carbon analysis relating to the classic Tiahuanaco period, which gave an approximate date of 500 A.D. One single date cannot tell us much; it is not a safe guide. The fact remains that at some sites at Tiahuanaco everything gives the impression of having been turned upside down. The Inca respected foreign gods, and treasure-hunters from early Spanish days would never have been able to continue the work of destruction so

FIG. 44 — *Polychrome clay jar with two small handles. The nose, ears and mouth of the face painted on the neck of the jar are rendered in relief. Typical Tiahuanaco features are the bisected eyes of the animal heads on the body of the jar, the S-shaped forms below the ears, and the N-shaped fangs on one of the heads. The large almond-shaped eyes of the human head point south, towards the Nazca region. Expansionist Tiahuanaco style. Said to have been found at Pachacamac. Museum für Völkerkunde, Berlin.*

systematically; it was not this that interested them. On the east side of the Calasasaya a stately stone stairway leads down into a smaller square, thought to have been surrounded even as late as Spanish times by walls into which stone human heads were inserted. It was here that several years ago Bennett excavated a large stone statue — the largest yet known. It was taken to La Paz, but another stone figure of more primitive appearance, likewise discovered by Bennett, was left at the site. Heyerdahl mentions it in his book *Kon-Tiki;* but he mistook a nose-ornament for the beard of the 'White God'.

'Palacio de los Sarcófagos', or 'Palace of the Sarcophagi' — this is the name given to the ruins of a building which used to stand in the western part of the Calasasaya. Today only the foundation-walls, buried under the earth, testify to its existence. It was 158 feet long by 131 feet wide. Bolivian archaeologists have carried out some careful excavations here in recent years, so that the ground-plan of the building can be made out clearly. A number of large and small chambers are arranged around a spacious inner court, and little immagination is required to see in this whole 'palace', as its size suggests, the residence of the high priest and his acolytes who once performed ritual functions in this city of temples. What manner of gods they served we do not know. Probably each temple was consecrated to a different deity. In the palace floors were found at various levels covered with a coating of white stucco — a helpful means of dating the potsherds discovered there. Perhaps during the excavation work the foundations of other priests' dwellings will be unearthed as well.

There are two diametrically-opposed points of view with regard to Tiahuanaco. In one camp are the patriotic romantics and dreamers who have called it 'the cradle of mankind' and maintain that the Garden of Eden must have been situated on the shores of Lake Titicaca. Some of them have claimed that this pagan place of worship is more than 10,000 years old. In the other camp are modern scholars, who endorse Bennett's theory that Tiahuanaco was a place of pilgrimage; the great lake close by, over 13,000 feet above sea level, was enshrouded in myth and legend. They assign classic Tiahuanaco to the second quarter of the first millennium A.D. This second interpretation, incomparably closer to the truth than the first, explains why Tiahuanaco came to be situated in barren mountain country which could never have provided the means of sustenance for a dense population.

When I myself for the first time set eyes on the numerous Indian peasant homesteads scattered over the plateau, with their extensive fields of potatoes and barley, I modified my views. Even today the plateau is still relatively densely populated. The peasants are deeply attached to this mountainous country and are accustomed to the severe climate. Where barley grows today there were once nourishing quinoa plants; barley was not introduced until the Spaniards arrived, but potatoes were known then, just as they are today. This is also the home of other tuberous plants, and ever since ancient times the Indian mountain folk have cultivated quinoa. Even maize grows at protected spots on the shores of Lake Titicaca, and it did so equally well in days of yore. Where sheep, llamas and even cows graze today, herds of llamas and alpacas used to pasture in bygone times. Even then this area had no lack of population.

When the Inca conquered the country several Aymara princes were ruling over northern Bolivia and the adjacent highland provinces of Peru. Even nowadays there are Aymara living on the plateau. Why should there be any doubt that the Aymara were the builders of Tiahuanaco? Already several decades ago Max Uhle and other writers established that many place-names that can easily be traced back to Aymara words are distributed throughout the whole of Peru, even in the remotest areas. In all probability this points to the expansion of Tiahuanaco culture in or about the 9th century A.D. The present-day Aymara are unjustly described by most travellers who have had no close contact with them as a dumb witted and untalented people. It is thought that their ancestors cannot have been capable of producing architectural works such as the Gateway of the Sun, or have possessed the artistic sense reflected in Tiahuanaco pottery. On two journeys in Aymara territory I came to know them as a

FIG. 45 — *Polychrome clay beaker (kero), of a characteristic Tiahuanaco shape. Typical features are the bisected eyes and what have been called 'traces of tears'. This is probably the figure in the centre of the Gateway of the Sun, though in a much cruder and more simplified form. Expansionist Tiahuanaco style. Pachacamac, near Lima. Museum für Völkerkunde, Berlin.*

most talented — and even quite sociable — people. Of course they have always been, and still are, a pastoral and peasant folk, with the reserve characteristic of all mountain-dwellers. But we have to bear in mind that ever since the Spanish conquest they have been oppressed and despised. On the other hand, it is true that already when they had their own princes, and during the time of the Inca Empire, a wide gulf developed between the high-born Aymara and the common people. Under alien rule the nobility declined or was completely eliminated.

VARIANTS OF EXPANSIONIST TIAHUANACO

Tiahuanaco culture does not really have a uniform style; one can speak rather of related styles, all of which have certain Tiahuanaco elements in common. The famous ruins on Altiplano that have posed so many riddles are certainly not the only centre from which Tiahuanaco culture was disseminated towards all points of the compass.

Many scholars nowadays see this expansion as having started at another ruined city that has been less well explored; this lies a considerable distance north of Lake Titicaca. At the village of Huari, near Ayacucho, there are to be found, as well as rough stone-masonry, typical Tiahuanaco stone cists with neatly-hewn slabs. Even if there is only a distant affinity between the few stone statues from Huari and the stone sculptures of classic Tiahuanaco, nevertheless the polychrome ceramic ware from Huari recalls very distinctly the style of the Nazca valleys, which was derived from Tiahuanaco. Perhaps some Peruvian coastal areas were inspired by new religious ideas emanating from Huari, which found expression in vase-painting, while from Tiahuanaco itself stimuli went out to reach more southerly areas, such as Arequipa (southern Peru), northern Chile and some parts of Bolivia. It is not impossible that some cultural influences may have been transmitted directly from the Bolivian highlands, by way of the Sierra, to central and northern Peru. For it seems, as most authors assume, that Bolivia. where supplies of tin are most plentiful, was also the country where tin and copper alloy was developed, and that from here bronze-casting spread out in all directions. But the T-shaped cramps used in Tiahuanaco architecture are mostly still of pure copper.

Tiahuanaco is one of the most difficult problems in all Andean archaeology, and may questions still await a convincing explanation.

Pucara ware

Much sought after by museums and private collectors is a rare ceramic ware that has so far been found only at one place, and in small quantities at that. Only isolated examples of this peculiar style, akin to that of Tiahuanaco, have been discovered intact. It originates from Pucara, a village on Peruvian soil north-east of Lake Titicaca, at approximately the same altitude as Tiahuanaco. Why this style of Pucara pottery should have been considered a predecessor of classic Tiahuanaco is a puzzle to

FIG. 46 — *Potsherds painted in red, black and orange with engraved contour lines and a beast of prey rendered plastically. Medallions similar to that affixed below the animal's head were found by the author on ceramic ware from lower strata at sites excavated in southern Bolivia in 1958. Pucara style (southern Peruvian plateau), approx. contemporary with the Tiahuanaco style of Bolivia. After a representation in 'Handbook of South American Indians'.*

me. Stratigraphic data are unfortunately not available, but the affinities with Tiahuanaco are obvious.

Pucara ware is characterized by a thick coat of yellow and black paint on a dark red slip. As in Early Paracas the outlines of the coloured areas are deeply incised. A characteristic feature are the heads of beasts of prey modelled *en face,* which project from the potsherds; the rims are occasionally decorated with a step pattern or with human heads in profile. Although the word *pucara* means 'fortress', there is no question of this site being a fortified point. A temple must once have stood there, overshadowed by a precipitous rock face; this is clearly evident from the ground-plan of the masonry that remains. In the middle of the building complex lay a sunken inner court.

FIG. 46

Stone statues found at Pucara have an individual style of their own. But there is an unmistakable affinity with the kneeling Tiahuanaco figures. This suggests the reflection that in evaluating ancient Peruvian art too little attention has so far been given to the question of individual workshops. The Pucara style in no way gives the impression of being more primitive than classic Tiahuanaco.

Pucara pottery is certainly not an early style: this could with greater plausibility be said of the potsherds and other objects which Bennett excavated from an inhabited mound on the very shore of the lake, on the south side. The old Spanish manor where this site lies was called 'Chiripa', and it has given its name to this style, in which only two colours occur: faded yellow and red. In contrast to Pucara ware this has, in addition to painted areas enclosed within engraved contour lines, simple painting without any incised lines. Stratigraphic evidence merely shows that Chiripa dates from an earlier period than expansionist Tiahuanaco.

As intensive excavation work is carried out in the area of Lake Titicaca and elsewhere in the Peruvian highlands, other variants of the Tiahuanaco style will no doubt be unearthed.

The Tiahuanaco gods must have held sway for several centuries over wide tracts of Inca territory, from Bolivia southwards as far as northern Chile and north-western Argentina, and northwards to the northern provinces of Peru. On the Altiplano in Bolivia they presumably still held sway during the Inca era.

At the turn of the 9th century, so far as can be inferred from emblems in the iconography of painted vases and textile designs, several peoples and tribal groups living very far away from one another came under the influence of a single religion. Not even tolerably accurate hypotheses can be advanced with regard to the form of state organization that existed during those centuries, or the process of intermarriage and assimilation of different peoples; despite their common religion, they seem to have undergone a time of disturbed political conditions, as has been deduced from the absence of large monuments and the collapse of the irrigation works in the coastal area.

More beautiful than anything else bequeathed to us by the craftsmen of that era are perhaps the lavishly-coloured textiles and tapestries, with their charming abstract ornamental compositions, in which Tiahuanaco elements lie mysteriously concealed. In the minor arts this distinction can be claimed by amulets and cult requisites, incrustations of coloured mussel-shell, gold and turquoise on precious wood, horn or bone, artistic containers for pulverized lime (used for ceremonial chewing of coca), four-pointed ceremonial caps with sacred symbols from some mystery cult, as well as many other splendid objects.

FIG. 47 — *Large clay jug painted in black on an off-white ground. Environs of Chancay, central Peru. Museum für Völkerkunde, Berlin.*

In the ensuing period we are once again best informed about the course of events in the coastal areas of the north. The traditional Moche style staged a revival after the influences from Tiahuanaco ceased to be felt; this coincided with a strengthening of the state authority under powerful regional princes. Sixteenth- and seventeenth-century Spanish chroniclers have familiarized us even with the names and titles of some of these princes. At first the mighty principality of the Chimú held sway over the homeland of the Moche culture, the northern river oases, and from there it conquered the territories to the north and south, from Piura as far south as the area of Lima.

The same sources mention a kingdom of Cuismancu, situated in the area around Lima, which controlled the oases of the River Chancay as far as the area south of the Rímac valley, in which the modern Peruvian capital lies. Its borders coincided with the area of distribution of a crude black-on-white pottery named after the locality of Chancay, whereas the area in which one finds the so-called Ica ceramic ware, which took the place of the Tiahuanaco style in the valleys near Ica and Nazca, coincided roughly with the boundaries of the state of the Chincha; (the Chincha later allied themselves with the Inca).

We are less well informed about the states that existed at this time in the plateau region. The Aymara principalities in the highlands of Peru and Bolivia have already been mentioned. But we do not know when they arose. The principality of Cajamarca in the northern Sierra was a powerful ally of the Chimú, who lived close by on the coast, and together they offered resistance to the Inca when they invaded in the middle of the 15th century. Cajamarca pottery comprises several periods, each with its own unmistakable style. One is at once struck by the light-coloured slip on which ornaments resembling written characters are painted in cursory fashion. This decoration distinguishes it clearly from all other Peruvian styles. Cajamarca potsherds are often as white as porcelain. The frequent occurrence of tripod bowls, which are not traditional in Greater Peru, suggests that they originated from the north.

The flourishing period of this and other Peruvian principalities may be dated to the 14th and 15th centuries, after the stylistic influences derived from Tiahuanaco had gradually weakened.

In the highlands the population was doubtless never so concentrated as it was in the oases of the coastal strip, where the density of population is thought to have increased steadily, until large settlements and finally towns were built. A classical example of this is Chanchán, the residence of Chimú princes and at the same time the seat of the ecclesiastical and secular lords of this mighty principality. Even today the ruins of the

FIG. 48 — *Double bodied clay vessel in black. The decoration, in relief, features a ray and a pelican. The face seems stereotyped by contrast with the more or less individualistic representation of the human face in Moche ceramic ware. Chimú culture. Environs of Trujillo. Museum für Völkerkunde, Berlin.*

brick buildings of Chanchán show that the layout of the city was planned, with streets and palaces, plazas and walled courtyards. Pyramids are scattered all over the city. Once they were crowned with temples and altars, but now they have been thoroughly stripped by treasure-hunters, for the graves of men of rank contain gold trinkets and tableware on a lavish scale.

The various districts of the city, some of them separated by high clay walls, were probably inhabited by various clans. This may also indicate social stratification. At one point there are remains of water reservoirs and vestiges of irrigated gardens.

The cemeteries outside the city walls give the impression of having been ploughed up, and sometimes at night, despite all prohibitions to this effect, treasure-hunters still carry out their acts of vandalism. No systematic excavations on a large scale have as yet been made, either in Chanchán or in other urban settlements of the Chimú realm. The ornaments in relief which embellished some clay walls, with designs like those of carpets, consisting of stylized fish, rows of birds and quadrupeds, lozenges, steps and other geometric patterns, have been almost completely destroyed by treasure-hunters or by the passage of time.

In other places, too, where sanctuaries existed, aristocratic metropolises developed. One such town is Pacatnamú, situated on the right bank of the River Jequetepeque where it discharges into the sea. Ubbelohde-Doering carried out excavation work here in 1938 and 1953, of the fore-courts in front of the pyramids and of some ancient graves. In later ages this may have been the seat of governors appointed by the Chimú rulers. According to Richard Schaedel, with the increase in population the large river valleys came to be devoted entirely to agriculture. Large peasant settlements grew up at strategic points, e.g. at the mouths of valleys, or at places that controlled their all-important water supply.

The concentration of population in urban settlements apparently led to mass production, with injurious effects upon artistic standards. Creative artists who had formerly worked for temples, for the dead or for the gods, now became artisans manufacturing goods for princes and nobles, and for export.

So far as form is concerned, the old Moche tradition probably underwent a partial revival, but on the other hand it was exposed to stifling extraneous influences, mainly from the northernmost provinces of Peru, which have not yet been thoroughly explored by archaeologists; according to legend foreign immigrants are said to have come here from overseas. Everything became much cruder in style. The old stirrup spout appears again, but cruder and more ungainly in form, decorated in a playful way with small conventional animal figures. Monochrome black or red ceramic ware prevails. On head vessels the facial features are schematized and cease to be individualistic portraits, as they had been in the hands of the Moche potters. Modelled genre scenes, too, are schematic, although they give a greater impression of vigour than the others. In short, we cannot resist the impression that this was mass-produced ware. Black Chimú pottery was exported as far afield as southern Peru and the highlands.

Within the coastal area the styles of textiles, so much easier to transport than pottery, now bear a greater resemblance to one another than they did in earlier times. Striped ornaments and fish and bird patterns predominate. In the centre and north blue and brown tints seem to be particularly popular.

In metal-working all the techniques of casting, alloying and gilding are known. In addition to morning-stars cast in copper and bronze, craftsmen produced knives decorated with delicate figures and small lime spatula for taking coca, as well as ornaments and ceremonial implements in all

Fig. 49 — *Jar with handle of light brown clay, painted in black in the Lambayeque style (northern Peru). The deeply incised ornamentation of the round base recalls that on metal objects, and gold jewellery has indeed been found most frequently in the Lambayeque region. The cursive painting forms a link between this ceramic ware and the Cajamarca style, as well as Moche painted vessels. Chronologically it follows directly upon the expansionist Tiahuanaco of the north and must in part be assigned to this period. Museum für Völkerkunde, Berlin.*

available metals, carved objects in bone and fine mosaic work of shells and feathers — chiefly profane objects, which for the most part possess none of the charm of the minor arts in earlier periods.

The so-called Ica culture on the southern part of the coast has bequeathed to us textiles which have an overall decoration of birds and fish ornaments, arranged diagonally as on a tapestry. Similar designs on painted vases seem to have been borrowed from textiles. Certain standardized forms appear here, too. Little remains of the almost fantastic wealth of the Nazca epoch. The old symbolism and profundity were superseded by decoration for decoration's sake. Rulers with a worldly outlook seem to have reduced the dominant part hitherto played by religion.

In the same period a crude ware was produced in the central coastal area, known after the village of Chancay. Simple painting in black on an off-white ground is typical of this pottery. Egg-shaped jars bearing schematized human faces on the necks of the vessels, as well as crudely painted beakers and bowls, seem to have been produced here *en masse*.

PLATE P. 194

In all provinces the regional styles blend with those of the Inca during the course of 15th century, if not before. This process no doubt took place only towards the end of the period of regional styles, which according to most authors lasted for several centuries. Led by Inca princes, a small highland people had now begun to extend their dominion over the whole country. They were destined to leave a lasting mark upon it.

THE INCA
EMPIRE

The Quechua Indians of the highlands surpassed the peoples of the coast in hardiness as well as in self-restraint. The capital of their small state, Cuzco, was situated in a fertile upland valley protected from cold winds. When the Spaniards arrived in this residence of the god-emperors in 1532, they marvelled at its temple gardens with maize-stalks and flowers of gold and silver, gold disks representing the sun and moon, and life-size gold figures. They melted down their golden beakers and bowls. We have official lists of all the gold objects taken to Spain after the conquest of Peru, but not one of the objects mentioned in these lists has survived. All the gold trinkets which are now in the hands of collectors originate from graves or depot finds.

With the beginning of the Inca period we gradually enter upon the era of recorded history and do not have to depend for our information exclusively upon sparse archaeological finds.

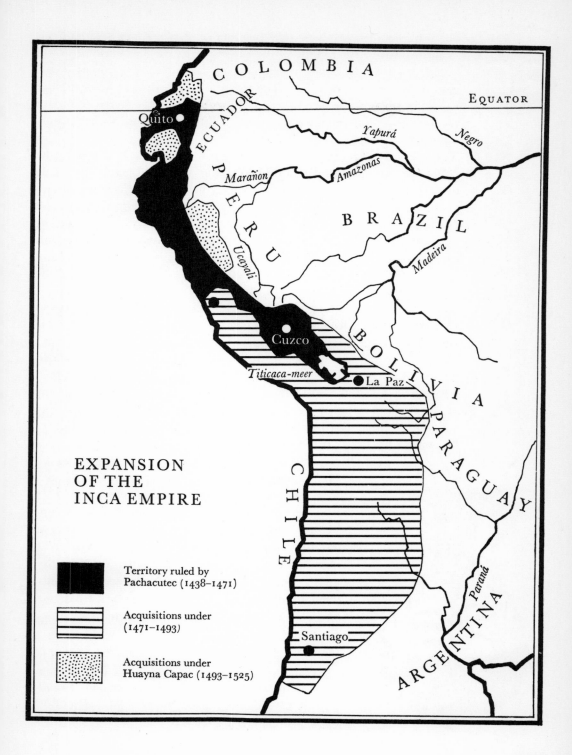

EXPANSION
OF THE
INCA EMPIRE

Territory ruled by
Pachacutec (1438–1471)

Acquisitions under
(1471–1493)

Acquisitions under
Huayna Capac (1493–1525)

Spanish eye-witnesses have left accounts of the brilliant splendour of 'Tawantinsuyu', 'the Empire of the Four Quarters of the World', as it was called. Such proud names were given by many ancient peoples to the empires of their divine rulers; they are proof of a feeling of self-assurance rooted in religious beliefs. In terms of world history the sacred empire of the Inca is one of the most recent of its kind. It begins in earnest only some 400 years ago.

The first full history of the Inca empire was written as early as 1550 by the noble Spanish crusader Cieza de Léon, who journeyed across the whole newly-discovered land when still a young man, keeping an open mind about what he saw. Some twenty years later, at the command of the Spanish viceroy, the learned Sarmiento de Gamboa wrote his history of the Inca empire, which 42 well-known Indian caziques authenticated with their signatures. He was followed by a large number of ecclesiastics and jurists, versed in the official Inca language, who have acknowledged the past greatness of this Indian civilization.

The name 'Inca' is wrongly used to denote the people as a whole. It was a title of nobility, which belonged first and foremost to the semi-divine ruler himself, the 'Sapay Inca'. The first part of the name 'Manco Capac', given to the first Inca prince in the list of rulers that has been handed down to us, seems to be another form of the Aymara word *malcu*, which means ancestor, and the assumption that the Inca clan sprang from one of the Aymara tribes is not by any means far-fetched. 'Capac' is simply the word in Quechua (the official language of the empire) for 'the mighty', 'the most illustrious'. It is a title of honour borne by all subsequent Inca

rulers as well as Manco Capac. According to legend Manco and his sister Mama Ocllo, whom he took as a wife (the saga legitimizes marriage between Inca who were brother and sister, although this was forbidden to ordinary folk) were the sole survivors of seven brothers and sisters. They subdued the fertile mountain valley of Cuzco; the natives fled at the ghastly sight of Mama Ocllo advancing towards them holding in one hand the lungs torn from one of their kin, and in her other hand swinging a sling.

FIG. 51 — *Inca aryballus, with decoration of maize plants. The aryballus, with its pointed base, two handles, plastically rendered animal's head, and two small loops below the wide mouth, is one of the standard forms of Inca ceramic ware. Realistic painting is rarer. There are geometric ornaments, too, that are typically Inca. After a photo in the Archaeological Museum at Cuzco, the Inca capital.*

Fig. 52 — *Clay plate with painted sheat-fish. Bowls such as these, like aryballi, are typical Inca forms. The handles are rendered either in the shape of a bird's head or, as in this case, an animal's head; sometimes they taper to a disk like a button. The protruberances on the opposite side are nearly always found. Environs of Cuzco. Museum für Völkerkunde, Berlin.*

The Inca no doubt owed their dominion over the peasants settled in the Cuzco valley to their cunning, courage and outstanding intelligence. The sixth ruler in the list, Inca Roca, is the first to bear the title 'Inca', and it is only with the ninth, Pachacutec Yupanqui, that authenticated history commences. This history was set down by Spanish chroniclers from the lips of local people who had heard tell of Pachacutec's deeds from their forefathers. There was no recorded history, as there was in Mexico, since the Peruvians were not versed in the art of writing. But the story-tellers had in their *quipu,* the so-called 'knot records', a mnemonic device by which they were able to re-member numbers, things and events and the sons of nobles were taught how to use them.

A large part of the sagas is taken up by historical reconstructions, such as are encountered among many peoples of antiquity, which served to legitimize political and religious conditions and to extol the glory of their rulers. The Inca emperors were venerated as sons of the sun god. The cog-nomen Pachacutec has been translated as 'world-improver' or 'reformer'. This reformer and saviour of his people embarked upon a great pro-gramme of systematic conquest, which was continued by his son Tupac and his grandson Huayna Capac. He had relief maps made in clay of the provinces he conquered, and the subjugated peoples, who had hitherto at the most been obliged to pay tribute in kind, were now firmly incorpor-ated into the Empire of the Sun.

Under Inca Tupac Yupanqui (1471—1493) the borders of the empire extended from what is now Ecuador southwards to the River Maule in northern Chile and beyond. Many of his conquests were achieved by means of diplomatic pressure, by taking advantage of the renown that surrounded the Inca name. Although the sun god cult was introduced, local deities were still allowed to exist.

The wealthy realm of the Chimú on the northern coast was, however, conquered by armed force; the Inca finally gained their victory by cutting off the water supply. The captured prince was taken to the Inca capital, along with goldsmiths and other craftsmen. Some authors hold that the Inca drew upon this coastal state for much of their political *savoir-faire*. According to the present state of our knowledge it seems certain that a large number of the buildings that are in characteristic Inca style and are ascribed to Inca architects originate from the time of Pachacutec at the earliest. For tradition has it that in 1440 the whole city was destroyed by a mighty earthquake. When the Great Inca ordered the sacred city of Cuzco to be rebuilt, use was apparently made of the stones that had survived from previous buildings. The giant polygonal blocks may originate from an earlier period, and the rectangular ones from later times. Porphyry, grey limestone and andesite were employed. The last-named stone, of volcanic origin, takes on a brownish hue when it weathers. Most of the palaces in Cuzco are built of rectangular blocks of andesite. Square-cut stones bulge forth like cushions from the flat surface of the walls, which in the dazzling sunlight produces a characteristic light-and-shade effect. Elsewhere trapezoid niches, windows and doors constitute the sole embellishment of the exterior walls. From the time of the Spanish conquest onwards the artistry of the stonemasons, who knew how to dovetail stones into one another without using any binder, has frequently been the object of keen admiration: "One could not even insert the blade of a knife between them", it has been said.

The prevailing impression produced by all fine Inca architecture is one of exquisite simplicity and restraint in the matter of additional ornamentation. But the conquistadors record that the interior walls of palaces and temples were adorned with draperies and embossed gold-plating. The Inca architects were familiar neither with the lavishly decorated façades of the Maya and the other peoples of Mesoamerica, nor with the modelled heads that embellished the exterior walls of monuments from the Chavín era, nor again with the reliefs on buildings in the coastal area. In many places the Inca affixed

FIG. 53 — *Carved wooden beaker. The Inca beakers known as 'kero' have vertical walls, which distinguish them from the Tiahuanaco vessels with their flaring mouths. This vertical form survived right into the colonial period. The beakers generally occur in pairs and were used at certain drinking ceremonies. In the colonial period they were usually decorated with scenes painted on with lacquer-like pastes. Ollantaytambo, near Cuzco. Museum für Völkerkunde, Berlin.*

FIG. 54 — *Figurine of a llama, in gold. Such figures, as well as human figures of precious metals, were used as sacrificial and votive offerings and mostly occur in the same standard form. In rarer instances they are composed of metals of varying colour. Inca style. Environs of Cuzco. Museum für Völkerkunde, Berlin.*

thorn-like projections asymmetrically to their buildings; these did not ful-fil any technical function, and their purpose remains a complete mystery. No roofs have been preserved. The ancient chroniclers expressed admira-tion for the way in which roofs were thatched to form artistic patterns. We know of a few gable-roofed houses. Some temples are said to have been open to the sky. This simple, yet at the same time magnificent arch-itecture expresses perhaps best of all the character of the mighty Inca empire. The finest workmanship was reserved to places of worship and official buildings. The most important of these, besides the remains of the Inca palaces at Cuzco, are the temples in the mountain strongholds of Sacsahuamán and Pisac. Another famous site is Ollantaytambo, also situated at the edge of the Urubamba basin; exquisite examples of the best Inca architecture have also been preserved in the vicinity of Cuzco, as well as on the islands in Lake Titicaca. The cyclopean masonry of the stronghold of Sacsahuamán, situated near Cuzco, is generally renowned; some of the polygonal blocks of stone measure more than 16 feet in length. Temples of the sun god may be identified in the whole Inca area by remains of fine masonry over an oval ground-plan.

Ordinary folk, on the other hand, lived in simple rectangular or round dwellings, with walls built of uncut stones and boulders embedded in clay, moulded clay or clay bricks. It may be assumed that the talent of the Inca architects and stonemasons derived from the Tiahuanaco tradition, but at the same time they developed an individual style of their own. The entire material culture of the Inca owed much to the achievements of older Peruvian cultures. It was these cultures that were responsible for the spread of the technique of working bronze. On the other hand, it has already been mentioned that the Inca summoned to their capital gold-smiths to do honour to the sun god and the Inca élite. The simple realism of the llama and human figures in gold and silver clearly distinguishes the work of Inca goldsmiths from the products of craftsmen from the coastal region. Inlays of various metals are also typical of this era. There was a predilection for decorating objects with a combination of gold and silver.

PLATE PP. 231 232, 233

PLATE P. 230

FIG. 54

FIG. 55

FIG. 55 — *Silver beaker, embossed over a wooden mould. Gold and silver beakers occur in the Inca period in different shapes, but always striking in their simplicity. Ica. Museum für Völkerkunde, Berlin.*

Beakers are simple in shape and devoid of any figured decoration.

In Inca pottery there are a considerable number of shapes that recur constantly; the aryballus, a pointed-based liquid-container, is probably the most characteristic. Disseminated by settlers from the highlands, it is to be found again at various places on the coast. In the area of the Chimú it appears true to form in black clay, but in the area around Lima in grey supplemented by application of modelled detail — apart from the small angular animal head at the base of the neck of the vessel, which is part of every aryballus: it serves a practical function as a sort of knob to which a strap may be affixed. Two vertical handles on the lower part of the body accentuate the perfect treatment of proportion in this vessel.

In addition to technical perfection all Inca products are characterized by a sure feeling for proportion, except in the rare instances when the human figure is portrayed.

Another very typical form of pottery is a flat plate with a handle affixed to the side in the shape of a loop or a bird's head. There are also jugs with handles, lidded cups mounted on a tall round stem and beakers with vertical walls. Many of these forms might well be called classical, for they are reminiscent of ancient Greek vessels. All of them are well-fired; the surface is highly burnished, the painting being polychrome more frequently than monochrome. The main colours are yellow, orange, purple red, black and white. Painted figures appear far less frequently than geometrical decoration.

FIG. 53 Only on the so-called *kero* do we find scenic compositions, often of persons wearing Inca costume in association with Indians from the backwoods; there are also Spanish soldiers, flowers and trees. These large wooden beakers, most of which date from colonial times, always appear in pairs, since they were used in certain drinking ceremonial. The contour lines of the figures, animals and plants are incised and filled in with colouring-matter containing resin like a viscous lacquer. The wooden beakers decorated with geometrical designs may also originate from an earlier date.

The bowls of hard stone were presumably used for ritual purposes. They are often flat, with vertical walls, and are decorated with modelled serpents; sometimes they take the shape of animals, e.g. llama heads or fish. They may be well-nigh perfect in their simplicity. Such great mastery

FIG. 56, 57

of the material makes the neglect of the human face and figure all the more striking.

Clay sculpture of human beings is relatively rare; even rarer in Inca times are stone figures or heads. The Spaniards may have destroyed a great many for political reasons. Idols in the proper sense of the word, a familiar feature in older cultures, are not to be found either. On another occasion I have suggested (perhaps even overstating the case somewhat) that the Inca rulers themselves may have been the only gods in human guise. For according to authenticated accounts from the reign of Pachacutec onwards their mummies were shown to the awe-struck populace on ceremonial occasions. Their faces were covered by gold masks. Since mummies of some of his predecessors were nowhere to be found, Pachacutec is said to have had artificial mummy packs made and have enthroned them in the Sun Temple instead. None of the gold masks they wore have been preserved. When Pachacutec's son, then sixteen years of age, appeared in public for the first time, his father instructed the foremost men of his empire to make offerings to this youth as though he were a god.

Small standing human and llama figures of gold and silver usually belong to a standardized type which varies only in points of detail. The human figures always have the same characteristic facial features. They stand there stiff and motionless, their hands on their chests. Equally numerous are llama figures of precious metal, likewise almost always represented in the same posture, standing rigidly with their ears pricked up. These figures are usually hollow.

FIG. 54

PLATE P. 229

Bronze objects were then used not only as ornaments but also for practical purposes; some of them bear figured decoration. The Berlin Museum houses a massive morning-star which served as a club-head and presumably belonged to an Inca; it contains approximately 18 ounces of fine gold. But none of the costly objects worked in gold and silver plundered by the Spaniards from the temples at Cuzco have been preserved.

The Inca artisans learnt some techniques in other applied arts, such as metal-working and weaving, from the older peoples of their empire. But

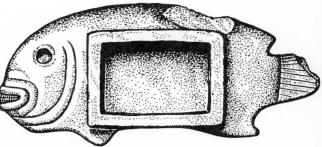

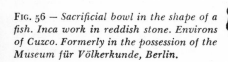

Fig. 56 — *Sacrificial bowl in the shape of a fish. Inca work in reddish stone. Environs of Cuzco. Formerly in the possession of the Museum für Völkerkunde, Berlin.*

FIG. 57 — *Small animal figure of light stone. The stylized mane enables it to be identified as an alpaca. The depression on the back was used to hold llama tallow or incense for sacrificial purposes. Even today similar animals are buried as magic votive offerings to the earth goddess under the threshold, in the fields or in the llama pens to encourage the propagation of animals. After Bennett.*

the number of really exquisite fabrics preserved is limited, for the privilege of wearing gold jewels and splendid robes was reserved to the nobility. We know of Inca tunics in bright colours with repetitive designs of small figures, mostly geometrical shapes. Wool and cotton were woven into tapestries, and for the Inca rulers tapestries were sometimes made that contained the fur of bats — or so one chronicler records. The silky wool of the vicuña, in particular, was reserved for the clothing of the ruler. Spaniards believed these fine fabrics to be silks, but silk was not

PLATE P. 228 known in Peru. The pleasing decorative designs of Inca textiles cannot vie either with the magic-charged embroidery on the Paracas shrouds or with the ceremonial robes of the Tiahuanaco era.

All the luxury of the Inca vanished when the Spaniards abolished the main privileges of the secular nobles and entirely suppressed the pagan priesthood in favour of the Christian church. The last occasion when the Peruvians gave expression to their feelings of awe for their ruler occurred forty years after Peru had been conquered, at the execution of the youthful Inca Tupac Amaru, whose court had led a phantom existence, hidden from the eyes of the Spaniards, in the wooded hills east of the Andes. In 1572, though he was guilty of no offence, he was beheaded at Cuzco. When his bloody head was impaled and put on public view in the cathedral square the crowd knelt down reverently to worship it. It seemed as though the muttering would have no end, and the viceroy was obliged to have the head removed the very same night. Even in our own day the word Inca still has a mystic ring about it for people in some parts of the ancient empire. But of the old artistic skill traces can now only be found, if at all, in weaving, which was encouraged — and exploited — for commercial purposes during the colonial period.

On the whole South American continent there are no works of art that reach the level of the best Maya products. This is above all true of architecture, but it also applies to sculpture.

Unfortunately only a few ancient Peruvian murals have been preserved. Those known to us tend to be of greater interest from the standpoint of cultural history than as works of art. South American stone sculpture is rarely carved free from the block. In stone-carving the best works are those in flat relief or engraving, and, moreover, those from a relatively early period, the Chavín era in Peru.

Rock drawings are to be found in different parts of the continent, but they have not yet been systematically collected or studied. Only a few have any real aesthetic value, and fewer still can be dated even approximately by comparison with painted vessels. There are examples of rock paintings in northern and southern Peru.

FIGS. 58, 61

What is the picture in the border areas of the Inca empire, before and during the period of their rule, and further afield in Colombia, Venezuela and Brazil? The history and archaeology of all these areas have been much less extensively studied than have the history and archaeology of Peru. The ancient art to be found here can be briefly sketched by singling out a few characteristic examples — with the proviso that many new discoveries can be expected which will make a more precise classification possible.

There are a large number of discoveries testifying to the fact that these two border areas, north-western Argentina and northern Chile, were ruled by the Inca for at least the final fifty years prior to the Spanish conquest, and were presumably under their influence for longer still. The cult of the sun god, recorded by several Spanish chroniclers, may be a heritage of Inca rule, and the remains of Inca dwellings and rest-houses provide testimony just as eloquent as stone morning-stars and bronze objects in familiar Inca shapes.

THE BORDER PROVINCES OF THE INCA EMPIRE: NORTH-WESTERN ARGENTINA AND NORTHERN CHILE

The earlier influences from Greater Peru no doubt date from the Tiahu-

FIG. 58 — *Demons locked in combat. Rock engraving in Chavín style from Alto de la Guitarra, between the Virú and Moche valleys. After a photo by the author.*

Fig. 59 — *Rock engraving from Cerro Mulato,
near Chongoyape, northern Peru. Tiahuanaco
style. After a photo by the author.*

Fig. 60 — *Masked dancers. Rock engraving
from the Majes valley, southern Peru. Of
uncertain date. After a photo by the
author.*

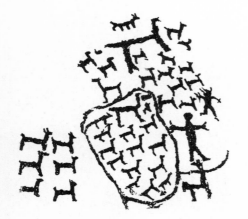

Fig. 61 — *Llama herdsman with his animals. The
enclosed area may denote a pen. Rock engraving
from the Majes valley, southern Peru. Probably
from the Inca period. After a photo by the author.*

anaco era. But the two most important indigenous peoples, the Atacameño and Diaguite, retained some individual characteristics up to recent times; their languages, however, have disappeared.

The ancient culture of the Atacameño centred upon the oases at the edge of the Atacama desert. In addition to the cultivation of crops known to us from ancient Peru, such as maize, capsicum pepper, beans and quinoa, the rearing of llama — also taken over from Peru — played an important part in their economy. The Atacameño had a reputation for being keen merchants. It is thus not surprising that in their territory pottery of the purest Tiahuanaco type should be found — e.g. at the oasis of Calama.

Owing to the wealth of wooden objects, excellently preserved in the dry soil in which they lay buried, the culture of the Atacameño has been termed a 'wood culture'. They made wooden tablets, used for mixing snuff for ritual purposes, which had artistically carved handles.

The Diaguite, the second largest people in the south, who lived in Argentina and Chile, made ornamental bronze plaques, which again have a FIG. 62 remote affinity with those of Tiahuanaco, but are nevertheless a native product. They probably obtained their knowledge of the technique of alloying bronze from Bolivia. On the whole they have left a richer heritage behind them than their northern neighbours. As well as the copper plaques mentioned, they made bronze bells with ornamentation on the rim at the bottom, sceptre-like bronze axes and other articles. In the case of the Calchaquí, an Argentinian branch of the Diaguite, their best-known ceramic products are urns of peculiar shape used in child burials. FIG. 63 They are painted in polychrome and decorated with stylized figures and geometric patterns.

Other forms of ceramic ware and ornaments display affinities with those

FIG. 62 — *Ornamental bronze plaque. Pectorals such as this, with one figure in the centre and two subordinate figures (in varying forms) are assigned to the Diaguite. This plaque was acquired at Tiahuanaco, where it may have been brought by traders. The shape of the axe dangling from the right hand of the figure in the centre enables this piece to be dated approx. to the Inca period. Diaguite culture. Formerly in the possession of the Museum für Völkerkunde, Berlin.*

225

FIG. 63 — *Large urn with painted figures, used for the burial of children. The form is typical of the Calchaqui people, a branch of the Diaguite who live in north-western Argentina. Museum für Völkerkunde, Berlin.*

of Bolivia and southern Peru (Arequipa dept.). But their monochrome bowls, painted in grey or black with incised decoration, have a thoroughly local flavour. We cannot as yet attempt to establish precise dates for the products of this whole area on the southern border of the Inca empire. The first step must be to correlate a whole number of local styles.

By and large the history and culture of this region evolved along independent lines. As Bennett put it once: "It reflects the course of development in the extensive province of the central Andes (Peru), but without being a part of it".

ECUADOR Ecuador is perhaps the area of South America that presents the art historian with the most unsolved problems — problems that are also of considerable importance. Its highland areas, like those of Bolivia and southern Peru, are still today pure Indian country. Although it was incorporated into the Inca empire only a few decades prior to Columbus' discovery of America, the Quechua, the official Inca language, still flourishes there in our own day. The Pacific lowland provinces, on the other hand, are inhabited by a mixed population consisting of Indians, negroes and whites.

FIG. 64 — *Clay figure with engraved decoration. Figures in the same style have also been found in the coastal area of Ecuador and in the adjacent coastal region of Colombia. There are a large number of variations. The projecting back of the head is of interest, since it indicates a certain ideal of beauty and intentional deformation. Environs of Tumaco, Colombia. Museum für Völkerkunde, Berlin.*

Man squatting, carrying an Inca aryballus on a strap. Painted clay. Inca style of the coastal region. Pachacamac. 15th century A.D. *Museum für Völkerkunde, Berlin. Height 8½ in.*

Sleeveless tunic with typical Inca design. The back has a similar design on a purple ground. Found in the burial-fields of Ancón, near Lima. 15th century A.D. *Museum für Völkerkunde, Berlin. Length 32¼ in.*

Male figure. A solid casting in silver with an admixture of gold. Venus shell, spondylus and gold inlays. Place of discovery not known. Inca style. *Museum für Völkerkunde, Berlin. Height 5¾ in.*

Gigantic fortifications. Sacsahuamán, above Cuzco. Approx. 1400 A.D.

View of the Inca ruins of Pisac, situated above the Urubamba valley.

Among the ruins of Pisac, in classic Inca style, those of the Sun Temple stand out on account of its oval shape.

Trapezoid gateway with flight of steps. Inca period. Sacsahuamán.

Death mask in embossed gold plate. Central part of Cauca valley, Colombia. *Museum für Völkerkunde. Berlin, Height 6½ in.*

But here too one comes across examples of Indian physiognomy, the basic type of which is the same as that found on the ancient clay figures and stone statues from the coastal area. It is a point of some interest that the wealth of clay figures buried in the soil is paralleled in Mexico. Although it would be wrong to ascribe their origin to the Maya, as some authors have done, Ecuador is nevertheless the South American country where the parallels with Central America are most marked; they are not apparent in Ecuador's northern neighbour, Colombia. We are therefore justified in assuming that maritime connections existed with Mexico. Archaeologists from Ecuador and the United States are said to have found potsherds in Ecuador which bear such a close resemblance to early Central American pieces that they could be mistaken for one another.

Immense areas on the archaeological map of Ecuador have still to be filled in. As is also the case in Peru, it is the coastal areas that are best known. Influences from the north, even from beyond Colombia, seem to predominate over those from Peru.

Despite the short time that the Inca ruled over the highlands, there are traces of their presence almost everywhere, whereas the indigenous tribes of the coastal area north of the modern border between Ecuador and Peru, who were in a state of almost continual revolt against Inca rule, display less evidence of Inca influence. There is no tradition going back to pre-Inca times, but the place-names indicate that most ancient peoples of Ecuador belonged to the linguistic stock of the Chibcha; at the time of the Spanish conquest many branches of this group were scattered over an area extending from Costa Rica to Ecuador.

The archaeological finds in the border area between the republics of Colombia and Ecuador pay no heed to present-day frontiers. The finest examples of the clay figures mentioned are authenticated in the Ecuador province of Esmeraldas. They have a large number of variants, but the basic type originates from the province of Tumaco in southern Colombia, as has recently been shown by the German scholar Horst Nachtigall. In the highlands, on the other hand, to either side of the River Ancasmayo on the border, the negative painting of the vessels is so similar that theoretically speaking they might have originated from the same workshop. Here we find deep shaft graves of which other examples do not occur until we reach northern Mexico.

FIG. 64

There are huge artificial mounds in the Ecuador highland provinces of Imbabura and Pichincha called *tolas*. These are partly burial mounds and partly substructures of temples, with varying ground-plans.

Finds of gold are so far known only from Esmeraldas on the northern coast and the highland provinces of southern Ecuador. The most notable objects are the embossed pectorals from Esmeraldas. The mythological animal figures resemble those from Panama. But more frequent are very small, and even minute, gold ornaments. In the highlands there were found, *inter alia*, headbands surmounted by gold plumes, such as were also produced by goldsmiths in northern Peru. Quite often there appear bells in gold, masks in gold and silver, an sizable copper disks with elegant animal heads, which may have served as gongs. Even platinum, which only fuses at a very high temperature, was alloyed with gold in Esmeraldas, long before the technique of melting platinum became known in Europe. And one must bear in mind that bellows were not invented anywhere in ancient America.

In Guayaquil, the second largest city of Ecuador, a 'Gold Museum' was opened a few years ago, where hitherto unknown treasures made by goldsmiths from the province of Guayas are exhibited; these include elegantly-shaped golden bowls with figures of aquatic animals, which are either embossed or encrusted with disks of red mussel-shell and turquoise. Although I was definitely promised them, I unfortunately failed to obtain coloured photographs of these treasures produced by the ancient Guayas goldsmiths, of which scholars were hitherto completely unaware.

It was not only in Esmeraldas that gold objects of various sizes very frequently fell into the hands of vandals. In Esmeraldas they are to be found in artificial mounds. The clay figurines already mentioned, which were also discovered there, bear a great resemblance to Mesoamerican prototypes, although it is easy to distinguish them from the latter owing to the peculiar deformation of the head.

The chronology of the dissemination of gold-working in ancient America

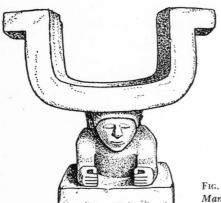

FIG. 65 — *Stone seat, supported by a recumbent human figure. Manabí province, Ecuador. Museum für Völkerkunde, Berlin.*

is by no means clear. There are some scholars who tend to ascribe all ancient American metal-working to intervention from the Old World, but their arguments, dazzling though they may appear, are not conclusive. Only one fact is certain, and that is that the earliest gold finds in America, which originate from northern Peru, must be assigned to the time of Christ, whereas Mesoamerican gold, so far as is known, appears at the earliest after the year 1000 A.D.

From the province of Manabí, which borders on Esmeraldas to the south, we have some peculiar human figures in stone, rigid and devoid of any ornamentation; the facial features are characteristic of some of the people living in the area today. There are also stone stools with arm-rests mounted on a base modelled in the shape of a figure, and slabs with figures and signs in flat relief.

The clay figurines which frequently occur here, as well as in Guayas, cannot claim to be so elegantly modelled as those from Esmeraldas, but there are stylistic affinities between them. For the most part they were mould-made in clay. They were already in use in Mexico about the beginning of our era. Further to the south, on the peninsula of Santa Elena, in association with these clay figures, there appear monochrome bases of vessels, partly decorated with modelled human faces in archaic style. They remind one forcibly of the well-known prototypes from Central America. Tripods are on the whole not typical of South America, and they occur only very sporadically in Peru.

By and large it seems as though contact was first established between the ancient cultures in a north-south direction, and later, with the discovery of metal-working, in a south-north direction. Ecuador undoubtedly played the role of an intermediary. One of the pieces in the mosaic of information about coastal navigation between Mexico and Ecuador may well be the fascinating affinity between some of the clay figures, which were discovered in Ecuador in strikingly large quantities such as we find nowhere else except in Mesoamerica — although there is no evidence of them in the intermediate areas, apart from the adjacent southern coastal province of Colombia.

We are still far from being in a position to assign tolerably accurate dates to the multifarious local cultures of Ecuador. Our ignorance becomes more pronounced the further we seek to go back in time beyond the few years of Inca rule.

III. THE EASTERN LOWLANDS

For several reasons we know even less about the ancient cultures to the east of the Andes. It is certain that these vast areas were settled by man before recent times. The advance of the Inca armies was greatly impeded by the tropical jungle. On the other hand very early strata of the Pacific coastal zone have yielded such typical elements of the jungle country as bark clothing and parrot-feather ·fans, as well as edible tropical plants such as manioc and ground-nuts.

It is already a long time since the great ethnographical museums of Europe and North America obtained specimens of beautifully decorated ceramic ware which had been excavated on the large island of Marajó, in the Amazon delta; they include anthropomorphic urns and figures. A little later the discovery was made of painted and engraved vessels with similar ornamentation originating from sites in eastern Ecuador, on the upper reaches of the River Napo, one of the tributaries of the Amazon and almost 3000 miles from the estuary of this 'king of all rivers'. In 1956 the American scholars Meggers and Evans carried out fruitful excavation work in eleven ancient settlements on the banks of the River Napo and one of its tributaries. The close affinity between the potsherds and clay vessels they found there and those from Marajó in the Amazon delta provide clear evidence that a certain phase of Marajó pottery originated from the rain-soaked slopes of the Andes; its centre has yet to be discovered. The area of the River Napo is probably one of several cradles of advanced culture from which influences radiated along the Amazon until they finally reached the Atlantic coast. This hypothesis is corroborated by evidence from the few sites hitherto known on the middle reaches of the Amazon.

FIG. 66 — *Large clay urn, engraved and painted. Marajó I., in the Amazon delta. After Palmatary.*

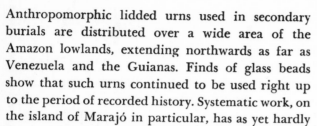

FIG. 67 — *A 'tanga', a kind of loin-board of fired clay worn by women like a fig-leaf. Marajó I. After Palmatary.*

Anthropomorphic lidded urns used in secondary burials are distributed over a wide area of the Amazon lowlands, extending northwards as far as Venezuela and the Guianas. Finds of glass beads show that such urns continued to be used right up to the period of recorded history. Systematic work, on the island of Marajó in particular, has as yet hardly begun. More than one hundred mounds — former dwelling-places — have been counted on this island, which is subject to periodic flooding. We may speak of an ancient Amazon style, although both local and chronological variants certainly occur. On his famous expedition eastwards from the Andes in 1542 Orellana did not come across any further large Indian villages. The American scholars mentioned above draw the conclusion that Napo ceramic ware must date from an earlier period than that of Marajó. In their estimation the earliest phases go back to the beginning of the 13th century.

Ancient Amazon pottery has a completely individualistic style which differs greatly from those of the Andean civilizations. Its wealth of ornamentation makes it worthy of display, and these urns, bowls and figures with modelled, painted, scratched or engraved decoration will always be treasured by collectors. A characteristic feature is the way in which broad and very fine lines are combined to form patterns, partly geometric and partly figured. In the same way curved and straight lines are combined to form a harmonious whole. The colours chiefly used are red, white and brown. Incision is often found in association with painting. Characteristics of a later period are manifest in the monochrome pottery from Santarém, an Amazon town at the mouth of the Tapajós. These vessels can almost be said to teem with human heads, frogs and so on, all fashioned in a primitive appliqué relief. Sparse linear ornamentation is incised in the soft clay before firing. Only in a few areas — e.g., in eastern Bolivia, where identifiable elements of expansionist Tiahuanaco were able to penetrate — is it as yet possible to establish links between the archaeology of the lowlands and the relatively precise chronology of the Central Andes.

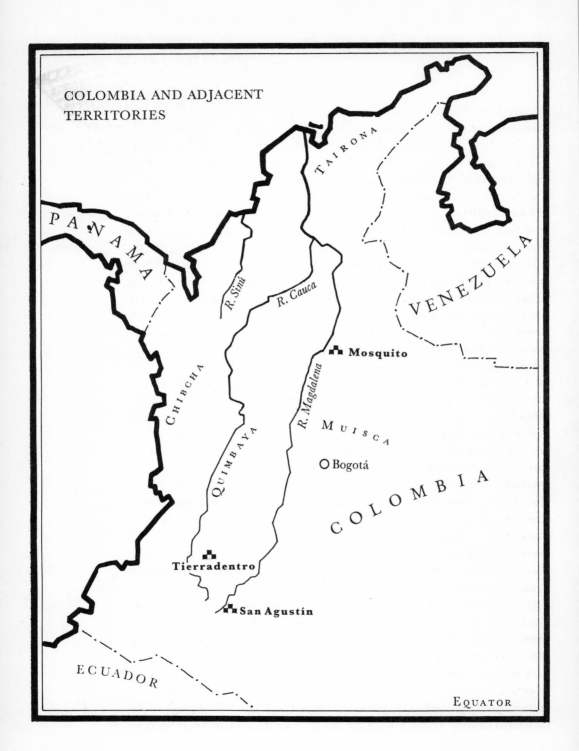

COLOMBIA AND ADJACENT
TERRITORIES

PANAMA

TAIRONA

VENEZUELA

R. Sinú

R. Cauca

CHIBCHA

QUIMBAYA

R. Magdalena

■ Mosquito

MUISCA

○ Bogotá

COLOMBIA

■ Tierradentro

■ San Agustín

ECUADOR

EQUATOR

IV. COLOMBIA

Ancient Colombia was, with Costa Rica and Panama, one of the principal 'lands of gold' in the New World. This was also the home of the 'Gilded Man', or 'El Dorado', one of the princes of the Muisca, a people belonging to the linguistic stock of the Chibcha. They spoke a language of their own which died out in the 18th century.

They inhabited the upland valleys near what is now Bogotá, a temperate and very fertile region. Even in antiquity this was the most densely populated area in the whole of Colombia. The legend of the 'Gilded Man', which spread beyond the borders of present-day Colombia and induced Spanish adventurers to undergo incredible hardships and to face calamity and even death, had its roots in a peculiar religious custom. For the prince of Guatavita, who like the Inca of Peru prided himself on having been begotten by the sun god, used on certain festival days to bathe in a sacred lake, after having sprinkled his whole body with gold-dust, so that when the sun rose he seemed to resemble a glistening idol. This was the particle of truth that lay behind the legends.

In 1536, when Gonzalo Jiménez de Quesada reached the Colombian plateau with his decimated army, the small state of the 'golden prince' had already been conquered by one of the two most powerful Muisca states, and had it not been for the Spanish invasion a united Muisca state would probably have been formed. Thus they would have gradually attained the more advanced phase of political organization reached by the Inca. Seen from the standpoint of cultural history the Chibcha civilization in Colombia found itself in a condition which Peru and Mexico had already overcome. At the time of the Spanish conquest the Chibcha were still at an early stage of development towards a veritable high culture.

Nevertheless the Muisca polity is often mentioned in the same breath as Mexico and Inca Peru. According to ancient Spanish accounts, in the political field they already had reached the stage of specialization of public offices, and had proper treaties and trade agreements, but on the other hand they lacked such characteristic features of high culture as stone monuments and buildings, urban settlements, and a written script or a substitute for one — although they had an oral historical tradition that dated back for more than two generations. The social stratification had both an economic and a religious basis. The princes commanded overwhelming authority, so that one may speak of a sacral kingship. The country owed its wealth chiefly to the flourishing trade that was carried on. The most

FIG. 68 — *Flat sacrificial figurine of gold, with a wire soldered on. Muisca style, Colombia. After Bennett.*

important exports were ready-made goods such as cotton blankets, etc., and in particular salt and precious stones. Raw cotton had to be imported, as well as gold-dust, coca leaves, and boy slaves for human sacrifice.

At a lower level of political and social organization stood the peoples of western Colombia, who practised cannibalism and differed little from their neighbours in the Caribbean. But the institution of chieftainship was already so well established that a Spanish priest, Castellanos (a chronicler who wrote in verse), was deeply impressed by the dignity of the princes of this area — although he had seen the prince of Nore travelling with his harem and using two of his wives as a bed, one as a pillow, while he consumed the fourth to obtain magic power. These chiefs, venerated as semi-divine kings, had themselves carried about in sedan-chairs in order not to lose their magic power by contact with the earth; they had large courts with nobles and slaves, interpreters and ambassadors. The external manifestations of their sovereign dignity were golden diadems and plumed sceptres, gold pectorals, long finger-nails and trailing robes. Cotton carpets were spread before their feet.

The most splendid gold objects are ascribed to the vanished Quimbaya people. They have been recovered from shaft graves on the middle reaches of the River Cauca and include heavy helmets, hollow figures cast in the *à-cire-perdue* technique, ornamental needles decorated with fine figures, knobs on staffs, masks and jars — all in gold. There are gold disks and breast-plates with eagles in relief, not unlike the gold objects from Costa Rica, as well as solid and hollow nose-ornaments with granulation and filigree — objects so exquisite that one is inclined to forget the barbaric nature of this kind of ornament. Even utilitarian implements such as fishing-hooks and (as in Peru) pincers for pulling out hairs are made of gold; all this entitles us to speak of a 'gold age' much as elsewhere we refer to a bronze age. Bronze was still unknown in Colombia at the

FIG. 69 — *Head of a large clay figure of the Muisca goddess Bachue. The decorative appendages recall the work of goldsmiths. Muisca style, Colombia. This figure was one of the earliest acquisitions of the Museum für Völkerkunde, Berlin.*

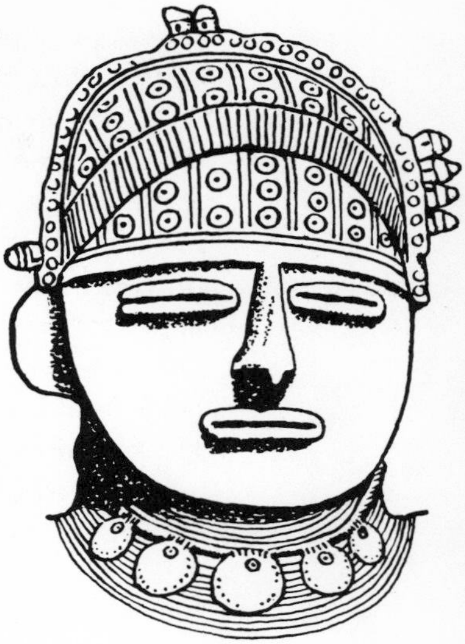

time of the Spanish conquest. The hollow figures from the Cauca valley, sometimes as much as two pounds in weight, have narrow eye-slits like dead or sleeping persons, with the result that they have been regarded (Georg Eckert) as effigies of interred chiefs. As in the case of artificial embalming of the dead elsewhere, their golden effigies were designed to ensure life after death in the manner of a 'living corpse'.

The richest collections of gold objects from the Cauca valley are contained in the 'Gold Museum' founded by the Republican Bank in Bogotá a few years ago, and the next richest are in the museums of Madrid and Berlin. But the gold the Colombians worked was not pure gold. Colombia is the home of *tumbaga,* an alloy of gold and copper, which usually contains a small percentage of silver. Probably this was preferred to gold with a heavy weight in carats since it was easier to work, and also on account of its colour. Several methods of gilding were employed, such as the *mise en couleur* technique, whereby an object was cast in an alloy of gold and copper, which was then treated with the acid sap of a plant which dissolved the copper, leaving a gold film on the surface. Gold ornaments stylistically akin to those of the Quimbaya originate from the north-eastern part of the country, from the Tairona, another extinct tribe whose name means 'goldsmiths'. Near the head-waters of the River Sinú lies the district of Dabeiba, where there stood a gilt-roofed temple dedicated to the goddess of the thunderstorm. The prince of Dabeiba — whom the Spaniards sought in vain — employed in his service about one hundred goldsmiths. So far as I am aware, not a single accurate inventory has been made of a grave containing gold objects so that an exact classification and attribution of them might be undertaken.

The gold objects produced by the Muisca can be distinguished at a glance from those of other Colombian peoples.

From the standpoint of craftsmanship and artistic quality they are inferior, although the legend of the 'Gilded Man' had its setting in their ter-

PLATE P. 234

FIG. 68 ritory. They produced in the main rather primitive flat angular human figures, with wires soldered on to suggest mouth, nose, eyes, hands and body ornaments. Small figures such as these were thrown into mountain lakes as sacrificial offerings to the deities who dwelt in them. Such votive offerings have occasionally also been found in clay jugs; these sometimes include whole groups of figures, as well as small serpents, sceptres, spear-throwers and so on. Flat nose-ornaments of astonishing size are also decorated with soldered-on wires.

Only a few shreds of Muisca fabrics with painted or printed designs have been found, located in dry caves where men of noble rank lie buried. Muisca pottery is simple and painted only in parts. Many figures and vessels are decorated with punched circles with dots in the centre, less frequently supplemented by application of detail. The coffee-bean eyes recall those on their gold figures. The most ornamental of all Colombian ceramics are pots and bowls with positive or negative painting in two or three colours; these originate from the department of Nariño, on the plateau near the border of Ecuador. In most cases they have geometric patterns, but there are also some stylized animal and human figures.

The inhabitants of the central part of the Cauca valley, who were famous for their gold-working, were also familiar with negative painting. Their monochrome human figures, with the tops of the heads reduced in size, appear very primitive. Some vessels have a decoration resembling filigree work incised deeply into the clay; this may have been influenced by designs used in metal-working.

FIG. 70 — *Clay figure of brown clay, painted in negative technique. Western Colombia. Museum für Völkerkunde. Berlin.*

Fig. 71 — *Clay bowl, painted in red, ochre and black in negative technique. Nariño dept., (Colombia). Museum für Völkerkunde, Berlin.*

From the wooded banks of the central reaches of the River Magdalena we have large cylindrical urns with rigid figures or human heads affixed to their lids; they belong to the Amazon style, as do several other elements from different parts of Colombia, such as secondary burials in urns, circular houses with wooden supports, stools with four legs, and much else besides.

Architectural remains have only been left by the Tairona, who dwelt in round houses of stone in large villages on the northern approaches of the Sierra Nevada de Santa Marta. The stone they used was not always carefully hewn. Paved roadways, bridges and flights of steps complete the picture of their settlements. The work of their goldsmiths has been mentioned above.

Fig. 72 — *Lid of a large urn of brown clay with traces of painting in a light colour. Mosquito style (named after a hacienda in north-eastern Colombia). Museum für Völkerkunde, Berlin.*

V. SAN AGUSTÍN

The culture of San Agustín in chiefly lithic; it is certainly the oldest of all the ancient Colombian cultures and presents us with many puzzling problems.

The little village of San Agustín is situated near the head-waters of the River Magdalena; the ancient culture to which it has given its name extends over a large, well-irrigated and fertile area. No one knows who the people were who built these megalithic shrines and sepulchral chambers, huge stone figures, and reliefs cut into the rock. They can hardly have been members of the Chibcha tribes who immigrated into the area in later times. The objects produced by this people cannot be traced; they are most likely to be found in the Peruvian and Bolivian highlands, but the idols from the San Agustín area do not bear sufficient resemblance to the monoliths of Tiahuanaco to justify the contention of some authors that San Agustín was the cradle of higher civilization in the whole Andean region. On the other hand, there can be no doubt that this megalithic culture must date from relatively early times. When the Spaniards arrived these highland shrines had long since been abandoned; they were found half-buried in the soil and overgrown with grass and brushwood.

Several years ago the Colombian Government made this an 'archaeological park' subject to official protection and control.

Some of the heavy stone statues in the shape of human beings and animals stood in ancient subterranean places of worship; from a stylistic point of view they can be classified into several phases, like the Tiahuanaco monoliths in Bolivia and Peru. Others served as caryatids; others again were placed on mounds. Stone sarcophagi measuring nearly seven feet in length were found, as well as stone cists.

Some of the huge statues bear traces of polychrome painting. As well as those crudely hewn out of the block there are others on which attention has been given to detail. The tallest measures over 13 ft. in height. Horst Nachtigall, an ethnologist from Mainz who has worked in southern Colombia, holds that some of the anthropomorphic monoliths were representations of human beings and that only some of them were idols. The human figures with fangs of beasts of prey, like those in Chavín and other ancient Peruvian cultures, may however be regarded with certainty as representations of deities.

The alae of the nose are always broad. The eyes have various shapes: they are either semi-circular, circular, almond-shaped, or even square. The figures generally bear little resemblance to one another. Some of them carry trophy heads in their hands, while others have sceptres or tools. There are also 'mother-and-child' figures. The ornaments include crescent-shaped nose-pendants, ear-plugs and necklaces. The heads are always disproportionately large; their massiveness must have made an even greater impression upon the native population of those days than they do upon modern man. They were carved from stone of volcanic origin. A total of 328 such statues have been counted so far.

FIG. 73

Remains of dwelling-houses are completely lacking. The very small number of ceramic finds confirms the facts that the megaliths in the environs of San Agustín were places of worship.

San Agustín is situated not far from the head-waters of the River Magdalena. At a place called Lavapatas, only a few feet below one of the hills where rites were performed, sculptures have been found on a rocky cliff-face in a gorge. Among them is a human figure wearing a plumed crown and with both arms raised, as well as serpents, lizards and aquatic animals. in high relief. The water of the stream that flows through the gorge can be diverted by means of basins and channels carved into the rock; in this way the figures would be sprinkled with water. Little imagination is required to conclude that this was a place where water and fertility rites were carried on. Similar places of worship are known in the Peruvian highlands.

It is as difficult to determine the age of Agustín culture as it is to assign these monumental statues and megalithic graves to any specific people. The finds of gold alone may indicate that the efflorescent period of this culture occurred in the not too distant past. The gold ornaments found are few in number and of inferior quality, but not much significance need be attached to this. For, as Horst Nachtigall has shown, the gold found in the Cauca valley and the Tierradentro area north of San Agustín displays stylistic and iconographic parallels with the stone figures of San Agustín. Tierradentro, 'the land in the interior', is situated in the highlands between the upper reaches of the River Magdalena and the River Cauca. The stone statues discovered there are less strictly stylized: the facial features are more human, but are less expressive than those of the Agustín culture; according to Nachtigall this came to an end in the 8th century A.D., but he gives no date for its origin. In any case the dating of Tierradentro to a later period is confirmed not only by several typological criteria but also by the more advanced stage reached in the development of metal-working technique.

A predominant characteristic of Tierradentro are the sepulchral chambers chiselled into the soft rock, with walls painted in white, black, yellow and red. The main motifs consist of intersecting parallel lines, lozenges, circles and other geometric patterns; less frequent are stylized human figures, woven into these paintings as though into a tapestry. From a typological point of view these spacious rock tombs, which are approached from above by steps and spiral stairways, are a development of simple shaft tombs with side-chambers. Besides these several painted sepulchral vaults have also been discovered in the central part of the Cauca valley. As archaeological exploration progresses throughout Colombia it will become possible to point to ever more parallels and links between the individual regional cultures, which today appear to be more or less isolated from one another. The same applies to the whole of ancient America. Perhaps even those scholars will be proved right who are inclined to ascribe all the impulses towards higher civilization in the New World during the millennia that preceded the Spanish conquest to links with and influences from the Old World. But there is as yet no evidence at all that this is so; there are still far too many large blank patches on the archaeological maps of Asia and America.

On the other hand the excursion we have made through the prehistoric art of South America has revealed characteristics that demonstrate in a spectacular way the originality and creativeness of the Indians before they had any contact with the blessings of the Old World. There are several indications that an Indian renaissance is now beginning; this will perhaps find expression less in the field of art than in other kinds of intellectual activity. But there can be no doubt as to the artistic talents of the early Indians. Some of the best-known modern European artists have personally said that they have a high appreciation of ancient Indian art and have drawn inspiration from it.

Fig. 73 — *Monumental stone figure. The enormous fangs indicate that it is a deity. San Agustin culture, Colombia. After H. Nachtigall.*

There is no telling how the ancient cultures of the New World would have developed had the Spaniards not invaded the country. The western hemisphere had neither iron nor glass, horses nor carts, nor even the potter's wheel; yet they had gold, silver and precious stones, knowledge of the stars and an expressive religious art. None of the other peoples of 16th-century Europe could have understood this strange civilization any worse or better than the Spaniards, who do not deserve gratuitous criticism on our part — for it is a fact that the laws they imposed upon the indigenous population were far better than those of the other colonial powers. The Spaniards, men of the Renaissance who had conquered the Moors, were unable to appreciate the wonders of the Indian civilizations they encountered; but the responsibility for this lay with the times in which they lived. Ubbelohde-Doering, a great friend of the Peruvian people, has put it pertinently: "If the Sumerians of the third millennium B.C. had found themselves before the brick pyramids of Peru, *they* would have understood the world into which they had stepped; and this ancient Peruvian world would have understood *them*." To generalize, for ancient Peru one may read: ancient America.

CHRONOLOGICAL TABLE

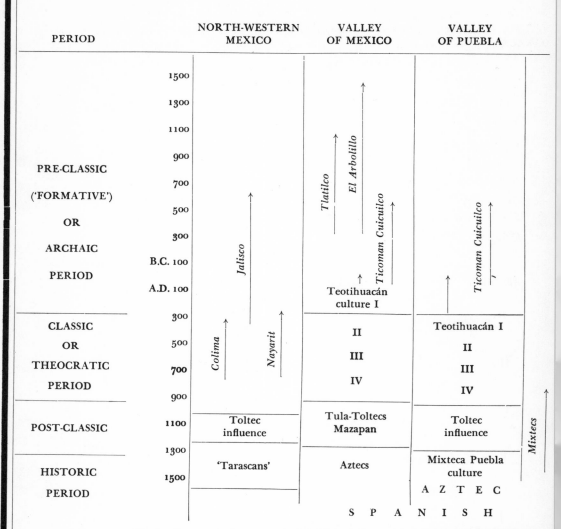

PERIOD		NORTH-WESTERN MEXICO	VALLEY OF MEXICO	VALLEY OF PUEBLA	
PRE-CLASSIC ('FORMATIVE') OR ARCHAIC PERIOD	1500 1300 1100 900 700 500 300 B.C. 100 A.D. 100	*Jalisco*	*Tlatilco* *El Arbolillo* *Cuicuilco* *Ticoman* Teotihuacán culture I	*Cuicuilco* *Ticoman*	
CLASSIC OR THEOCRATIC PERIOD	300 500 700 900	*Colima* *Nayarit*	II III IV	Teotihuacán I II III IV	
POST-CLASSIC	1100 1300	Toltec influence	Tula-Toltecs Mazapan	Toltec influence	*Mixtecs*
HISTORIC PERIOD	1500	'Tarascans'	Aztecs	Mixteca Puebla culture	

A Z T E C

S P A N I S H

Mexico has a past but no recorded history. Some dates can be established by means of radio-carbon analysis, but many further tests would be necessary in order to build up a reliable chronological table. This would be fairly costly, and it would be still more difficult to obtain material of which precise information is available with regard to the circumstances of its discovery. The chronological table given here should be regarded merely as a provisional sketch.

OF MESOAMERICA

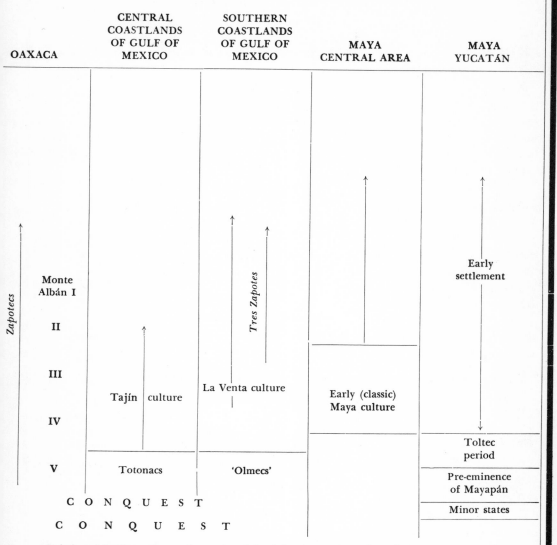

	CENTRAL COASTLANDS OF GULF OF MEXICO	SOUTHERN COASTLANDS OF GULF OF MEXICO	MAYA CENTRAL AREA	MAYA YUCATÁN
OAXACA				

Zapotecs

Monte Albán I

II

III

IV

V

Tajín | culture

Totonacs

Tres Zapotes

La Venta culture

'Olmecs'

Early (classic) Maya culture

Early settlement

Toltec period

Pre-eminence of Mayapán

Minor states

C O N Q U E S T

C O N Q U E S T

It is based in the main on the works of the following authors: S. K. Lothrop, Gerdt Kutscher (chronological tables in catalogues to the exhibitions of Pre-Columbian Art of Mexico and Central America held in Munich, Zurich, Berlin, Vienna and Frankfurt-on-Main in 1959–60) and Wigberto Jiménez Moreno (in *Esplendor del México Antiguo*), who in turn has consulted the most eminent Mexican archaeologists.

CHRONOLOGICAL TABLE OF THE ANDEAN LANDS*

	NORTH	CENTRE	SOUTH
3000			
2500		*Beginning of plant cultivation*	
2000		CHAVIN HORIZON	
1500		COASTAL CHAVIN	
1000			
500		Beginning of metal-working: gold	Polychrome ceramic ware
400			Early Paracas
300	Bichrome ceramic ware		Paracas Necropolis
200	**Salinar** (white on red)		
100	Gallinazo (negative)		
0			
100			
200	Moche (development		Nazca
300	of metal-working:	Early Lima	
400	gold, copper, silver)		Classic Tiahuanaco
500			
600			
700		*Spread of bronze-working*	
800		EXPANSIONIST TIAHUANACO	
900			
1000		MINOR KINGDOMS AND CITY-BUILDERS	
1100			
1200	Chimú	Chancay	**Ica**
			Rise of the Inca
1300			
1400		INCA EMPIRE (1440–1532)	
		Subjugation of Aymara princes on the plateau	
		Conquest of Chimú principality (northern coastlands)	
1450			
1500			
	Struggle for succession between Inca brothers Huascar and Atahualpa (1527–1532)		
1532	Pizarro's march to Cajamarca		
1533	Assassination of Atahualpa		

* Although some radio-carbon datings are available, the chronology of Ancient Peru can by no means as yet be ascertained with precision. Any chronological table must therefore be regarded as tentative.

APPENDICES

GLOSSARY

adobe
> Sun-dried clay brick. Its use as a building material in Mexico dates back to prehistoric times, and it is still employed even today. Unfortunately *adobe* does not stand up to time and wet weather, and easily turns to earth again. Since *adobe* occasionally contains artefacts from earlier cultures, it may happen that those from more recent cultures are found below those from an earlier one.

alpaca
> South American species of llama *(q.v.)*.

atlantes
> Figures or half-figures supporting an entablature or cornice in place of a pilaster.

atlatl
> (Mexican: 'something to throw spears with'): an ancient American spear-thrower, consisting of a short flattened wooden stick with a groove for the spear-shaft and a hook to accommodate the butt of the spear. A very ancient hunting weapon, found not only in Mexico but also in Australia, New Guinea, among the Eskimo and in many parts of South America.

Axayacatl
> ('water face'): the 6th Aztec priest-king (1469–1483), father of the kings Moctezuma, Xocoyotzin and Cuitlahuac. Axayacatl is said to have introduced the Xipe Totec cult into Mexico, and he himself is also depicted wearing a Xipe skin.

Aztecs
> (Mexican: *azteca,* the people from the 'white place', the island of Aztlan): the great Mexican warrior people at the time of the Spanish conquest. They called themselves *mexica* or *mexitin,* but they were also referred to as *tenochca* after their tribal ancestor, Tenoch — hence the name of their capital, Tenochtitlán.

ball-game
> (Mexican: *tlachtli*): ritual game with a heavy rubber ball which the players endeavour to put through a stone ring, using their backs and hips.

C-14
> cf. *radio-carbon dating*

caryatids
> (Greek: *karyatides*): female figures supporting an entablature or cornice, like *atlantes.*

Castilla del Oro
> (Gold Castile): a territory corresponding approximately to present-day Panama.

cazique
> An Indian chief or prince.

cenote
> A lake formed by a subterranean river (Yucatán).

Centéotl
> (or Cintéotl): god of maize, son of the Mother of God Tlazoltéotl, first of the five guardians of the first Venus period, fourth of the nine lords of the night. Originally a Totonac deity; he is also known as Xochipilli, 'prince of flowers'.

Chac Mool
> 'the reclining god' (*chac*: Mexican for 'god'): a Maya name given by the French scholar Désiré Charnay to a Toltec figure.

Chalchhuitlicue
> or 'the goddess with the cloak embellished with precious stones': the goddess of water and rain.

chicha
> Fermented beer made from corn, manioc, quinoa, ground-nuts, etc.

Chichén Itzá
> 'at the well of Itzá': cultural centre in Yucatán founded by a group of Toltecs who had emigrated from Tula.

Cholula
> The pyramid of Cholula resembles a mountain with a church on the summit. An archaeological investigation made in 1931 established that it consisted of five pyramids superimposed upon one another.

Chorotega
> The primitive population of Nicaragua.

cire-perdue
> ('lost wax' process): a technique of casting. A model of the work is first prepared in wax and then a clay coating is applied. When the hot molten metal is poured in the wax melts; when the metal becomes solidified the clay cover is broken away. If the object is intended to be hollow a core of clay is also used.

Ciudadela
> A square in Teotihuacán used for festivals and ceremonies.

cloisonné
> A term derived from enamel painting; actually the enamelling of strips of gold. Gold strips are affixed upon a gold plate in such a way that they form the design and thin strips of metal (*cloisons*) into which the enamel is placed and then melted. After firing the sur-

face is burnished and polished. Used here to denote a specific kind of ornamentation on ceramic ware.

Cóatl
Ser₊ent: the fifth Mexican day-sign.

Coatlicue
'serpent skirt': an article of clothing consisting of plaited snakes, worn by the Aztec earth goddess, mother of the war god Huitzilopochtli.

corbelled arch
An arch between two parallel walls, in which the inner faces of both walls are carried inward by means of overlapping courses until the gap in the middle can be bridged.

Cuicuilco
The round pyramid near Cuicuilco is the oldest American monument yet discovered. It was built in approx. 500 B.C.

danzantes
Ritual dancers.

Guetár
Ancient inhabitants of the central plateau lands of Costa Rica.

Huaca Prieta
Archaeological site at the mouth of the Chicama valley in northern Peru. *Huaca* means sanctuary in the Quechua language; *prieta* (Spanish for dark-coloured) denotes the dark colour of the large mound, caused by the weathering of the refuse of which it is composed.

huaqueros
Grave-robbers.

Huaxtecs
An isolated Maya tribe living on either side of the River Pánuco and in the eastern part of the state of San Luis Potosí.

Huehuetéotl
(Aztec: 'the old god'): god of fire and light and 'father of the gods and men'. The oldest identifiable Mexican deity, and also, like Xiuhtechtli, 'lord of turquoise'. Huehuetéotl had many functions to fulfil, particularly in connection with the calendar. Huehuetéotl has been found by archaeologists under a layer of lava near Cuicuilco in his customary guise of an old man bent with age.

Huitzilopochtli
Tribal and principal god of the Mexicans, who appears in the guise of a humming-bird.

ik
Maya hieroglyph for 'day'.

ikat
(literally, 'to tie'): a technique for decorating fabrics with designs. The threads are grouped and tied with thin fibre before dyeing, so that the dye into which they are dipped cannot penetrate to the bound parts.

interlocking style
American term for a style of ceramic ware found mainly in the central part of the Peruvian coastlands and dating from the 1st millennium A.D.

jadeite
Another term for jade, a translucent light green or yellowish mineral. This word is also used to denote related types of stone, usually very hard. Real jade is rare and costly.

Jívaro
Head-hunters in Ecuador.

Kaminaljuyú
Ruins near Guatemala City.

kero
Large wooden beaker with scenic representations. The outlines of the human beings, animals and plants are incised and filled in with resinous colouring matter (Inca period). The term is sometimes also used for clay beakers of a similar shape (e.g., in the Tiahuanaco period).

La Venta
Village on the border between the states of Veracruz and Tabasco where the 'La Venta' culture was found.

llama
Camel with no hump, the size of a stag, native to the Andean lands. To this species also belongs the vicuña; the alpaca is a domesticated llama.

maguey
agave atrovirens, also *americana*. It blossoms approximately once every ten years. The large bud is cut off just as it is ready to emerge and the heart of the plant scooped out. The sap (*agua miel*) is collected (this plant yields about 55 gallons in three to four months). It is then stored in distended ox-skins that have not been tanned, where fermentation takes place, yielding a slightly sour beverage with a 5—6% content of alcohol: *pulque* (Mexican: *octli*). It was probably produced already in the Teotihuacan period. *Pulque* was mentioned by Hernando Cortés in 1524 in a letter to Emperor Charles V.

mangrove forests
Evergreen deciduous forests in tropical coastal areas. The trees (e.g., the common mangrove) adapted themselves to the natural

environment (marshy land, frequent flooding) by means of air roots.

manioc
Nutritious tropical plant. The flour obtained from the tuberous roots was used by the Indians to make gruel and cakes, as well as intoxicating beverages.

mantos
Woollen and cotton shrouds embroidered with figures on the hem or all over. Found in the Paracas peninsula and the Ica region (southern Peru).

mastodon
(Greek: *mastodontes* = animals with long teeth): extinct species, related to the elephant of the present day.

Maya
'the Greeks of Mexico': a people who originally came from Guatemala and Yucatán.

Mesoamerica
Cultural and geographical term comprising Mexico and the areas formerly inhabited by the Maya.

metate
stone (Mexican: *metlatl*) upon which, even today, boiled maize is ground with a *metlapilli*.

metlapilli
'Son of metate': a cylindrical pestle used for grinding maize on a *metate*.

mise en couleur
Method of gilding. An object of gold and copper alloy is dipped into the sap from acid-bearing plants, leaving a gold film on the surface.

Mixtecs
(Mexican: *mixteca*): 'the people from the land of clouds', who exerted a strong influence upon the Nahua people and their last descendants, the Aztecs, through their religion (i.e. the wisdom accumulated and transmitted by their priests) and their art (especially codices, gold-working, sculpture and mosaics).

Moctezuma
(Mexican: *Motecuzoma*), altered by the Spaniards into Montezuma, which they found easier to pronounce. Derived from Aztec *Mo tecuh zoma*, 'the raging prince'. Moctezuma I Ilhuicamina ('the support of heaven') reigned from 1440 to 1469. Moctezuma II Xocoyotzin ('the younger') was born in 1468 and died in 1520.

mollusca
A sub-kingdom of soft-bodied invertebrates, including snails and mussels.

monolith
(Greek: *monolithos*): a commemorative stone erected as a single slab, or a major detail on an architectural monument; it may be either worked or not worked.

mould
A hollow form in clay, stone or wood.

Nahua
Tribes linguistically related to the Aztecs.

Nahuatl
(literally: 'mouth', 'opening', 'ring'): the Aztec language.

nephrite
A kind of greenstone.

Nezahualcóyotl
('the fasting coyote'): king of Texcoco, poet and statesman. He was a great architect and built the large dam in Lake Texcoco as well as the enormous aqueduct extending from the springs near Chapultepec to the centre of Tenochtitlán-Mexico.

Nicarao
A people who emigrated from Tula in 1168 (or earlier) to Nicaragua ('the water of the Nicarao').

Oaxaca
(Mexican: *huayacac*): 'the beginning of acacia trees', a state in Mexico and the capital city of this state.

obsidian
(Mexican: *itztli*): vitreous volcanic rock with sharp edges, used for sacrificial and other knives, spear- and arrow-heads, etc.

Olmecs
(Mexican: *olmeca*): the people from Olman, the land of rubber in the east, on the coast of the Gulf of Mexico.

petrography
Description and systematic classification of rocks.

plangue
Technique in textile designing. Motifs are drawn or stamped upon the fabrics, and are then carefully tied off. When the fabric is dipped into a dye vat the colour is unable to penetrate to the tied-off parts, thus forming the design.

pulque
Intoxicating drink made by Mexican peoples from the fermented sap of the agave.

puma
Large species of feline animal, found all over America from Canada to Patagonia.

quauhxicalli
(Mexican for 'eagle's bowl') vessel in which

were deposited the heart and blood of the victims of human sacrifice.

quechquemitl

Short cape worn by women.

quetzal

(*pharomacrus mocinna*): an exceptionally fine bird with four curious brilliant green tail-feathers some three feet in length.

Quetzalcóatl

'The plumed serpent', god of wind, heaven (the feathers) and earth (the serpent), creator of mankind, etc. One of the most ancient gods of Mexico. In Teotihuacán (Ciudadela) he served as a water deity. Later this was the title given to rulers in Tula.

quinoa

(*chenopodium quinoa*): ancient Indian kind of corn, which only thrives on the plateau and is full of nourishment.

quipu

So-called knot-records, in which knots tied in cords were used to express numbers in the decimal system and colours to express different materials. It was employed by the Inca to keep numerical records and for mnemonic purposes.

radio-carbon dating

The radio-carbon dating method is based on the following principles: at high altitudes part of the nitrogen in the air is transformed by cosmic rays into C-14 (the radio-active isotope of carbon). This radio-active carbon is absorbed by plants in the form of carbon dioxide, which in the course of time disintegrates. This disintegration of radio-carbon takes place at a constant rate, with a 'half-life' of 5568 ± 30 years. By comparing the radio-activity of the carbon with that found in a living plant, the age of the material in question can be established. According to the calculations of the Bureau of Standards, Washington, D.C., the 'half-life' is not 5568 but 5760 years. This means that all dates obtained by C-14 analysis should be set back by 192 years. At the moment (June 1961) this point remains open.

spectroscopy

The measurement of wave-lengths by means of spectroscopes, optical instruments designed to produce and examine spectra. Spectral analysis is the determination of the elements contained in matter by means of spectra. This method is extremely precise: for example, the occurrence of 1/10,000,000 mg. of sodium can be clearly perceived.

spindle-whorl

The clay or stone disks affixed to a hand-spindle which keep it moving.

spondylus

A kind of sea-mussel.

stele

A large upright stone slab or column decorated with reliefs or inscriptions. Found particularly in the Maya and Zapotec cultures, but (very rarely) in other ancient Mexican civilizations as well.

stratigraphy

Branch of science concerned with geological and archaeological strata, enabling finds to be dated.

Tajin

(Totonac for 'lightning', i.e. the god of rain): called by the Zapotecs *Cocijo*, by the Maya of Yucatán *Chac*, and in the Valley of Mexico *Tlaloc*.

techichi

or *tepescuintli*: a fattened hairless dog, an Aztec table delicacy.

Tenochtitlán-Mexico

'cactus on the rock': the Aztec capital built on islands in Lake Texcoco. On its ruins the Spaniards built a city that has disappeared completely. Today it is the centre of the modern capital of Mexico.

Teotihuacán

'the place where one becomes God': an ancient cultural centre from the pre-Aztec period, 31 miles north-east of the capital, the only really ancient city in the country; it has pyramids said to be dedicated to the sun and moon.

Tezcatlipóca

The god of obsidian and the sacrificial knife. In some codices he is described as the god with knives in place of feet. Also the god of evil.

thermoluminescence

A new method of dating. Details of it have not yet been given in archaeological journals.

tillandsia

Plants with no roots but having many ramifications, which lie loose on the desert sand.

tlachtli

cf. *ball-game*.

Tlaloc

'the rain god who causes the sprouting': the deification of water. In more ancient times the guardian of water, in the guise of a serpent. One of the oldest deities of ancient Mexico.

Tlalocan
　　The paradise of the rain god, the beautiful land of the dead.

Tlamimilolpan
　　One of the largest complexes of houses explored at Teotihuacán; it was excavated in 1934—5 by the second expedition from the Ethnographical Museum of Sweden.

Tlatilco
　　Brick-works south of the Mexican capital. *Venus Tlatilco* was the ideal of female beauty to the peasants of those ancient times, and was a symbol of growth and fertility.

Tlazoltéotl
　　'The goddess of earth' and 'eater of dirt', who could take upon herself the sins of mankind and absolve them; mother of Centéotl.

tolas
　　Artificial mounds erected for burial purposes or as temple bases (Ecuador).

Toltecs
　　(Mexican: *tolteca*): a people from Tollan (Tula).

totemism
　　In ethnology, the concept that there exists a mystical connection, between a group of men on one hand and an animal, more rarely a plant or natural phenomenon, on the other. The totem is the object, animal or plant concerned.

Totonacs
　　A people on the central and northern coastlands of the state of Veracruz.

Tres Zapotes
　　Village in the district of Tuxtla, Tabasco, noted for the archaeological finds made there of the 'La Venta' culture.

vigesimal system
　　Numerical system used by the ancient Maya, in which each unit is twenty times larger than the one inferior to it.

volute
　　Spiral scroll in ornamentation.

Xipe Totec
　　'The Flayed Lord', god of growth and vegetation, who obtained his power from the skin of the human victims sacrificed to him. He was 'the great atoner' and the fierce god of penance, of fallen warriors and of sacrificial stones, and was also the special god of goldsmiths.

Xiuhtecutli
　　(Mexican: *xiuh* = turquoise, *tecutli* = lord, prince): 'lord of turquoise' and god of fire. Cf. *Huehuetéotl*, 'the old god', the father of gods and men.

Xochipilli
　　('prince of flowers'): the god of growth and vegetation, the young god of maize, as well as of games, singing and dancing. In songs he is also invoked as Centéotl.

Xochiquetzal
　　The 'flower quetzal feather': goddess of flowers and love. Spouse of Tlaloc. Raped by Tezcatlipóca and made goddess of love.

Xolotl
　　('page', 'servant'): the dog-headed god Xolotl accompanied the setting sun on its way through the nether world. His twin brother, the wind god Quetzalcóatl, led the sun up again into the heavens. A statue in the Stuttgart Museum represents him as a skeleton. He personified the planet Venus as the evening-star. Xolotl was also the god of the ball-game. As the god of lightning he cleft the earth and opened up the way to the nether world in order to carry out his function of accompanying the dead. From Hades he or his twin brother brought the bones of the dead out of which men were created.

Yacatecutli
　　(Mexican: 'the lord of the nose', 'the prince who goes before'): the god of travelling merchants.

Zapotecs
　　(Mexican: *zapoteca*): an ancient civilization in the state of Oaxaca. One of the largest tribes, not only in Mexico, but in the whole of America.

BIBLIOGRAPHY

I. THE ART OF MEXICO AND CENTRAL AMERICA

Aguilar, P., Carlos, H.: La orfebrería en el Mexico precortesiano, in Acta Antropologica, II: 2, Mexico City, 1946.

Armillas, Pedro: Teotihuacán, Tula y los Toltecas, in Runa, Vol. 3, Buenos Aires, 1950.

Bovallius, Carl: Nicaraguan Antiquities, Stockholm, 1886.

Burland, Cottie A.: Art and Life in Ancient Mexico, Oxford, 1948.

Bushnell, G. H. S. and Digby, Adrian: Ancient American Pottery, London, 1955.

Caso, Alfonso: Las estelas zapotecas, Mexico City, 1928.

Caso, Alfonso: El pueblo del Sol, Mexico City, 1953. English translation: The Aztecs, People of the Sun, University of Oklahoma Press, 1958.

Caso, Alfonso and Bernal, Ignacio: Urnas de Oaxaca. Memorias del Instituto Nacional de Antropología e Historia, 2, Mexico City, 1952.

Castillo, Bernal Díaz del: The Discovery and Conquest of Mexico, 1517—1521, London, 1928.

Covarrubias, Miguel: Mexico South, New York, 1947.

Covarrubias, Miguel: Indian Art of Mexico and Central America, New York, 1957.

Dahlgren de Jordán, Barbro: La Mixteca, su cultura e historia prehispánicas, Mexico City, 1954.

Disselhoff, Hans-Dietrich: Geschichte der altamerikanischen Kulturen, Munich, 1953.

Drucker, Philip: La Venta, Tabasco: a Study of Olmec Ceramics and Art. Smithsonian Institution, Bureau of American Ethnology, Bulletin 153. Washington, 1952.

Dürer, Albrecht: Albrecht Dürers schriftlicher Nachlass, ed. Ernst Heidrich, Berlin, 1918.

Enciso, Jorge: Sellos del Antiguo México, Mexico City, 1947.

Esplendor de México Antiguo, 1—2. Centro de Investigaciones Antropológicas de México, Mexico City, 1959.

Feriz, Hans: Zwischen Peru und Mexico. Koninklijk Instituut voor de Tropen, Amsterdam, Mededeling CXXXIV, Afd. Cult. en Phys. Anthropologie, No. 63. Amsterdam, 1959.

Gamio, Manuel: La población del Valle de Teotihuacán, Vol. 1—3, Mexico City, 1922.

van Giffen-Duyvis, Guda E. G.: De Azteken, Amsterdam, 1957.

Groth-Kimball, Irmgard and Feuchtwanger, Franz: Kunst im alten Mexico, Zurich—Freiburg i. Br., 1953.

Hartman, C. V.: Archaeological Researches in Costa Rica, Stockholm, 1901.

Hartman, C. V.: Archaeological Researches on the Pacific Coast of Costa Rica. Memoirs of the Carnegie Museum, Vol. 3, No. 1. Pittsburg, 1907.

Heine-Geldern, R. and Ekholm, G. F.: Significant Parallels in the Symbolic Arts of Southern Asia and Middle America, in: Selected Papers of the XXIXth International Congress of Americanists, I, Chicago, 1951.

Heine-Geldern, R.: Die asiatische Herkunft der südamerikanischen Metalltechnik, in: Paideuma, Vol. 5, Bamberg, 1954.

Holmes, William H.: Archaeological Studies among the Ancient Cities of Mexico. Field Columbian Museum, Publ. 8, Anthropological Series, Vol. 1, No. 1. Chicago, 1895, 1897.

Joyce, Thomas Athol: Mexican Archaeology, London, 1914.

Joyce, Thomas Athol: Central American and West Indian Archaeology, London, 1916.

Joyce, Thomas Athol: Maya and Mexican Art, London, 1927.

Kelemen, Pál: Mediaeval American Art, 1—2, New York, 1946.

Kidder, Alfred V., Jennings, Jesse D. and Shook, Edwin M.: Excavations at Kaminaljuyú. Carnegie Institution of Washington, Publ. 561. Washington, 1946.

Kidder II, Alfred and Samayoa Chinchilla, Carlos: The Art of the Ancient Maya, New York, 1959.

Krickeberg, Walter: Märchen der Azteken und Inka-Peruaner, Maya und Muisca, Jena, 1928.

Krickeberg, Walter: Altmexikanische Kulturen, Berlin, 1956.

Linné, S.: Darien in the Past, Gothenburg, 1929.

Linné, S.: Archaeological Researches at Teotihuacán, Mexico. The Ethnographical Museum of Sweden, Stockholm, New Series, No. 1. Stockholm, 1934.

Linné, S.: El valle y la ciudad de México en 1550. The Ethnographical Museum of Sweden, Stockholm, New Series, No. 9. Stockholm, 1948.

Linné, S.: Treasures of Mexican Art, Stockholm, 1956.

Lothrop, S. K.: Pottery of Costa Rica and Nicaragua. Contributions from the Museum of the American Indian, Heye Foundation, Vol. 8: 1—2. New York, 1926.

Lothrop, S. K.: Coclé: an Archaeological Study of Central Panamá, 1–2. Memoirs of the Peabody Museum of Archaeology and Ethnology, Harvard University, Vol. 7–8. Cambridge, Mass., 1942.

Lothrop, S. K.: Archaeology of Southern Veraguas, Panamá. Memoirs of the Peabody Museum of Archaeology and Ethnology, Harvard University, Vol. 9, No. 3. Cambridge, Mass., 1950.

Lothrop, S. K.: Pre-Columbian Art. Robert Woods Bliss Collection. New York, 1957.

MacCurdy, George Grant: A Study of Chiriquian Antiquities. Memoirs of the Connecticut Academy of Arts and Sciences, Vol. 3. New Haven, Conn., 1911.

Marquina, Ignacio: Arquitectura Prehispánica. Memorias del Instituto Nacional de Antropología e Historia, 1. Mexico City, 1951.

Maudslay, A. P.: Archaeology. Biologia Centrali-Americana, Vols. 1–5. London, 1889–1902.

Morley, S. G.: The Ancient Maya, 3rd ed., Stanford University, Calif., 1956.

Noguera, Eduardo: La cerámica arqueológica de Cholula, Mexico City, 1954.

Nowotny, Karl A.: Mexikanische Kostbarkeiten aus Kunstkammern der Renaissance, Vienna, 1960.

Peterson, Frederick A.: Ancient Mexico, London, 1959.

Piña Chán, Román: Las culturas preclásicas de la Cuenca de México, Mexico City, 1955.

Pinã Chán, Román: Tlatilco. Instituto Nacional de Antropología e Historia: Serie investigaciones, 1–2. Mexico City, 1958.

Proskouriakoff, Tatiana: An Album of Maya Architecture. Carnegie Institution of Washington, Publ. 558. Washington, 1946.

Proskouriakoff, Tatiana: A Study of Classic Maya Sculpture. Carnegie Institution of Washington, Publ. 593. Washington, 1950.

Rivet, Paul: Cités Maya, Paris, 1954.

Ruppert, Karl, Thompson, J. Eric S. and Proskouriakoff, Tatiana: Bonampak, Chiapas, Mexico. Carnegie Institution of Washington, Publ. 602. Washington, 1955.

Saville, Marshall H.: The Goldsmith's Art in Ancient Mexico: Indian Notes and Monographs. Museum of the American Indian, Heye Foundation. New York, 1920.

Saville, Marshall H.: Turquois Mosaic Art in Ancient Mexico. Contributions from the Museum of the American Indian, Heye Foundation, Vol. 6. New York, 1922.

Saville, Marshall H.: The Wood-Carver's Art in Ancient Mexico. Contributions from the Museum of the American Indian, Heye Foundation, Vol. 9. New York, 1925.

Seler, Eduard: Gesammelte Abhandlungen zur amerikanischen Sprach- und Alterthumskunde, Vols. I–V, Berlin, 1902–23.

Seler, Eduard: Codex Borgia: eine altmexikanische Bilderschrift der Bibl. der Congregatio de Propaganda Fide (Roma), 3 vols., Berlin, 1904–9.

Séjourné, Laurette: Un palacio en la Ciudad de los Dioses (Teotihuacán). Instituto Nacional de Antropologia e Historia. Mexico City, 1959.

Soustelle, Jacques: La vie quotidienne des Aztèques à la veille de la conquête espagnole, Paris, 1955. German translation: So lebten die Azteken am Vorabend der spanischen Eroberung, Stuttgart, 1956.

Soustelle, Jacques and Bernal, Ignacio: Mexico: Pre-Hispanic Paintings, New York, 1958.

Spence, Lewis: The Gods of Mexico, London, 1923.

Spinden, Herbert Joseph: A Study of Maya Art, its Subject Matter and Historical Development. Memoirs of the Peabody Museum of Archaeology and Ethnology, Harvard University, Vol. 6. Cambridge, Mass., 1913.

Spinden, Herbert Joseph: Ancient Civilization of Mexico and Central America. American Museum of Natural History Handbook Series, No. 3. 3rd ed., New York, 1928.

Spinden, Herbert Joseph: Maya Art and Civilization, Indian Hills, Col., 1957.

Spratling, William: More Human than Divine, Mexico City, 1960.

Stirling, Matthew W., Stone Monuments of Southern Mexico. Smithsonian Institution, Bureau of American Ethnology, Bulletin 138. Washington, 1943.

Termer, Franz: Die Mayaforschung, in: Nova Acta Leopoldina, N.F., Vol. 15, No. 105. Leipzig, 1952.

Thompson, J. Eric S.: The Rise and Fall of Maya Civilization, Norman, Oklahoma, 1954.

Toscano, Salvador: Arte Precolombino de México y de la America Central, 2nd ed., Mexico City, 1952.

Trimborn, Hermann: Das alte Amerika. Grosse Kulturen der Frühzeit, Neue Folge. Stuttgart, 1959.

Ubbelohde-Doering, Heinrich: Altmexikanische und peruanische Malerei, Berlin, 1959.

Vaillant, George C.: Aztecs of Mexico: Origin, Rise and Fall of the Aztec Nation, Garden City, N.Y., 1944.

Villagra Caleti, Augustín: Bonampak, la ciudad de los muros pintados. Anales del Instituto Nacional de Antropología e Historia, Vol. 3. Mexico City, 1949.

Westheim, Paul: Arte antiguo de México, Mexico City, 1950.

Woodbury, Richard B. and Trik, Aubrey S.: The Ruins of Zaculeu, Guatemala, Vols. 1—2, Richmond, Va., 1953.

II. THE ART OF THE ANDEAN LANDS

Bennett, W. C. and Bird, J. B.: Andean Culture History, New York, 1949.

Bennett, Wendell C.: Ancient Arts of the Andes, New York, 1954.

Bushnell, Geoffrey H. S.: Peru, London, 1956.

Carrión Cachot, Rebeca: Paracas Cultural Elements, Lima, 1949.

Cieza de León, Pedro: Segunda parte de la crónica del Peru que trata de la señoría de los Incas Yupanquis y de sus grandes hechos y gobernación (1550), Madrid, 1880.

Collier, Donald: El desarrollo de la civilización peruana, Bogotá, 1959.

Disselhoff, H.-D.: Tahuantinsuyu: das Reich der Inka, in: Saeculum I, Fribourg-Munich, 1950.

Disselhoff, H.-D.: Geschichte der altamerikanischen Kulturen, Munich, 1953.

Doering, Heinrich: Altperuanische Gefässmalerei, Marburg/Lahn, 1926.

Engel, Frédéric: Sites et établissements sans céramique de la côte péruvienne, in: Journal de la Société des Américanistes, N.S., XLVI, Paris, 1957.

Engel, Frédéric: Algunos datos con referencia a los sitios precerámicos de la costa peruana, in: Arqueológicas, Vol. 3, Lima, 1958.

Hissink, Karin: Gedanken zu einem Nazca-Gefäss, in: Mexico Antiguo, Vol. VII, Mexico City, 1949.

Hissink, Karin: Motive der Mochica-Keramik, in: Paideuma, Vol. 5, Bamberg, 1951.

Horkheimer, Hans: Historia del Perú: Epoca prehispánica, Trujillo, 1943.

Ibarra Grasso, Dick: Tiahuanaco, Cochabamba, 1956.

Keleman, Pál: Medieval American Art, 2 vols., New York, 1946.

Kidder II, Alfred: Some Early Sites in the Northern Lake Titicaca Basin, in: Peabody Museum Papers, Vol. 27, Cambridge, Mass., 1943.

Krickeberg, Walter: Amerika, in: Bernatziks Grosser Völkerkunde, Vol. 3, Leipzig, 1939.

Krickeberg, Walter, Altkolumbianisches Gold, in: Atlantis, Pt. 10, Berlin-Zurich, 1931.

Krickeberg, Walter: Felsplastik und Felsbilder bei den Kulturvölkern Altamerikas, Berlin. 1949.

Krickeberg, Walter: Spätperuanische Kleinplastik, in: Baessler-Archiv, N.F., VI, Berlin, 1958.

Kroeber, A. L.: Peruvian Archaeology in 1942, New York, 1944.

Kutscher, Gerdt: Chimu: eine altindianische Hochkultur.

Kutscher, Gerdt: Nordperuanische Keramik: Figürlich verzierte Gefässe der Früh-Chimu. Monumenta Americana I. Berlin, 1954.

Larco Hoyle, Rafael: Cronología Arqueológica del Norte del Perú, Buenos Aires, 1946.

Linné, Sigvald: The Technique of South American Ceramics, Gothenburg, 1925.

Linné, Sigvald: Darien in the Past: The Archeology of Eastern Panama and Northwestern Colombia, Gothenburg, 1929.

Linné, Sigvald: Prehistoric Peruvian Painting, in: Ethnos, Vol. 18, Stockholm, 1943.

Lothrop, S. K.: Altamerikanische Kunst, Olten-Fribourg, 1959.

Mason, J. Alden: The Ancient Civilizations of Peru. Pelican Books A 395. Harmondsworth, 1957.

Montell, Gösta: Dress and Ornament in Ancient Peru, Gothenburg, 1929.

Muelle, Jorge C.: Muestrario de arte peruano precolombino, Lima, 1938.

Nachtigall, Horst: Tierradentro: Archäologie und Ethnologie einer kolumbianischen Landschaft, Zurich, 1955.

Nachtigall, Horst: Die amerikanischen Megalithkulturen, Berlin, 1958.

Nordenskiöld, Erland: The Copper and Bronze Ages in South America, Gothenburg, 1931.

Palmatary, Helene: The Pottery of Marajó Island, Brazil, in: Transactions of the American Philosophical Society, N.S., Vol. 39, Philadelphia, 1949.

Preuss, Konrad Theodor: Monumentale vorgeschichtliche Kunst, Vols. 1—2, Göttingen, 1929.

Reiche, Maria: Mystery on the Desert, Lima, 1949.

Reiss, Wilhelm and Stübel, Alphons: Das Totenfeld von Ancón in Peru, 3 vols., Berlin, 1880—7.

Rydén, Stig: Archaeological Researches in the Highlands of Bolivia, Gothenburg, 1947.

Sarmiento de Gamboa, Pedro: Geschichte des Inkareiches (1572), Berlin, 1906.

Schmidt, Max: Kunst und Kultur von Peru, Berlin, 1929.

Seler, Eduard: Gesammelte Abhandlungen, Vols. 1—5, Berlin, 1902—23.

Soldi, Pablo: Chavín en Ica, Ica, 1956.

Steward, J. H. (ed.): Handbook of South American Indians, Vol. 2: The Andean Civilizations, Washington, 1946.

Stübel, Alphons and Uhle, Max: Die Ruinenstätte von Tiahuanaco im Hochland des alten Peru, Breslau, 1892.

Strong, William Duncan: Paracas, Nazca, and Tiahuanacoid Cultural Relationships in South Coastal Peru, in: American Antiquity, XXII, Salt Lake City, 1957.

Tax, Sol (ed.): The Civilizations of Ancient America, Chicago, 1951.

Tello, Julio C.: Discovery of the Chavín Culture in Peru, in: American Anthropologist, Vol. 9, Menasha, Wis., 1950.

Trimborn, Hermann: Vergessene Königreiche: Studien zur Völkerkunde Nordwest-Kolumbiens, Brunswick, 1948.

Trimborn, Hermann: Das alte Amerika, Stuttgart, 1959.

Ubbelohde-Doering, Heinrich: Auf den Königstrassen der Inka, Berlin, 1941.

Ubbelohde-Doering, Heinrich: Kunst im Reiche der Inka, Tubingen, 1952.

Uhle, Max: Wesen und Ordnung der altperuanischen Kulturen, Berlin, 1959.

Valcárcel, Luis E.: Historia de la Cultura Antigua del Perú, 2 vols., Lima, 1943.

Willey, Gordon E.: Prehistoric Settlement Patterns in the Virú Valley, Washington, 1953.

Willey, Gordon E.: A Functional Analysis of 'Horizon Styles', in: A Reappraisal of Peruvian Archaeology, assembled by W. C. Bennett, Menasha, Wis., 1947.

Willey, Gordon E.: The Chavin Problem: Review and Critique, in: Southwestern Journal of Anthropology, Vol. 7, Albuquerque, 1951.

INDEX

The numerals in italics refer to the plates and figures. The letter (G) indicates Glossary.

Acapana 149
Acolman 21
adobe (G), 13, 23, 25f., 34, 46, 64
agate 42
agriculture 13, *19*, 61, *67*, 88, 108, 109f., 122, 132, 133, 135, 157, 169; cf. maize, plants
alabaster 42
Alta Verapaz *109*
altar 47, 51, 56, 66, 149, 156
Altiplano 200, 202, 208, 209
Alto de Guitarra 223
Amazon, R. 238ff., *238*
America, Central 18, 39f., *85*, *76*, 122-130; South 39f., 83, *76*, 131-248; contact between Central and South 18, 118, 122f., 125, 129, 157, 235, 237; contact between Mexico and South America 17f., 83, 131f., 160; cf. Mesoamerica, Asia and Oceania
amethyst 75
amulet 150, 161, 210
Ancasmayo, R. 235
Ancón 161, 200, *216*
andesite 201, 211
Andrews, E. W. 120
animals 14, 16, 126, 156f., 160f., *168*, 171, 174, 177, *182*, *195*, 197f., 203, 213, 217, 221, *224*, *236*; alligator 124f.; alpaca (G), *136*, 153, 207; ape 76, 124, *128*; armadillo 29; bison *14*; camel 14; cattle 207; coyote 77, 87f.; dog *24*, 29; fox *164*, *179*, *192*; guanaco 148; horse 14, 60, 147; mammoth 14; mastodon (G), 14; opossum 65; puma (G), *187*, 203; sheep 207; stag *178*, 181; vicuna 132, *136*, 147, 153, 222; cf. jaguar, llama
appliqué work 127, 239
architecture: Aztec 87ff.; Chavin 159f.; Colombian 241, 245; Inca *215*, *216*, *217*, 218f., 225f., 225; Maya 111ff., *114-5*, 117f., 119ff.; Mixtec 57; Moche 173, *175*, 175f., 181; Nazca 199, *200*; Paracas 151; Teotihuacán 30ff., 57; Tiahuanaco 201ff., 205f., 208f.; Toltec *46*, 77, 77, 79, 118; Zapotec 52ff., 57ff., 58; cf. burial-places, columns, forts, pyramids, temples, corbelled arch
Arequipa 208, 226
Argentina 135, 210, 223-6
aryballus *211*, *216*, 217, 220
Asia and Oceania 10f., 83, 129, 138, 204
Asia (Peru) 149

astrology 110f.
astronomy 63, 103, 107, 108ff., *110*, 116
Atacama 225
Atacameno 225f.
atlantes (G), 77, 79
atlatl (G); cf. weapons
Axayacatl (G), *74*
axe 115, *178*, 232; 'ceremonial axe' 60, *61*, *62*
Ayacucho 208
Aymara 200, 207f., 211, 216
Azcapotzalco 105
Azteca 86
Aztecs (G), 10, 15, 33, 37, 41ff., *49*, *50*, 53, 59, *60*, 61, 63, *68*, 79, *79*, 81, 84-106, *88*, *89*, *91*, *92*, *94*, 113, 122f., 126, 199
Aztlan 86

Bachue *243*
Balbao, Vasco Núñez de 130
ball-game (G), 52, 60f., *63*, *92*, 112, 118
batik 173
Batres, L. 33
beads 26, 126, *146*, 177, 239
beans 15, 148, *154*, 155, 225
bells 174, *180*, *192*, 203, 225, 236
Bennett, W. C. 157f., 202, 206f., 209, 226
Bird, J. 148ff., 152
birds *45*, 56, *64*, 124, 154, 156, *175*, *180*, 183, *191*, 197f., 199, *212*, 213f., 217; *ara* parrot 47; colibri *179*; condor., 158f., 201, 202, *203*, 203; duck 29; eagle 2, 77, 119, *157*, *182*, 201, 242; goatsucker 198; humming-bird 198; parrot 47, *166*, 198, 238
Boca del Monte 62
Bogotá *243*
bolas 170
Bolivia 135, 200ff., 207f., 210f., 226, 246
Bonampak 114
bone 58, 81, 83, *83*, 111, 132, 147, 148f., 161, 214
Bovallius, C. *123*, 125f.
bronze 129, 147, 177, *192*, 199, 208, 213, 219, 221, 223f., 225, 242
Bronze Age 147
burials 14, 26, 51, 177, 184, 200, 225, 239, 245; burial-places 36ff., *39*, *40*, 51, 53, *55*, 56f., 58, 65, 115f., 126, 128, *129*, 131, 136, 138, 149ff., 160f., 177ff., 184f., 205, 214, *216*, 235, 242, 247f.; cf. gloves, Monte Albán, Paracas, urns
Burland, C. A. 83

INDEX

Cachot, C. 151

Cahuachi 186, 198

Cajamarca 211, 213

Calama 225

Calasasaya: cf. Tiahuanaco

Calchaquí 225, 226

calendar 60, 63, 83, 110f., 118, 121, 155, 202;
'Calendar Stone' 104f.

Callejón de Huaylas 173

Campeche *94, 113*

caryatid (G), 77, 123, 246

Casas, B. de las 8

Casma 159, *159*

Caso, A. 55, 57, 81, 83

Castellanos 242

Castilla del Ora (G), 128

Castillo, Bernal Díaz del 10, 90f., 102

Cauca, R. *218*, 242ff., 247f.

cavernas: cf. Paracas

Cellini, B. 81

cenote (G), 117, 120

Centéotl (G), 67

Cerro de las Mesas *17*, 65

Cerro Montoso 65

Cerro Mulato 224

Cerro Sechin 159

'Chac Mool' (G), 46, 77f., 118

Chalchihuitlicue (G), 33

Chancay, R. 211, *213*, 214

Chanchán *192*, 211, 212

Chapultepec 88f.

Charles V, Emperor *50*, 81, 88f., 100, 106, 147

Chavín 131, 150-171, *143*, *160-2*, 172, 200, 218, *223*, 223, 249

Chavin de Huántar 156ff., *156*, 159

Chiapas 61, *92*, 114

Chibcha 122, 127, 235, 241, 246

Chicama, R. 148, 16of., *162*, *163*, *171*, 172f., 177, *177*, 18of.

chicha (G), 182

Chichén Itzá (G), 46, 77f., 80, 86, *95*, 117ff., *123*

Chiclayo 146

Chicomecóatl 104

Chile 14, 135, 148, 208, 210, 217, 223-6

chilli 15

Chimú *176*, *192*, 211ff., *212*, 217

China 83

Chincha 211

Chincultic 61, *92*

Chiripa **209**

Chiriquí *98*, 123, *127*, 127

Cholula (G), 78, 83, 85

Chonogoyape *224*

Chorotega (G), 122

Christianity 33, 147; Christian churches 89, 158, 201, 203

chronicles, chroniclers 56, 83, 86ff., 211, 217f., 223, 242

Cincatlán 62

cire perdue (G), 130, 177, 242

city-states 86f., 114ff., 211

clay 138, 149, 183, 195f., 200, 219, *239*; clay sculpture: archaic 15, 15f., *18*, *19*; Chavín 156; Colima 27, 28ff., *29*; Colombia and Ecuador 226, *226f.*, *236*; Jaina *94*; Jalisco 27, 29; Maya *94*, 119f.; Mzaapan 79; Michoacán 27; Mixtec *48*; Muisca *243*, *244*; Nayarit 21, 27, 28ff.; Teotihuacán 35f., *40*; Tiahuanaco 203f.; Zapotec *44*, *48*, 53, 54, *54*; cf. pottery, portrait heads, vessels

climate 52, 85, 120, 137, 161, 173, 207

cloisonné (G), 156, 186

clothing 21, *64*, 90, *94*, 109, 111, 135, 147, 148, 152f., 161, 174, 178, *180*, 18off., *216*, 220, 222, 238

cóatl (G), 56

Coatlicue (G), 103

Coatlinchán 35

coca 15, 175, 210, 213, 242

Coclé *98*, 128f., *129*, *140*, 128f.

codices 83, 86, 110f.

coiling technique 196

Colhuacán 86

Colima *18*, 27ff., 174

Colombia *98*, 126, 130, 135f., *139*, 153, 226, *234*, 235, 241-5, *242*, 245, 246, 248

columns 46, 77, *78*, 79, *82*, 118f., 120

Condor House 159

copal: cf. incense

Copán **38**

copper 126, 129, *164*, *165*, 174, 177, 180, 208, 214, 225, 236, 243

corbelled arch (G), 111f., 114f., 120

Cortés, H. 10, *50*, 66, 79, 81, 88ff., 99f., 106

Costa Rica 83, *96*, *98*, 122f., *124-5*, 126f., *139*, 235, 241

cotton 18, 148, *149*, *151*, 151ff., 185, *189*, 199, 222, 242

Cuicuilco (G), 17f.

Cuismancu 211

INDEX

cults 67, 82, *102*, 103, 197, 210

culture hero 102, 103

Cuna-Cuna 127

Cupiznique' 160

Cuzco 214, *216*, 216, 217, *218*, 218f., *219*, 221, 221; Sun Temple 221, *232*

Dabeiba 243

dance 55, 76, 154, *180*, 182, *182*, 198, 224

'Danzantes' (G), 54, 160

deities 15, 29, 33, *36*, 39, *45*, 46, 62, *64*, 76, 84, 110f., 115, 116, 119, *151*, *157*, 160, 162f., 175, .176, *180*, 182, *195*, *196*, 197, 202, 203, 204, 210

Dzibilchaltun 120f.

demons 29, 114, 126ff., *129*, 133, *152*, 155, *155*, 177, *178*, *181*, 182f., 185, *187*, *195*, 197, *198*, 223; cactus-spine demon *197*, 198

Diaguite 225ff., *225*, 226

'Diosa del agua' 35

Dongson 83

Dürer, A. 81, 106

Easter I. 205

Eckert, G. 243

Ecuador 40, *123*, 126, 131, 135f., 153, 217, 226, 226, 235ff.

Egypt 116, 132, 179

Ehecatl 104

'El Dorado' 241, 243

El Salvador 78, 120

embossed work 159, *164*, 199, 228, 236

embroidery *142*, 149, 152, *152*, 154, 184, 197, 199, 222

Engel, F. 148f., 160

engraving 159ff., *161*, *169*, 185, 200, 203, 209, *226*, 238, *238*

Esmeraldas 235ff.

Etén *146*

Europe, Europeans .50, 57, 85, 100, 138, 174

Evans 238

'Fasting Coyote' 87f.

feathers 2, *45*, *53*, 56, *69*, 77, 81f., 99f., 105, 111, 119, 149, *196*, 213f., 236

filigree work 242, 244

fish 25, 29, 81, *139*, *149*, 154, 156, *167*, 174, *189*, 197, 212; fishing 15, 147f., *183*, 242

'Flayed Lord': cf. Xipe Totec

flowers 38, 40f., 105, *175*, 214, 220

Folsom *14*

food-gatherers 14, 78, 181

fort 177, *230*

friezes 77, 201, 202

fruit 14f., *148*, 161, 177, *185*

Gaffron 186

Gallinazo *171*, *172*ff.

Gamboa, S. de 216

Gateway of the Sun: cf. Tiahuanaco

gloves, funerary *193*

gold *50*, 57f., 81f., *78*, 90, *98*, 100, 105f., .117f., 123, 126f., 128f., *129*, 131f., *139*, *140*, 146, 147, 153f., 159, 162f., *164*, *165*, *170*, 173, 177, *193*, 199, 202, 214, 217f., 219ff., 229, 234, 235ff., 241ff., 247

Goodman 107

Grande de Nazca, R. 199

granulation 242

'Grave 7': cf. Monte Albán

graves: cf. burial-places 62

greenstone 62

ground-nuts 15, 238

Guanajuato 76

guano 183

Guatavita 241

Guatemala 30, *109*, 117, *118*, 120f.; Guatemala City 38, 120f.

Guayaquil 236

Guayas 236

Guerrero 26, 27, 28, 35, 75, *75*, 82

Guetar (G), 126ff.

haematite *64*

Hartman, C. V. 126

head-dress 36, *42*, 55f., *66*, 92, 99, 115, *176*, *180*

helmet 29, 128, 147, 242

Heyerdahl, T. 205, 206

Hidalgo *46*, 76, 77

hieroglyphs *60*, 61, *63*, *91*, 92, *93*, 107, 110, *110*, 115, 127, 135, *176*, 198, 203

Higueras *18*

Honduras 30, 38, *96*, 122

Hoyle, L. 16off.

Huaca del Loro 199

Huaca del Sol 175f.

Huaca Prieta (G), 148f.

huaquero (G), 57

Huari 208f.

Huaxtecs (G), 63f.

Huayna Capac 217

INDEX

Huehuetéotl (G), 30, 33, *101*

huehuetl: cf. musical instruments

Huitzilopochtli (G) , 86, 90f., 102, 104f.

hunters 11ff., *46, 50,* 181; hunter culture 14, 78, 85, 138ff.

Ica *141,* 152f., 184f., *194,* 211, 214, *232*

ik (G) , *110*

ikat (G) , 136

Imbabura 235

implements 14, 16f., 34, 58, 82, 100, 116, 120, *124,* 126, 129, 147ff., 154, 162, 177, 213f., 242

Inca 25, 123, 130, 132, 135, 138f., 153, *180,* 186, 200, 205, 207, 210f., 214, 214-226, *216, 217, 219, 224, 225,* 227, *232, 233,* 235, 238, 241

Inca Roca 217

incense *45,* 90, 222; burners *95,* 119f.; vessels *168, 169,* 203f.

inlay work *49,* 81, 90, 100, *124, 147, 165, 188,* 220, 223

insects 41, 76

'interlocking style' (G) , *200,* 200

Iztapalapa, Mt. 100

jadeite (G), 58, 75, *75, 76,* 115, 117, 120, 131

jaguar *2, 44,* 58, 66, *75,* 77, *98,* 119 *124,* 124, 126f., 158, 160, 174, *178*

Jaina I. *94*

Jalisco 25, 27, 28, 38, 76

Jequetepeque, R. 159, 175, 212

jewellery *21,* 58, 81f., 90, 105, 111, 117, 123, 128, 132, *146,* 150, 177, 221f., 242, 247; cf. ornaments

Jivaro (G) , 126

Juárez, B. *44*

Kaminaljuyú (G) , 38, 120f.

kelim 149, *189, 190*

kero (G) , 207, *218,* 220

Knopoff, L. 11

knot-records: cf. *quipu*

Krickeberg, W. 18, 62

Kroeber 155, 196

'Kuntur Wasi' 159

Kutscher, G. *203*

La Paz 204, 205f.

'La Venta ' (G) , 54, 65ff., *66,* 131

Lacandones 108, 116f.

Lambayeque 159, *213*

languages 30, 63, 84, 86, 105f., 119f., 122f., 127, 132, 138f., 241

Las Aldas *160*

Las Balsas, Rio de *75*

Lavapatas 247

legend *25, 42, 90*

Léon, C. de 216

Lewisville 11

Lima 161, 186, 200, *207,* 211, *228;* Early *167,* 200

limestone *92,* 116f., 218

Lothrop, S. K. *75,* 128, *129, 173*f.

Magdalena, R. 126, 245ff.

magic *15, 19,* 30, 83, 115, *133,* 153, *167,* 179, 181, 198, 220, 222, 222

maguey (G), *32*

maize *15,* 17, *31,* 40, 67, 84, *90, 95,* 103 117, *124,* 148, 150, 162f., 175, 207, 214, 225

Majes, R. *224*

malcu 216

Mama Ocllo 216f.

Manabí *236*

Manco Capac 216

mangrove (G) , *66*

manioc (G) , 15, 238

mantos (G) : cf. shrouds

Marajó I. 238f., *238, 239*

Maranón, R. 159

marble *75*

Martinez 107

mask *26,* 35, 36, 60, *68, 70, 75,* 82, 99f., 104, 114, *165,* 198 ,221, *224, 234, 236*

Maule, R. 217

Maya (G) , 30, *46,* 61ff., *75,* 77, 84, 85, *93, 94,* 107-121, *109, 110, 113, 114,* 122, 124ff., 131f., 135, 158, 218, 222f., 235

Mayapán *95,* 119f.

Mazapan 78, *79, 95*

Megalithic 205, 246f.

Meggers 238

Mérida 120

Mesoamerica (G) , 131, 135, 150, 157, 159, 172, 178, 181, 218, 236f.

Mestizos 200f.

metal-working 83, 129, 131, 138, 159; Aztec 90, 100, 105; Central America *98,* 126, 129 *139, 140;* Chimú 213; Colombia 241ff., 247; Ecuador 235ff.; Inca 214, *219,* 219ff., *229;* Maya 117f.; Mixtec 81f., 100, 105; Moche *146, 164,*

165, 177, *179*; Nazca 199; Salinar 173; Virú 173; Zapotec 57f.; cf. bronze, copper, gold, silver

metate (G),   17, *124*
metla-pilli (G),   17
Mexica   86
Mexico 10-121, 124f., 126, 129, 131, 135, *139*, 153, 174, 205, 235, 237, 241
mica   *36*
Michoacán   27, 77
Mictlantecuhtli   *102*
Midland man   11f.
mirror   *64*, 90, *112*, 149
Misantla   62
mise en couleur (G),   243
Mitla   38, 58f., *58*, 82
Mixteca Puebla   49, *69*, 81-3
Mixtecs (G), *46*, *48*, *50*, 53, 57ff., *70*, *81*, *82*, 83, 86f., *98*, 100, 129
Moche *145*, *164*, *165*, *171*, *172*, 173-184, *175*, *177*, *179*, *180*, *182*, *183*, 196, 211, *212*, 213, *213*, 223; Moon Pyramid *165*, 176; Sun Pyramid 176
Mochica: cf. Moche
Moctezuma (G),   66, 79, *81*, 88ff., 99f.
molcajete   88
monoliths (G),   *58*, 201, 204, 246
Monte Albán 18, *44*, 51, 52f., *54*, *55*, 56f., 57ff., 62, 81, 123, 129, 160; 'Grave 7' 57f., 81f., *83*, 129
Montezuma: cf. Moctezuma
Moon Pyramid: cf. pyramids
Moore, H.   106
Morelos   *47*, 80
Morley, S. G.,   94
mosaic   26, 58, *69*, 81, 100, *112*, 177, 214
Mosquito   245
mother-of-pearl   49, 58, 100
Mozna, R.   157
Muisca   241ff., *242*, *243*
mummification, mummies 151ff., .*179*, *188*, 221
music 105, 114, 182, *182*; musical instruments *49*, 114
myth, mythology, mythical creatures *25*, 37, 79, *142*, 154, 156, 159, 169, 195, 196, .198, 199, 203, *209*, 211, *236*

Nachtigall, H.   235, 246f.
Napo, R.   238f.
Narino   244, *245*
Navaho (Navajo)   10
Nayarit   *21*, *27*, 28, 29
Nazca 152, 184-201, *200*, 203, *206*, 208, 211, 214;

classic *185*, 185f., *186*, 194f.; *195-6*, 198, 199, Late *166*, 187, *197-8*, 198; proto-Nazca 185, 195
Nebaj   *109*
Nepena   159, 175
Nahuatl (G),   86, 105f., *123*
nephrite (G),   *91*
Nezahualcóyotl (G),   *32*, 87f., 89
Nicaragua 78, 85f., *96*, *123*, 123; Lake 122, 125
Nicarao (G),   122, 124
Nicoya   *96*, 124, *124*
nopal cactus   *32*
Nordenskiöld, E.   128f., *129*, *140*
Nore   *242*

Oaxaca *21*, 28, 30, 38, 51, 52, 54f., *54*, 58, *62*, 75, *82*, 82, 83, 103ff.
obsidian (G),   14, 75, *101*, 153, *155*
Ocucaje   153
Ollantaytambo   218f.
Olmes (G),   *44*, 54, *65*, *66*, 75, 150, 157
onyx   58
Orellana   239
ornaments *45*, 58, 61, *62*, 75, 81f., *98*, *112*, 115, 127f., 149, 159, *165*, 173, 177, *180*, 202, 206, 221, *225*, *236*, 242, 244, 247
Otátes   *48*

Pacatnamú   212
Pachacamac 186, *189*, *190*, 200, 205, *207*, 227; Sun Temple 200
Pachacutec Yupanqui   217f., 221
'padlocks'   60
painting, negative *96*, 156, 173ff., *183*, 235, 244, *244-5*; cf. vase-painting, wall-painting
palaces 31, *39*, *58*, 87, 88ff., 114f., 120, 212, 218
Palenque   *93*, 115
'palmas'   60, *61*
Panama 83, *98*, 122f., *127*, 127f., *129*, *140*, 241
Pánuco, R.   63
Paracas 150ff., 161, 173, 184f., 195, 197, 199; Early *151*, 155f., 161, 185f., 209; Late *154*, 156, 185f.; Cavernas *141*, 152, 155f.; Necropolis *142*, *152*, 152ff., *154*
Paradise of the Rain God: cf. Tlalocan
Pearl Is.   128, *129*, *131*
pearls   81, 90
pepper   17, *88*, 148, *195*, 197, 225
Peru 16, 18, *25*, 28, 57, 83, *98*, 126, 129, 131f 135-237, *139*, 241, 246
Pichincha   235

Pisac 219, *231, 232*
Piura 211
Pizarro, F. 131
plangue (G), 136
plants *178-9*, 181, 197f., *197*; cultivated 15, 18, 30, 90, 147f., 150, 174, 177f., *189*, 199, 207; cf maize, tillandsia
plaque *170*, 225
platinum 236
porphyry 218
portrait heads 138, 175, 179
potsherds 36, 161, 209f., 211, 235
pottery *17*, 51, *65, 76*, 136, 147; Aztec *88, 89*, 100; Central American *96*, 123, 124f., 127f., *127-8, 130-2; 140;* Chancay 214; Chavin *140*, 150, 154, 156ff., *156-9, 161-2;* Chimú *212*, 212; Colima 27f., *28;* Diaguite 226, *226;* Huaxtec 64; Ica *194*, 214; Inca *216, 217*, 220, 220, *221;* Lambayeque *213;* Lima (Early) 200; Marajó 238f., *238;* Maya 64, 93, 108f., *109, 112-3*, 114, 120f., 123; Mixtec *81*, 81-3; Moche *171-2*, 176ff., *175-6, 177-9*, 181-2, 186, *212, 213;* Mosquito *245;* Musica 244, *245*, 248; Nazca *166*, 184ff., *185, 186, 195-6, 197-9*, 200, 208; 'Olmec' *17;* Pucara 208f., *209;* Recuay *144*, 173ff.; Salinar 172f.; Teotihuacán 35ff., *37-41, 64*, 79, 120f.; Tiahuanaco *167, 168, 169, 187*, 202ff., 202, *203*, 206-7 207f., 223f.; Tlatilco 15f., *16-17;* Toltec 78, 82; Virú *171*, 174; Zapotec *45*, 52, 55f., *55;* cf. incense-vessel, urn, aryballus, *kero*, 'interlocking style', vessels
priest 30, 32, 42, *48*, 63, *63*, 67, 74, 82, 90, 101, 103, 110f., 116f., 119f., 153, 155, 180, 198, 206; priest-king 32f., *58*, 63, 66, 87, *93, 109*, 111, *113*, 115, 118, 127, 181, 241
'prince of flowers': cf. Xochipilli
Pucara 208f.
Puebla *23*, 82, 85, 105
pulque (G),
pyramids 28, 30f., 33f., 52., 62f., 77, 80, 89f., 102, 104, 114, 116, *117*, 118f., 131, 174, 176ff., 181, 200, 205, 212; Sun, Moon Pyramids: cf. Moche, Teotihuacán
pyrite *49, 70, 100, 112*

quauhxicalli (G), 2
quechquemitl (G), 35
Quechua 214, 226
Quesada, G. J. de 241
quetzal (G), 56, *71*, 119

Quetzalcóatl (G), 33f., 56, 77, *78*, 79, *80, 83*, 94f., *94-5*, 99f., *133*
Quimbaya 242f.
quinine 15
quinoa (G), 207, 225
quipu (G), 217

radio-carbon dating (G), 10ff., 51, 54f., 107, 148, 157, 185f., 202
Raimondi Stele 157
Ratinlinul *118*
Recuay *144*, 173ff., 180
Reiche, M. 198
relief 34, 36, 47, 61, *63*, 64, 77, *77*, 80, 92, 111, 115, 119, *157*, 157f., *159*, 159f., 174, 195f., *202*, 202, 204, *212*, 223, 247
religion 15, 15f., 28f., 30ff., 37, 51, 52f., 54, *55*, 56f., 61, *62*, 63, *71*, 83, 84, 95, *102*, 105, 110f., 113, 119ff., 133ff., 150, 162f., 176, *178*, 184, 199, 208, 210, 214, 216, 217, 241; cf. priest, rites, cults, sacrifice (human), Christianity
reptiles: crocodile *128;* lizard 90, 247; cf. serpent
Rímac, R. 211
rites 63, 83, 114, 131, 155, 183, 206, 221, 225, 247; death rites 26, 56, *74*
rock-crystal 58, 75, 81f., 100
rock drawings and engravings 223, *223-24*
Rowe, J. H. 195
Rydén 202

sacrifice, human 2, *74*, 84, 90f., *101*, 101, 104f., 117, 119, *181*, 183, 242
Sacsahuamán 219, *230, 233*
Sahagún, Fray B. de 67
Salinar *171*, 172ff., 186
San Agustín 246-49, *248*
San Isidro General *98, 139*
San Lorenzo Albarradas 54
San Vicente Chicoloapan 14
sandstone 204
Santa, R. *144*, 173f.
Santa Elena 237
Santa Maria de Guadalupe 104
Santa Marta, Sierra Nevada de 245
Santarém 239
Santiago de Tlatelolco 53
Sapay Inca 216
sapota 40
Schaedel, R. 212
schist *64, 112*

Seler, E. 83, *91*, 197

serpent 29, 34, 38, 56, 60, 77, 90, 103, 118f., 124, *149*, *151*, 153f., 157f., *157*, 174, 182, *183*, 244, 247; plumed *46*, *47*, 56, *71*, 77, 78, *78*, 79f., *80*, *82*, 102, 103, 126

shell *26*, 34, *36*, *70*, 100, 111, 123, 131, 147ff., *164*, *165*, *170*, *181*, *188*, 210, 213f., *229*, 236

shrouds (G), *142*, 151ff., *152*, 184f., 195, 222

silver 58, 81, 90, 128, *146*, *164*, *165*, 177, 188, 214, 219f., *220*ff., *229*, 243

Sinú, R. 243

snake: cf. serpent

Spanish chroniclers 56, 211, 216f., 223, 242

Spanish conquest: of Mexico and Central America 10, *50*, 59, 61, 75, 79, 81, 88ff., 100, 102, 120, 128, 130; of South America 147, 175, 200, 205, 207f., 214f., 220ff., 241ff., 249

Spinden, H. J. 107

spindle-whorl (G), *90*, 100

stamp 60, 100

stele (G), 75, 108f., 111, *156*, 157, *159*

stone-carving: Aztec *68*, *70*, *71*, *74*, 84, 92, 102ff.; Central American *124*, *125*, 125; Chavin *156*-8, 157ff., *159*, 162; Colombia 246f., *248;* Ecuador 235, *236*, 237; Inca 221-2, 221f., 223; 'La Venta' 66f., *66;* Maya 108ff., 119; Moche 183; Olmec 66f., *66;* Recuay 174; Teotihuacán 35, *36;* Tiahuanaco 201ff., *202*, 203ff., 207ff.; Toltec *46*, 77, 77, 80, *82;* Totonac 60f., *65;* cf. frieze, relief

stone implements 82, 147ff., 183

Stone Age 34, 66, 107, 111, 126, 147

'Stone of Tizoc' 104f.

Strong, W. D. 153, 155, 185ff., 197f., 199

Sun Pyramid: see Pisac, Teotihuacán, Moche, Cuzco

Tabasco 65

Tairona 243, 245

Tajín (G), 30, 61f., *63*

tanga *239*

Tapajós *239*

tapestry *191*, *203*, 210, 222; cf. *kelim*

'Tawantinsuyu' 216

techichi (G), *24*, 29

Tello, J. C. 135, 138, 151ff., 155, 159, 195

temples 15, 17f., *23*, 28, 30, 33f., *46*, 52f., 58, 67, 70, 77, 87, 89ff., *93*, 101f., 104f., 115, 116, *117*, 118, 119f., 125, 131, 157f., 159f., *159*, 162, 177f., 186, 201, 205, 209, 212, 213f., 218f., 221f., 235; Temple of Warriors 118

Tenayuca 89

Tenocha 86

Tenochtitlán-Mexico (G), 10, *24*, *25*, 32f., 81ff., 86ff., 101f., 123

Teopancaxco *42*

Teotihuacán (G), *23*, 30, *31*, *36*-42, *43*, *44*, *46*, 51, 54, *55*, 57, 62, 62, *64*, 69, 76, 78ff., *79*, *82*, 83, 85, 86, *90*, *113*, 120f., 195, 205f.; Moon Pyramid 34; Sun Pyramid *23*, 34

Tepantitla 40, *43*

tepescuintli: cf *techichi*

Tepexpan 14

teponaztli: cf. musical instruments

Texas 11

Texcoco 32, 35, *74*, 85f.; Lake 10, 84ff., 87

Texcotzingo 87

textiles *60*, 105, *139*, 131f., 135f., *141*, 147ff., *151*, 151ff., 161, 182, *190* *194*, 197, 199ff., 202, *203*, 204, 209, 210, 213, 222, 242; cf. tapestry, shrouds, weaving

Tezcatlipóca (G), *90*, 100, 102

Thompson, J. E. 107f., 116, 121

Tiahuanaco 178, 184, 199, 200-210, 211, *218*, 223f., 224, 225, 246; classic *168*, *169*, 202, 204, *204*, 204; Early 202; expansionist *167*, *170*, *187*, 202, *203*, 206, 208f., 209, *213*, 239; Late *191;* Calasasaya 205; Gateway of the Sun 201ff., *202*, 206, 207; Palacio de los Sarcófagos 206f.

Tierradentro 247

Tikal *117*

tillandsia (G), *178*-9

tin 208

Titicaca, L. *138*, 200f., 202, 206, 208, 209, 219

Tiwanaku: cf. Tiahuanaco

tlachtli: cf. ball-game

Tlaloc (G), 32ff., 37f., *39*, 40f., 56, 60, 89, 100, *101*-2, 102, 105, 121, 158

Tlalocan (G), 40, *43*

Tlamimilolpan (G), 32, 36, *39*, *41*, 51

Tlatelolco 89, 99f., 102

Tlatilco (G), 15f., *17*, 18, *19*, 29, 75, 85

Tlaxcala 30, *41*, 49, 82

Tlazoltéotl (G), 67, 103

tobacco 15, 175

tolas (G), *235*

Toltecs (G), 33, 37, 41, *46*, *50*, 72, 76-80, 77, *82*, 83, 86f., *95*, 105, 117ff., 126

tombs: cf. burial-places

totem-pole 108f.

Totonacs (G), 61f., *64*, *65*

trade 38f., 81, 123, 131, 213, 242
trees 40, *189*, 220
Tres Zapotes (G), 65
tridacna *170*
Trimborn, H. 162
trophies 35, 81, 126f., 154, *155*, *166*, 174, 181, *187*, *196*, 198ff., 201, 247
Trujillo *175*, *179*, 212
Tula 33, 38, *46*, 76, 77, 77f., *78*, 79, *82*, 83, 86f., 117f., 122f.
Tule Springs 11
Tumaco *226*, 235
tumbaga 243
Tupac Amaru 222f.
Tupac Yupanqui 217
turquoise 26, 58, 81, 100, 147, 177, 210, 236

Ubbelohde-Doering, H. 135, 155, 186, 198, 212, 249
Uhle, M. 135, 178, 186, 207
urn *45*, *54-5*, 55ff., 124, *230*, *238*, 239, 245; funerary 39, *45*, 55f., 95
Urubamba, R. 219, *231*
Uxmal 117

Vaillant, G. C. 78, 79
Valley of Mexico 11f., *15*, 16, *17*, *18*, 30, 41, *46*, *67*, *68*, *69*, *71*, *74*, 75f., *78*, 84, 86, *90*, *91*, 100, 104, 117
vase-painting 135, *178*, 184, 204, 208f.
Vega de la Torre 64
Venus (planet) 77, *91*
Venus Tlatilco 15
Veracruz *17*, *48*, 60, 62, *63-4*, 77, 79
Veraguas 98, *129*
vessels: double-bodied *171*, 212; double-spouted *167*, *185*, *195-6*, 196, 197; effigy 176; figure *171*, 173ff., 198; head 197, 199, 239; portrait *145*, 179; stirrup-spouted 161, *161*, *171*, 173, *175*, 176, *178-80*, 180, *182*, *213*; tripod 35, *40*, 121, 124, 211; in shape of animals 64, *96*, 156, 173, *216*, 220; of bird 16, *17*, 39, 173, 220; of fish 16 *17*, 220, *221*; of house 161, *171*, *172*, 173; cf. incense-vessel, *kero*, aryballus

vigesimal system (G), 111
Virú, R. 159, *171*, 172, 173f., *223*

wall-painting 34, *42*, *43*, 54, 57, 84, 132, 183, 223
warfare, warriors 29, *69*, 83, 84, 114, 116f., 119f., 154, *177-8*, *180*, 183, 198
weapons 14, 106, 126, 129, 132, 147, 150, 176, 182; bow and arrow 90, *166*; club and club-head 29, *124*, 126, *159*, *166*, *170*, 176, *177*, 180, 222; cuirass 106; dart *109*; javelin 14, 83, *112*; shield *69*, 106, *177*, 180; spear and spear-head 11f., *14*, 17; spear-thrower (*atlatl*) 14, *50*; spear-thrower *112*, *166*, 181, 244
weaving 111, 135, 162, 173, *181*, 204, 221f.; cf. textiles, shrouds
white-on-red style: cf. Salinar
wood 111, 131, 147, 149, 183, *188*, 210, 225
wool 136, 147, 152f., 221f.
writing 81, 83, 86f., 105, 135, *190*, 198, 217, 241; cf. hieroglyphs

Xipe Totec (G), *48*, *68*, *74*, 79, 82, 103
Xiuhtecutli (G), 103
Xochicalco *47*, 80, *80*
Xochimilco 88
Xochipilli (G), *102*, *104*
Xochiquetzal (G), *101*, *102*, 104
Xolalpan *31*, *32*, 37, *38*, 38ff., *39*, *41*, *43*, 79
Xolotl (G), *91*, *102*, 103

Yacatecutli (G), 33
Yagul 59
'yokes' 60, 62
'Youth of Tamuín' 64
Yucatán *31*, 78, 80, 85f., *95*, *98*, 116f., 119f.
Yucatec 116f.

Zacuala 32
Zapotecs (G), *21*, 30, *45*, *48*, 51, 52-59, 56, 61
Zapatera I. *123*
Zócalo 103